MEASURING, MARKING & LAYOUT

A BUILDER'S GUIDE

MEASURING, MARKING & LAYOUT

A BUILDER'S GUIDE

JOHN CARROLL

The Taunton Press

COVER PHOTO: **Scott Phillips**

PUBLISHER: **Jim Childs**
ACQUISITIONS EDITOR: **Steve Culpepper**
EDITORIAL ASSISTANT: **Carol Kasper**

TECHNICAL EDITOR: **Andrew Wormer**
EDITOR: **Thomas McKenna**
DESIGNER: **Henry Roth**
LAYOUT ARTIST: **Lynne Phillips**
ILLUSTRATOR: **Vince Babak**

TYPEFACE: **Stone Serif**
PAPER: **70-lb. Somerset Matte**
PRINTER: **Quebecor Printing/Hawkins,
Church Hill, Tennessee**

Taunton
BOOKS & VIDEOS

for fellow enthusiasts

Printed in the United States of America
10 9 8 7 6 5 4 3 2 1

For Pros / By Pros™: Measuring, Marking & Layout
was originally published in 1998 by The Taunton Press, Inc.

For Pros / By Pros™ is a trademark of The Taunton Press, Inc.,
registered in the U.S. Patent and Trademark Office.

The Taunton Press, Inc., 63 South Main Street,
PO Box 5506, Newtown, CT 06470-5506
e-mail: tp@taunton.com

Library of Congress Cataloging-in-Publication Data

Carroll, John (John Michael), 1949-.
    For Pros / By Pros™: Measuring, marking & layout :
a builder's guide / John Carroll
       p.   cm.
    Includes index.
    ISBN 1-56158-335-9
    1. Building layout. I. Title.
TH385.C37   1998
690—dc21   98-18115
                                      CIP

To my parents, Denny and Micky Carroll,
who raised a couple of girls and a half-dozen boys
and somehow made each of us feel special

ACKNOWLEDGMENTS

As a builder, I've always appreciated the hard work of my subcontractors, particularly the drywall finishers, painters, and others who come in toward the end of the project—just when my energy and enthusiasm are starting to wane. These trusted craftsmen not only supply an essential, last-minute burst of energy, but they also fix mistakes and put the finishing touches on my job. They make me look good, and for that I am ever grateful.

As a writer, I feel the same sense of gratitude toward the people who have taken my rough and imperfect manuscript and turned it into a finished book. First, I want to thank Julie Trelstad, who encouraged me to take on this project, helped me form a plan of action, and guided me through the first draft. Next, I want to thank Andrew Wormer, who helped edit the manuscript and provided most of the text that accompanies the drawings. Andrew's questions and suggestions caused me to rethink and change many parts of the book, and his talent as a wordsmith directly improved the organization and flow of the text. I am also deeply indebted to Vincent Babak, who produced the clear, well-wrought drawings that are such a vital part of this book. For applying the finishing touches to the manuscript, I want to thank Tom McKenna. And for overseeing the process by which the manuscript and drawings became a published book, I want to thank Steve Culpepper.

Because of the technical nature of this book, there were hundreds of details and thus hundreds of chances for me to make mistakes. To ferret out those errors, I enlisted the support of four very talented friends, who served as technical readers. I deeply appreciate the time and effort they so freely gave. They not only found and corrected mistakes, but they also offered encouragement and made insightful suggestions. These readers were: Steve Lockwood, a draftsman and carpenter; Andy Hudak, an architect; Sky Ludwig, a structural engineer and builder; and Tom Jochum, an electrical engineer. I especially want to thank Tom, who painstakingly checked the accuracy of every mathematical problem. On top of that, he waited patiently for over a year for me to finish the book before I began his addition. It's loyal customers like Tom who make being a builder such a rewarding profession.

I also want to thank another loyal customer, Professor Harold Layton, who provided the proportional tables in the Appendices. Like Tom, Harold has been patiently waiting for me to find time to remodel his kitchen.

Finally, I want to thank all the craftsmen who have shared tips and techniques with me during the last 30 years.

CONTENTS

INTRODUCTION

On a warm Maryland morning during the summer of 1966, I followed my older brother up a ladder to the bare plywood deck of a roof. I was 16, eager to learn, and totally inexperienced in roofing and most other things. My brother talked me through our first task, which was rolling out, cutting, and nailing down roofing felt. After an hour or two of hard work, we had all of the bare wood covered.

Then my brother unfolded his carpenter's ruler, held it flat on the roof deck and scratched V-shaped marks in the felt with a roofing nail. He explained the measurements as he worked, and as I watched and listened, I was impressed by the simplicity and logic of it. After marking off the roof, he told me to hold one end of a string, and as he unwound it from a scrap of wood, he rubbed a half-round chunk of red chalk on it. The blue chalk favored by carpenters, he explained, would fade in the sun. Holding the chalked string on the marks, we struck horizontal lines every 10 in., stopping after every fourth line to rechalk the string. To keep the grooves of the shingles straight, we snapped two vertical "bond" lines 6 in. apart on each section of the roof. Over the next two days, we nailed off an asphalt shingle roof by following those lines.

By now, those shingles have worn away and been replaced. The lessons I learned from working on that roof, however, have stayed with me through three decades of building. The most important lesson I learned is that careful measuring and marking are vital parts of craftsmanship and that those who do things "by eye" invariably produce inferior-quality work. Another lesson I learned is that careful measuring and marking don't take that much more time. Like other building skills, measuring and marking techniques can be improved and made more efficient through practice.

Unfortunately, many builders never develop good measuring and marking skills because they believe that careful layout isn't as important as production. If they're not moving forward, they feel like they're wasting time. But whoever asked, "Why is there never enough time to do the

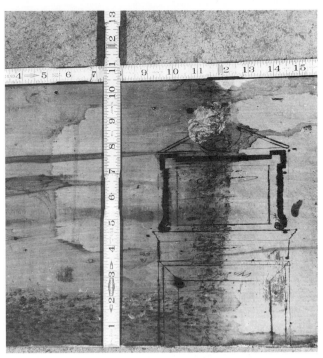

*The two 18th-century drawings reproduced here were discovered on the back of boards installed on the Belle Farm, Gloucester County, Virginia. One of them was incised with a knife or an awl; both were built essentially as drawn. It is reasonable to conclude that the same callused hands that worked the wood also executed the drawings. (*The Eighteenth-Century Houses of Williamsburg, *by Marcus Whitten; rev. ed. 1984, pp. 42 and 43. The Colonial Williamsburg Foundation, Williamsburg, VA.)*

plexity and tolerances of the job. Sometimes I put together detailed drawings at home before I go to the job; other times, I draw the job full scale on the floor where it will be built. But in many cases, a simple, freehand sketch on a scrap of wood is all I need. Whichever kind of graphic representation you use, the goal is the same: You want to see, understand, and show clearly to others what will be built.

Drawing has long been an essential part of building (see the photos above). Historians have identified the plan of a group of dwellings on a wall painting that dates back before 6000 B.C. (about 2,500 years before the invention of the wheel). They have documented the existence of architects prior to 2000 B.C. and know the names of many of the architects who designed the pyramids of Egypt and the temples of Greece and Rome.

It's easy to see why drawing has always been so intimately connected to the art and business of building. For one thing, drawing is an inexpensive way to experiment and create. Completed drawings can be reviewed by the interested parties—owners, inspectors, builders, special trade contractors, and bankers—who can then revise the plan with a pencil and an eraser, a process that is infinitely preferable to the sledgehammer and reciprocating saw that must be used later. Because they depict what will be built far better than words can, drawings are the centerpiece of most building contracts. They are also a vital part of books like this one.

The act of drawing serves as a warm-up period for craftsmen, a time to become familiar with the job at hand and, hopefully, to spot and revise awkward or unworkable details. Unfortunately, in this day and age, craftsmen generally do not draw as well or as often as our pre-decessors did. The fact is we don't have to. Much of what we build and install today has been designed and manufactured by others. Yet, to paraphrase Mark Twain, rumors of the demise of drawing have been greatly ex-aggerated. In the shop and on the job site, a drawing is a formidable—sometimes indispensable—layout tool. In many circumstances, drawing is a vital part of both the business and craft of building. It protects craftsmen and their clients from misunderstandings and keeps crafts-men in the thick of the creative process.

Work with full-scale layouts

Although a drawing or sketch is just about essential for some jobs, it isn't the only way to visualize a project. For example, to lay shingles, roofers rarely need to make a drawing or even look at a blueprint. However, by laying out the job full scale on the roof deck, they can make sure they end up with straight, even courses. Instead of a drawing, roofers use a full-scale layout to review the job before beginning the installation.

Of course, it isn't always possible to lay out right at the point of installation. Frame carpenters sometimes lay out rafters or stair stringers full scale right on the ply-wood deck of a house. In doing so, they can review their work and be satisfied that it is correct before cutting into expensive lumber.

Sometimes the best way to see the layout and thus make sure that it will work is to use the material itself. Brick-layers and tilesetters, for instance, frequently lay out their units dry and establish the proper spacing before installing them with cement. This "dry run" is usually faster and more accurate than using a ruler.

See the finished job

Few things are more frustrating for craftsmen than to do first-class work all the way through a job, only to find at the last minute that they forgot to allow for a piece of trim, the thickness of a mortar joint, or another small detail. Seemingly insignificant things like drywall, un-

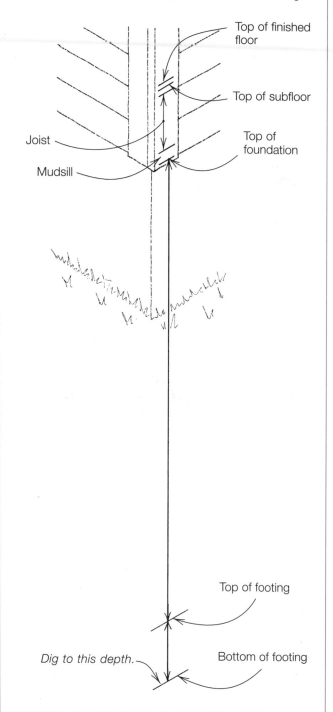

Laying Out Details before Digging

Before digging the footing for an addition, mark on the exterior of the existing house the required finished floor elevation. Then draw the framing details of the addition and use them to determine the proper overall height of the foundation and the starting elevation for the footing.

Top of finished floor

Top of subfloor

Top of foundation

Joist

Mudsill

Top of footing

Bottom of footing

Dig to this depth.

derlayment, and trim details pile up, raising the level of floors and enclosing openings. When this buildup goes unnoticed, unpleasant surprises can follow: A cabinet might not fit in a given space, a staircase might end up with an odd-size riser, or a roof might not overlap the final trim along a gable. It's very important to include small details in drawings, sketches, and full-scale layouts, even when they don't seem to be directly related to the job at hand.

Before I begin digging the footing for the foundation of an addition, for example, I draw a detailed elevation directly on the side of the existing house. This sketch typically indicates the exact height of the finished floor, the thickness of both the finished floor and the subfloor, and the sizes of the floor joists and mudsills (see the drawing on the facing page). After figuring out where the top of the foundation should be, I measure down to determine where the top of the footing should be. After accounting for all of the details, I begin digging.

In this and most other layout tasks, it's important to see the finished product and work back from that point. Because it is often necessary to look far ahead and anticipate in detail the finished project, the builder has to do some groundwork before plunging into the job.

The first task is to get the pertinent information. This often means nailing down the homeowner or architect as to precisely what the job entails, then calling suppliers or subcontractors to confirm the exact dimensions of those materials. The second task is to remember to allow for those items. From painful experience, I can attest that small details are easy to forget, and so I rarely try to "keep in mind" the many items that go into a project. I am much more comfortable when I can see them in tangible reminders, such as drawings, detailed layouts, story poles, or in some cases, actual mockups. The very process of making these reminders helps me keep the details firmly in mind.

WORK FROM CRITICAL TO NONCRITICAL DIMENSIONS

About ten years ago, my youngest brother built a brick walkway behind my parents' house. The walkway connected a patio with a storage shed and had to curve around a heat pump. Working freehand, he built a graceful S-shaped walkway. Unfortunately, it missed landing square with the door of the shed by about 3 in. An experienced craftsman most certainly would have started at the door of the shed, where precise alignment was visually critical. By working toward the patio, where the walkway could have landed several inches one way or the other without looking bad, he would have avoided the mistake my brother made.

The success or failure of a design often hinges on the craftsman's ability to recognize and then achieve critical dimensions. This is not always an aesthetic matter. Sometimes dimensions are critical for quite mundane reasons. A bathroom tub surround, for example, has to be 60 in. wide to accommodate a standard tub. When I lay out the walls for a house or an addition, therefore, I start with the bathroom, making sure there is sufficient room for the tub-surround framing. If ½ in. has to be lost, I'd much rather lose it in the living room or a bedroom, where it isn't critical.

Dimensions can be critical for other reasons as well. Knowing and satisfying the requirements set forth in the building code is absolutely essential. Once in a while, customers have special requests (making sure a piece of furniture will fit in a given space, for instance). Recognizing and sticking to critical dimensions is also an essential part of being a proficient craftsman. For example, laying out masonry so that it results in full, uncut bricks not only makes that job look better but also makes it go faster. In fact, most building tasks have multiple critical dimensions (see the drawing on p. 8).

AVOID CUMULATIVE ERROR

When laying out the frame of a house, carpenters routinely pull a steel tape measure from one end and mark every 16 in. or 24 in. (the standard framing increments). They do this rather than stepping off measurements using a framing square or a spacing block, even when these other methods might be safer and more convenient. The reason for this is simple. Prudent carpenters are concerned about cumulative error.

Working from Critical to Noncritical Dimensions

Dimensions can be critical for visual, functional, and safety issues. A fireplace, for example, needs to be built to the proper dimensions to function well. The positions of adjacent windows and shelving in the room are also important.

Critical dimensions

1. Fireplace centered in room: visually critical
2. Carefully dimensioned firebox, throat, smoke chamber, and flue: critical for proper functioning of fireplace
3. Sufficient clearance to combustibles: critical for safety and code compliance
4. Even brickwork: critical for productivity and visual appeal
5. Windows centered between fireplace profile and corner: visually critical
6. Large lower shelf to accommodate large books: critical to comply with special request from homeowner

In laying out the top plate of a wall, for example, it would seem logical to cut a block of wood at 14½ in. to space rafters (which are 1½ in. thick) 16 in. on center (o.c.). In many cases, this would certainly be easier than climbing up on a wall and pulling a tape measure. The problem with using a spacing block, however, is that if its length is just ¹⁄₁₆ in. too long, the layout will end up with a cumulative error: It will grow by 1 in. over 21 ft.

Another problem with using a spacing block might be the exact thickness of the rafters. If humidity has been high, the rafters could be as thick as 1⅝ in., which would cause the layout to grow by 1 in. in just 10 ft. Let's say further that one of the rafters has a lump or a burr where the spacing block engages it. If either of these goes unnoticed, it would push everything ahead

of it out of whack. In this day and age, when house frames are covered inside and out with precisely dimensioned sheets of sheathing and drywall, a cumulative error of 1 in. can be a major headache. To avoid it, frame carpenters measure once from a single fixed reference point rather than measuring numerous times from several different reference points.

The standard framing increments of 16 in. and 24 in. are highlighted on most tape measures, either by red boxes, arrows, or some other easily seen reminder. Many of the other increments that craftsmen work with vary from job to job. There is no such thing as a standard stair-riser dimension, for example. Whether working with these custom increments or the standard increments, there is the same basic concern: that a small error consistently repeated can multiply into a significant error. In subsequent chapters I'll take a closer look at how craftsmen use spacing rulers, dividers, calculators, and common sense to control this "growing" problem. I will also show you how craftsmen can tame this beast and use cumulative gain or loss to their advantage.

WORK WITHIN PRACTICAL TOLERANCES

As I write this, I am working on an addition in which the architect has specified the center of a kitchen window to be 2 ft. $8^{11}/_{16}$ in. from the outside corner of the house. I find this to be somewhat amusing. Even if, by some miracle, I had been able to build the foundation within a $^1/_{16}$ in. tolerance and had managed to create an opening precisely where it was specified, there is no guarantee that these things would stay that way. Building materials, particularly wood, shrink and expand, and the frame carpenter who needlessly worries about $^1/_{16}$ in. torments both himself and those around him.

Let's pretend that somehow I built the perfect foundation and window opening and that the framing remained absolutely stable. If the window isn't perfectly square, finding the center within $^1/_{16}$ in. will prove impossible anyway. And, the truth is, as I hang a window, my primary concerns are not to drop it, that it operates properly, and that it looks good in relation to the nearest other window once it's in place. If the center of the window is still 2 ft. $8^{11}/_{16}$ in. from the outside corner after installation, it is due only to divine intervention. But let's pretend a little further and say that, miraculously, the window is centered exactly according to plan. How will that 2-ft. $8^{11}/_{16}$-in. center change once the corner is covered, inside and out, with finishing materials?

Builders—at least those who wish to remain sane and financially solvent—have to work within practical tolerances. Once in a while, $^1/_{16}$ in. or even $^1/_{32}$ in. is significant; it can cause a door to stick, for example. For most residential construction, however, $^1/_{16}$ in. is meaningless. The anguished soul who should have been a machinist but ended up as a carpenter deserves our pity.

Building materials are selected and produced for their strength, their beauty, and their ability to withstand the environmental insults that Mother Nature hurls at them. They are large, heavy, and—compared to most of the goods produced by our industrialized economy— unstable and imprecise. They shouldn't be treated like the gears of a watch. Part of being a builder is adjusting to imperfect conditions and knowing when $^1/_{16}$ in. does or doesn't matter. Make compromises, "split the difference" between perfection and affordability, and learn how to make something that is neither perfectly uniform nor absolutely straight look crisp and neat. Fooling the eye is a big part of being a builder.

READJUST AND STRAIGHTEN OUT PERIODICALLY

One of the most gratifying things about building homes for a living is that you begin afresh with each new project. Indeed, builders usually have the opportunity to start over several times during the same project. The foundation crew pours 80,000 lb. of concrete and ends up with a structure that is, remarkably, just $^3/_4$ in. out of square and $^1/_2$ in. out of level. By using shims and hanging the floor slightly over one side, the framing crew can build a floor that for all practical purposes is square and level. As the frame goes up, the carpenters use strings and chalklines again and again to straighten out walls, line up ridge beams, and cut crisp, straight eaves.

Still, somehow, the frame is never quite perfect, and when tilesetters, trim carpenters, roofers, siders, and others arrive, they too have to strike new lines and start over (see the drawing on p. 10). These craftsmen have at least one thing in common: They don't assume that an earlier step has been done so perfectly that they can or should build off it. By striking a new baseline, they can leave prior mistakes and imperfections behind and work toward increasingly refined tolerances as they install the finished surfaces of the house.

THINK MODULARLY

In 1938, a group of forward-looking industrialists—now called The American Standards Institute—met to discuss the idea of modular coordination of building materials. The results of that initial meeting and a subsequent project to establish a standard modular format for construction materials have been far-reaching.

Today, homebuilders use a wide variety of materials that are divisible by 4 in., the base unit for modular coordination. In unit masonry, for example, two standard modular bricks with mortar joints are 16 in. long, the length of one concrete block with a mortar joint. The 8-in. height of three bricks with mortar joints, furthermore, equals the height of one block with a joint. Sheathing, drywall, and plywood are manufactured in 4-ft. widths and are usually 8 ft. long. As a result, joists, studs, trusses, and rafters are laid out in standard increments of 16 in. or 24 in.

Many building practices, which have been standardized in building codes, follow the 4-in. format (see the drawing on the facing page). A concrete footing in my area, for instance, must be 8 in. thick and 16 in. wide (to carry an 8-in.-thick foundation). Under a chimney, a footing must be 12 in. thick. The standard thickness for a concrete slab is 4 in. The standard height of a door is 80 in.; the standard floor-to-ceiling height is 96 in.; the tops of wall cabinets are usually 84 in.; and so on.

Modular coordination offers several benefits to those in the building trades—including savings in time and materials—because pieces fit better. Critical dimensions are easier to remember (multiples of four) and work with, and it lends a degree of order and predictability to a process that tends toward chaos. While many craftsmen take it for granted, modular coordination is now an integral part of residential construction, and they need to think in terms of these modules when laying out their work.

LOOK FOR SIMPLE SOLUTIONS

Builders have to make an untold number of tactical decisions as they assemble and install the materials that make up a house. These decisions can become complex issues that involve precise measuring devices, but this isn't always necessary. Invariably, the simple and tangible solution is the best one.

To figure out the angle of the top cut for a shed roof, for example, carpenters don't need to employ geometric calculations. They can simply hold the rafter in place and, using a scrap of wood, scribe the angle (see the top drawing on p. 12). Experienced builders use a variety of similar techniques to simplify the process of measuring and marking. Instead of taking a measurement and then transferring that measurement to the material, craftsmen routinely hold the material in place and mark it directly. Or they run things long, then cut them in place. They use dividers, bevel squares, and scraps of wood to transfer angles and shapes without ever knowing—or caring about—the underlying geometric relationships.

One of the most effective ways to simplify a measuring and marking task is to break it down into separate components. Sometimes this simply means doing one thing at a time. To lay out a foundation, for example, builders often first set up batter boards with a builder's level to

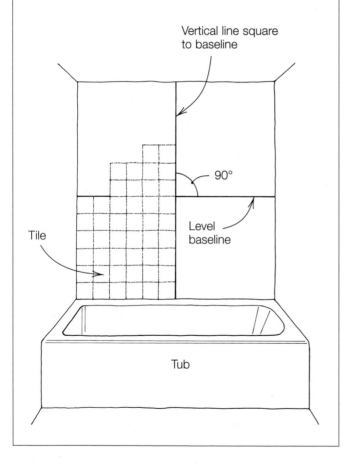

Readjusting and Straightening

Professional tilesetters don't assume that a tub has been set perfectly level. They establish a new level horizontal baseline and a plumb vertical baseline before doing their layout. This process of checking and reestablishing level and plumb occurs over and over again in all construction trades.

Vertical line square to baseline

90°

Tile

Level baseline

Tub

Think Modularly

Most of today's construction materials and design specifications are based on the 4-in. module. Modular coordination makes the construction process more efficient and makes it easier to remember important dimensions, like the standard height of wall cabinets or the proper thickness and width of footings.

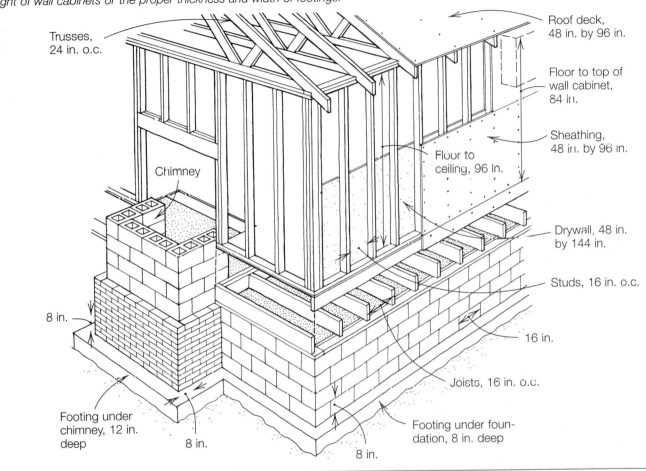

Trusses, 24 in. o.c.

Chimney

Roof deck, 48 in. by 96 in.

Floor to top of wall cabinet, 84 in.

Sheathing, 48 in. by 96 in.

Floor to ceiling, 96 in.

Drywall, 48 in. by 144 in.

Studs, 16 in. o.c.

16 in.

Joists, 16 in. o.c.

8 in.

Footing under chimney, 12 in. deep

8 in.

Footing under foundation, 8 in. deep

8 in.

establish a level plane. Then they use a tape measure and a calculator to lay out the corners and other linear measurements of the foundation.

Craftsmen cannot always do one thing at a time, however, and sometimes must deal with two or more things at once. Still, these complex tasks can often be thought through and laid out separately. The compound cuts needed for valley-jack rafters (the rafters running from the valley to the ridge beam), for instance, are made with one pass of the saw, but they are set up in two separate operations. The carpenter first lays out the miter with a straightedge and a pencil and then sets his saw

to get the correct bevel angle (see the bottom drawing on p. 12). As in other areas of life, the ability to break down complex problems into manageable components is a vital part of building. And the elegantly simple solution is often the mark of a seasoned craftsman.

WORK IN A LOGICAL SEQUENCE

For centuries, competent builders have understood the importance of doing things in their proper order. Sequence has a huge impact on quality and productivity and plays a major role in measuring and marking. Craftsmen sweat out and sometimes quarrel over the best possible sequence because a simple task can become

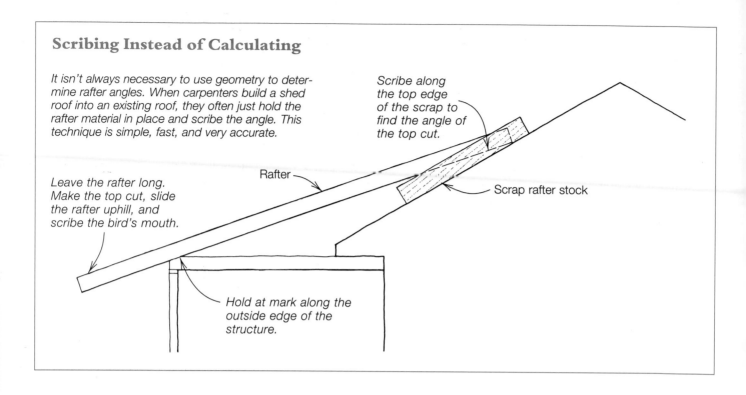

Scribing Instead of Calculating

It isn't always necessary to use geometry to determine rafter angles. When carpenters build a shed roof into an existing roof, they often just hold the rafter material in place and scribe the angle. This technique is simple, fast, and very accurate.

Scribe along the top edge of the scrap to find the angle of the top cut.

Rafter

Scrap rafter stock

Leave the rafter long. Make the top cut, slide the rafter uphill, and scribe the bird's mouth.

Hold at mark along the outside edge of the structure.

difficult if it is done out of order. Take, for example, the case of a stonemason and a drywall contractor. If the stonemason lays up the profile of a fireplace before the drywall is hung, the drywall contractor must painstakingly measure and fit the drywall around the irregular edges of the stonework. If the drywall contractor goes first, on the other hand, the stonemason can easily overlap the drywall by a few inches to get a nice, finished joint (see the drawing on the facing page).

Sequence is not just a factor in scheduling the various trades. It is also an important consideration within individual trades. Carpenters, in particular, have to worry about the order in which they carry out tasks. They often build one section of a job, then measure off that section to lay out the next. For example, when adding a gable roof onto an existing roof, I first set the addition's trusses or common rafters (see the drawing on p. 14). Then I extend through that structure with a straightedge (or stringline) to locate the valley (see Chapter 6 for more on roof framing).

Sequence can be nudged or tweaked slightly, but it shouldn't be ignored. Charging forward without paying due respect to sequence often costs impatient builders

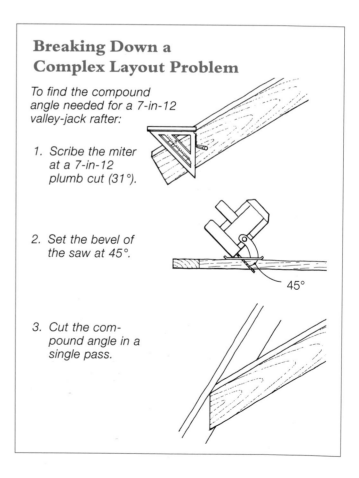

Breaking Down a Complex Layout Problem

To find the compound angle needed for a 7-in-12 valley-jack rafter:

1. Scribe the miter at a 7-in-12 plumb cut (31°).

2. Set the bevel of the saw at 45°.

45°

3. Cut the compound angle in a single pass.

more money correcting mistakes and usually results in a ragged-looking job.

BE CONSISTENT

One of the easiest ways to work efficiently and avoid mistakes is to do things consistently. For people who produce things for a living, consistency plays a vital part in everything from brewing beer to serving up a predictable burger to making reliable mortar. For builders, consistency is both a means and an end. It is a means because working in familiar patterns reduces confusion, speeds up production, improves quality, and above all, helps avoid mistakes.

For example, I've learned the hard way to work consistently in inches. On more occasions than I care to remember, I've looked at a plan with a window opening specified at, say, 3 ft. 4 in. and proceeded to build it at 34 in. As a result of this mental lapse, of course, I would have to revise my neat and orderly frame with a saw, a hammer, and a prybar. This process not only tends to ruin the looks of my frame but also has an equally dis-

agreeable effect on my sense of humor. Now, when I take possession of a floor plan or a window specification chart, I immediately cross out the foot-and-inch designations and convert them to inches only.

In a similar vein, I follow a strict routine when I lay out three-tab roof shingles. For reasons that will be discussed in detail in Chapter 9, I always mark the horizontal lines in increments divisible by 10 in. I have routines for finding the center of any given span, for estimating concrete, and for figuring the total rise for a staircase. The procedures I habitually follow aren't mindless rituals; instead, they are calculated efforts to avoid mindless mistakes.

Consistency not only reduces confusion and moves the job along smoothly, but it is also one of the most sought-after goals of craftsmen. Even courses, consistent grout joints, and precisely matched stair risers are hallmarks of fine workmanship. There are, of course, those who admire randomly placed bricks and deliberately wavy courses of shingles. Their point of view raises im-

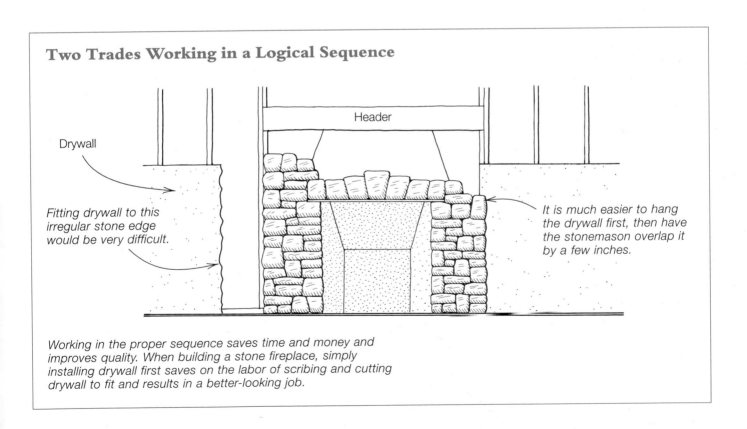

Two Trades Working in a Logical Sequence

Drywall

Header

Fitting drywall to this irregular stone edge would be very difficult.

It is much easier to hang the drywall first, then have the stonemason overlap it by a few inches.

Working in the proper sequence saves time and money and improves quality. When building a stone fireplace, simply installing drywall first saves on the labor of scribing and cutting drywall to fit and results in a better-looking job.

Locating Valleys for a Gable Roof Addition

Laying out the complex angles of an addition roof can be a thorny problem, but working in a logical sequence simplifies it. Installing the new ridge beam and common rafters first is relatively straightforward and makes it easier to find the location of the valleys where the new and old roof connect.

To locate the valley:
1. *Install a level ridge beam.*
2. *Install the common rafters.*
3. *Extend through the rafters with a straightedge (or string) and mark the valley.*

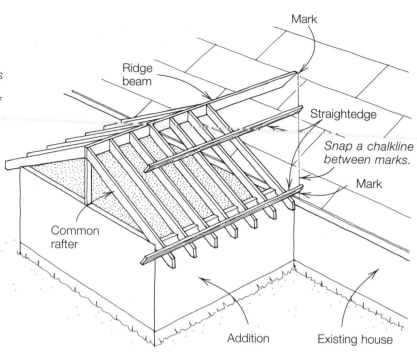

Mark

Ridge beam

Straightedge

Snap a chalkline between marks.

Mark

Common rafter

Addition

Existing house

---

portant questions in a book like this one. Why do we worry about straight lines and consistent, even courses (see the sidebar on the facing page)?

There's no easy answer. In many cases, neat work simply makes economic sense because it speeds up efficiency and production. In some cases, it touches on safety issues. To be safe, stairs need to be as consistent and predictable as possible, so stairbuilders work within a narrow range of acceptable riser and tread dimensions. Their driving force is precision rather than creativity.

Along similar lines, doors must be precisely installed so that they don't stick, since few people consider doors that work improperly to be serendipitous or charming in any way. On the exterior of a house, materials should fit together tightly, not just because of appearance but also because tight joints keep weather and insects out of the building. On the inside, tight joints keep crud and vermin from collecting and make the day-to-day functioning of the household smoother and safer. Yet, in some cases, the primary reason we install our materials

in neat, straight lines is simply because our customers like the way it looks.

LEARN FROM YOUR MISTAKES

There's one thing I hate to see done consistently on a construction site: the same mistake made over and over again. Strange as it may seem, I've known many hardworking individuals who have made the same mistakes year after year for 20 or 30 years. Consistency means approaching a job in an orderly, deliberate fashion. It doesn't mean slavishly repeating a technique learned when a person is a teenager, especially if the technique is flawed.

There is a saying that a house is a work in progress, meaning that modifications, repairs, and maintenance continue throughout the life of the house. In a similar vein, the people who build and repair houses should be works in progress, perpetual students who continue to learn until the day they lay down their tools for good. Those content with C-minus workmanship and those not interested in learning new and better tech-

Why All the Fuss about Straight Lines and Right Angles?

We ask a lot of houses. They have to be structurally sound and be an effective barrier against the weather, insects, and other uninvited guests from the outdoors. They also need to be durable, safe, and convenient for their human occupants, as well as pleasant to look at and be in. They should be all these things and still be affordable. The shortest route to this difficult and multilayered goal is the straight line, which is why the vast majority of houses are dominated by straight lines and right angles. The inescapable fact is that a house goes together faster and better—and with less expense—when the designers stick to the right angle and when builders take the time to use a line or a straightedge.

One of the reasons that this is so is because, overwhelmingly, building materials themselves are rectangular in shape. It's easy to see why: rectangles are efficient (thus, economical) to manufacture and transport. Bricks, blocks, boards, plywood, drywall, and a host of other building materials arrive at the job site with four square corners. And the materials, of course, affect how houses are built. As a house goes up, builders try to keep things straight and square so that the structure will conform to the straight and square edges of the materials that will be installed in succeeding stages. There is economy in square foundations and straight eaves because the plywood that will cover them is straight and square.

Not surprisingly, people sometimes rebel against the tyranny of the right angle. Curves, arches, and angles other than the tired, old 90° angle break up the monotony and provide for individual expression. Sometimes courses are deliberately made wavy or jagged and rough. Sometimes materials are left unfinished to celebrate their natural beauty (or simply to vent an architectural primal scream).

Yet, because the straight line is the fastest route to building economy, many of these organic, rustic, or otherwise unorthodox treatments occur mainly on the surface of the building. The structural and working parts of these unusual houses are rarely very different from conventional houses and are built using the same basic principles.

But setting aside the stringline and the straightedge doesn't mean that consistency and craftsmanship should also be cast aside. Joints still need to be tight for practical reasons, and even randomness must be consistent. Wavy siding, for example, will not look good unless it is consistently wavy. One section that is noticeably straighter than the rest of the house will stand out like a sore thumb. Ironically, houses that are meant to look spontaneous often require more work and more planning than houses designed to look as if no detail were overlooked.

niques never really become craftsmen. Unfortunately, they miss out on some of the most fulfilling parts of the profession: the quiet confidence gained from taking on challenging problems and finding elegant solutions; the simple pleasure of discovering a new tool or technique; the deep satisfaction that results from doing a job really well.

Craftsmen develop and improve by reviewing the work of their own and of others, looking for mistakes and correcting them. Other craftsmen are great sources of information, and most are proud of their techniques and more than happy to discuss them with anyone who shows interest. Even craftsmen who don't have the time or inclination to explain what they are doing can be a rich source of information. It's often possible to learn simply by watching them carefully as they work.

At the end of a job, take a look at the areas where things could have gone more smoothly. Not infrequently, the problems—and the solutions—lay in the layout or in the way measurements were taken and transferred.

Chapter 2
PLUMBING, LEVELING, AND MEASURING

TOOLS FOR MAKING THE JOB PLUMB AND LEVEL

TOOLS FOR TAKING AND TRANSFERRING LINEAR MEASUREMENTS

MEASURING AND MARKING TECHNIQUES

On today's construction sites, electronic measuring devices share space with measuring tools that would have been familiar to Socrates (who earned a living as a stonecutter, by the way). Craftsmen continue to use tools that date back thousands of years because those tools continue to be effective. After 5,000 years of snapping a line, the only difference between today's technique and that of the Egyptians is the material used to coat the string. The Egyptians used wet red or yellow ochre. Like the Greeks, we use chalk.

Tools like the chalkline will probably never be replaced because they are inexpensive, uncomplicated, and get the job done. But there have also been countless refinements of old tools and the invention of many new ones through the centuries as well. While not all of these innovations have been successful, many of them are incredibly clever and effective, and there is a place for both kinds of tools. Builders face a wide range of problems that can best be solved by using a combination of the simple and complex, the old and the new.

When masons arrive to lay out a foundation, for example, they might use a transit, which is a combination of the theodolite (a precise base with increments representing the degrees of both a horizontal and vertical circle), the telescope, and the spirit level. These were all invented between 1570 and 1670 and combined into a surveying instrument shortly thereafter. The masons would also probably use a stringline and a plumb bob, which both go back at least to the Egyptians. To calculate the diagonal of the building (to ensure squareness), they could use the tables on a metal rafter square (developed in the mid-19th century) or a handheld calculator (first available in the 1970s). The geometry compiled on the tables and stored in the calculator was devised in the 6th century B.C. by the ancient Greeks, who inherited the 360° circle and much of their mathematics from the Babylonians. For linear measurements, the masons would undoubtedly use a steel tape measure (first produced in the United States in the 1890s) and might find it convenient to use a simple stick ruler (which goes back at least to the Sumerians) as well. It's no exaggeration to say that today's masons would have 50 centuries' worth of tools at their disposal.

When it comes to tools, this generation of craftsmen has an embarrassment of riches. We have scores of squares, levels, and tools for taking and transferring linear measurements, and they're often better and far less expensive than they were for preceding generations. While it would be impossible to discuss all of the measuring and marking tools on the market, I've selected what I consider to be the most important ones. With a few exceptions (which I indicate in the text), I own and regularly use all of the plumbing, leveling, and measuring tools discussed here.

TOOLS FOR MAKING THE JOB PLUMB AND LEVEL

Most builders get their first lesson in structural engineering well before their third birthday. As building tykes, we eventually learn that the way to overcome gravity is to stack our blocks up plumb. The life expectancy of buildings at this point in our careers is short—about 30 seconds—and we delight in the sudden catastrophic effect that gravity has on them. As adult builders, of course, we know that structural failure is no laughing matter. As most of us would agree, gravity is a very serious concern. It's important to build structures that are both plumb and level.

Plumb bob

Gravity is not just a structural concern. It also affects how a building looks and feels, how water flows, and how things like doors operate. Fortunately, builders have been able to measure the precise direction of gravity's pull—called plumb—for thousands of years (the word plumb comes from the Latin *plumbum*, which means lead). They've done this in an elegantly simple

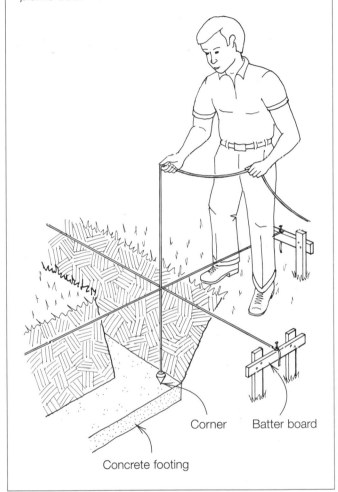

Marking a Foundation Corner

After establishing the corner of a foundation using stringlines attached to batter boards, you can transfer the layout vertically to the concrete footing using a plumb bob.

Corner   Batter board

Concrete footing

manner: by attaching a weight to a length of string. The first plumb bobs were made of stone, but by 2680 B.C., Egyptian builders were using lead bobs. Almost 3,000 years later, the Romans were still using lead bobs.

A very simple and accurate tool, the plumb bob just isn't used as much as it should be today. Aside from its great accuracy, it has two distinct advantages over its closest rival, the spirit level. First, a hanging plumb bob is

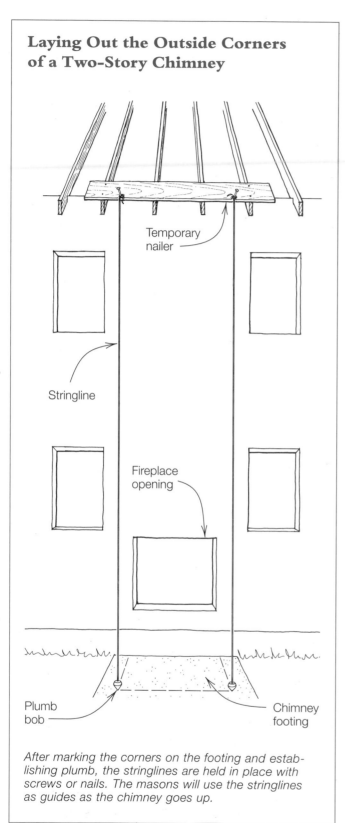

Laying Out the Outside Corners of a Two-Story Chimney

Temporary nailer

Stringline

Fireplace opening

Plumb bob

Chimney footing

After marking the corners on the footing and establishing plumb, the stringlines are held in place with screws or nails. The masons will use the stringlines as guides as the chimney goes up.

plumb from all directions, while a spirit level can measure plumb from just one direction at a time. The ability to establish plumb from all directions at once is particularly useful for marking the corner of a foundation. With a level, you would have to plumb down from each stringline, but with a plumb bob, you can simply plumb down from the intersection (see the drawing on p. 17).

The second advantage of the plumb bob is that it can be used for much longer distances than the spirit level. By using a straightedge, a spirit level's useful range can be extended, perhaps, to 18 ft. But with a plumb bob, it's easy to plumb down 25 ft. or more. Because a plumb bob is accurate over such long distances and shows plumb from both sides of a corner at the same time, masons use it to establish the outside corners of a two-story chimney (see the drawing at left).

The main drawback of the plumb bob is that it needs to be held from above. Because of this, the plumb bob is more commonly used by surveying and foundation crews, who frequently transfer plumb measurements down, than it is by frame carpenters, who generally measure and build from the foundation up. For carpenters, the plumb bob is not very useful until after much of the framing is in place. But I think the tool gathers a lot of undeserved dust on modern construction sites.

I've heard carpenters complain both about the difficulty of holding the bob in place and about the time it takes to get the bob to stop moving, particularly if there's any wind. But these problems can be mitigated with a good, heavy bob, braided string (which spins and stretches less than the twisted kind), and a few minutes of preparation. For outdoor use, where an occasional breeze can be expected, a 16-oz. or heavier bob is necessary, particularly when plumbing down more than 8 ft. You can overcome the problem of holding the bob steady by devising some mechanical means of holding it. I use a small eyebolt or a nail to hold the string, and I rig up a simple cleat with two nails to tie the string off once the bob is lowered into position.

To keep a plumb bob from acting like a pendulum, first steady it near the top, then slowly lower it into place (see the drawings on the facing page). Tie the string off to a cleat, leave the bob, and do something else as it comes to a standstill. There's no need to wait for the bob

employed a plumb bob at the end of each arm (see the left drawing below).

The plumb-bob level reached its zenith with the invention of the theodolite (ca. 1570), which provided for precise measurement of angles in both the horizontal and vertical planes (see the right drawing below). Ironically, this ingenious building device was first used to help artillery crews find the range to castles and other fortified buildings and destroy them.

Roman sight level

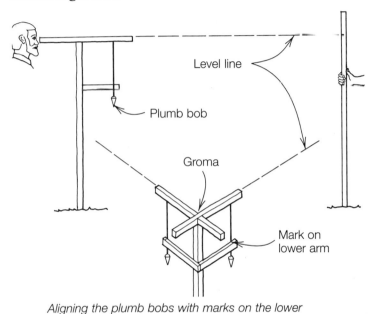

Aligning the plumb bobs with marks on the lower arms levels the instrument.

16th-century theodolite

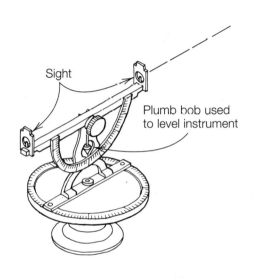

Though the theodolite lacked a spirit vial for leveling and a telescopic sight, it otherwise functioned like a modern transit.

And in contrast to the delicate process by which a plumb bob is coaxed to a standstill, the level can be tapped, pulled, or pushed into place yet still provide an instant reading. Because the level is rectangular in shape, moreover, it is compatible with the rectangular materials that dominate building sites. This means that a level can be used to straighten out rows of bricks or can be set snug against a wall as it's braced. It can also sometimes be temporarily clamped to the material, leaving both hands free for other tasks.

The main shortcoming of the spirit level is that it is short. For the larger leveling tasks of construction work, such as leveling the top of a foundation, some means must be found to extend the level's reach. Up to a certain point, this can be accomplished by resting a spirit level on a longer straightedge—a straight board, for instance. While this works tolerably well for distances up to 16 ft., what do you do when you have to lay out a structure that will be 40 ft., 60 ft., or even 75 ft. long? Fortunately, a level line can be extended over such long distances in at least three ways (see the drawings on p. 22): the sight level, transit level, and laser level (for alternatives to these tools, see the sidebar on p. 23).

Sight level

The first method of leveling over a long distance is to simply sight down the top edge of the level or (the more accurate method) peer through a peep hole drilled horizontally down the length of the level. The sight level, as it is called, was commonly used well into the first part of this century, often mounted on a tripod and equipped with a leveling screw for making fine adjustments.

Using a sight level is a little like aiming a rifle, and its accuracy is limited by the eyesight of the person looking down or through the level. It also requires a coworker to mark precisely where you see the level pointed.

Transit

The second way to level over an extended distance is a refinement of the sight level. Affixing a telescope that is exactly in line with the level provides a very exact and controlled level for distances exceeding 75 ft.

In the 1570s, before the invention of either the spirit level or the telescope, inventors developed the theodolite. Artillerists used this instrument to help calculate the range of their targets. Combined later with the spirit level and the telescope, the theodolite has become the modern surveying instrument commonly called a transit. However, because of its expense, the instrument was

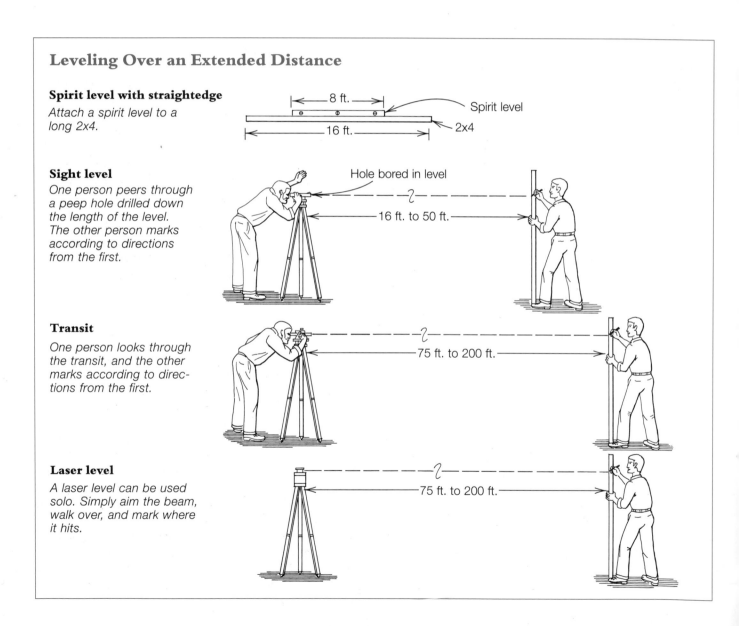

Leveling Over an Extended Distance

Spirit level with straightedge

Attach a spirit level to a long 2x4.

8 ft.

Spirit level

16 ft.

2x4

Sight level

One person peers through a peep hole drilled down the length of the level. The other person marks according to directions from the first.

Hole bored in level

16 ft. to 50 ft.

Transit

One person looks through the transit, and the other marks according to directions from the first.

75 ft. to 200 ft.

Laser level

A laser level can be used solo. Simply aim the beam, walk over, and mark where it hits.

75 ft. to 200 ft.

not widely available to most builders until this century. Generally speaking, a telescopic instrument that swivels horizontally but does not tilt is called a builder's (or dumpy) level, while an instrument that swivels horizontally and tilts vertically is called a transit. (An expensive, high-quality transit is often called a theodolite.)

Like the sight level, the transit is usually mounted on a tripod and leveled with adjusting screws, but it's more accurate and has a longer range than a sight level (see the drawings on p. 24). To use a transit, look through the scope (it has crosshairs like the scope of a rifle) and have a coworker mark in response to your commands.

A transit mounted in a level position on a tripod can rotate 360° and thus provide what amounts to a level plane. It can also be tilted up and down and thus provide a plumb plane. On many instruments, furthermore, the swiveling base is divided into precise gradations that represent the degrees of a circle. This means

Alternative Leveling Tools

Several alternatives to the spirit level, the transit, and the laser level deserve mention. The bull's-eye level is an obscure type in which a bubble is floated in a bowl-shaped vial to indicate level in all directions. The only time I've dealt with one of these was when it was mounted on a transit that belonged to someone else. I found it difficult to adjust, perhaps because of my inexperience using it. Invented in 1777, its lack of presence on construction sites may say something about the practical worth of the bull's-eye level.

Another more technologically advanced alternative to the spirit level is the digital level. Like the spirit level, the digital level uses a liquid to determine level. But unlike the spirit level, it uses a microprocessor to "read" the bubble and digitally display the results. A big advantage to this type of level is that it not only indicates level but also how far out of level it is (in either degrees or pitch). In other words, a digital level could be placed on a roof to determine

its pitch. I don't own a digital level, but it does seem to offer some practical advantages. Digital levels are expensive, though, and I can't help but wonder how well their electronics will hold up in the day-to-day punishment of construction work.

The line level is basically a small, lightweight spirit level vial with clips attached directly to a stringline. This setup is just about worthless, though, because the level makes the stringline sag and gives unreliable readings.

Another alternative, called a Locke level, looks like a spyglass. As you look through it, you can see the leveling vial and thus know when you're holding it level. Taking several readings from the same spot can get you a rough idea of how the land is sloping. Requiring virtually no setup, a Locke level is often used by excavators, though the instrument doesn't provide the kind of precision that masons and carpenters generally need.

Finally, there is the hose or water level. The first written reference to this tool occurred in 1629, a generation before the spirit level was invented, but it didn't become a practical tool until the development of vulcanized rubber in the 1830s. The water level operates on the principle that water always seeks its own level. By either attaching glass tubes at the ends of the hose or using a clear hose, you can see and mark the level of the water, which will always be equal at both ends.

Some water levels have a reservoir at one end, making them practical for one-man operation. And unlike other kinds of levels, a water level can easily level around corners or through small openings in a wall, making it a good choice for interior work. The water level has many staunch defenders because it is inexpensive and reliable. I've found this instrument to be time-consuming to set up and adjust, though, and prefer my transit and laser level.

you can shoot the instrument in one direction, mark a straight line, then turn the instrument exactly 90° and establish a right angle. The pivot that allows transits to tilt up and down is also frequently fitted with precise gradations. By locking the transit at a slight incline, workers can use it to maintain a precise grade when installing things like storm drains.

Do you need an expensive transit? Maybe not; in 20 years, I've had very few occasions to use the tilting mechanism in mine, and a less-expensive builder's level would probably have been sufficient.

Laser level

The third way to level over an extended distance is to affix a device that emits a laser beam that travels in a level line. The greatest advantage of a laser level is that it isn't necessary to work with a second person. The person aiming one can simply walk over and mark where the beam hits.

A laser level often has precisely positioned mirrors that deflect part of the laser beam at a 90° angle. Some laser levels shoot a beam that is split into 90° angles right, left, up, and down—all at the same time—while others come equipped with a motor that continuously rotates the beam, thus providing a level plane. This specialized laser level is commonly used by crews who install suspended ceilings in office buildings.

While recent innovations in laser technology have enhanced the performance of the basic transit, residential builders continue to prize most the ability of these instruments to shoot a level plane—the first and most important reference for the measuring and marking process. But, again, do you need an expensive instrument to do the job? I use my laser level, which has a leveling adapter plate and a tripod, exactly as I use my transit. The only difference is that I can operate the laser level without a second person, so if you do a lot of work by yourself, you might consider it.

Uses of a Transit and Laser Level

Level plane

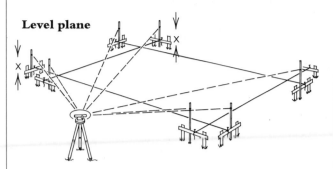

Rotating a transit or laser level horizontally establishes a level plane to measure against. Here, batter boards are set up at a distance x below the level plane.

Plumb plane

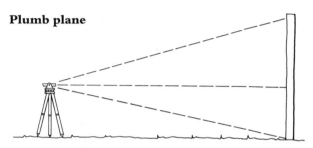

Tilting a leveled transit vertically establishes a plumb plane.

Right angle (plan view)

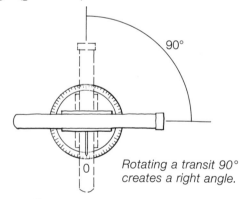

Rotating a transit 90° creates a right angle.

Consistent grade

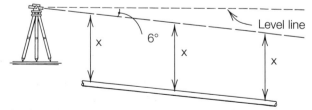

Locking the instrument at a slight incline will allow you to maintain a precise grade to measure against, useful for installing storm drains.

TOOLS FOR TAKING AND TRANSFERRING LINEAR MEASUREMENTS

The earliest known measuring standard, a half-cubit ruler, can be found in the lap of a statue of King Gudea of Sumeria (ca. 2050 B.C.). While the units on the ruler have varied from place to place and over time, the concept of the ruler—a basic straight stick divided into equal units—has remained the same. One of the few modifications to the ruler that I can think of was the inclusion of hinges so that it could be folded. This first occurred in Roman times, but the folding ruler was rare until the 18th century. The 6-ft. brass-tipped zigzag ruler that many carpenters are familiar with was first introduced in Stanley's 1900 catalog.

Because the divisions on rulers were painstakingly cut by hand far into the 19th century, rulers were expensive—and short. Prior to the Civil War, rulers were usually 2 ft. or less in length, far too short for many of the demands of house builders. Carpenters were expected to arrive on the job with a 10-ft. measuring rod, which was a straight strip of wood they carefully marked off with smaller rulers. For distances longer than 10 ft., carpenters either stepped off their measurements with their 10-ft. sticks or marked the distance with a rope or chain, later using their measuring stick to determine the length. To measure distances, today's carpenters use rulers, measuring sticks, as well as tape measures.

Rulers and measuring sticks

I've used the classic 6-ft. folding ruler for many years. It lies flat, so I can hold it with one hand while marking with the other. This has made it my tool of choice for laying out roofing or siding courses and for certain framing layout chores.

In recent years, however, I've regressed even further than the folding ruler, for I now use a straight ruler, the same basic tool the Sumerians used. My 24-in., 48-in., and 72-in. metal rulers are very handy around the job site, both for measuring and as straightedges, and they're especially useful when I'm working alone. The only problem with my rulers is that they are sometimes too short. So I do what colonial carpenters did: I make a measuring stick out of scrap lumber.

A measuring stick doesn't need to be fancy. I've found that a spare length of trim or 1x stock ripped to about 1½ in. works fine. A measuring stick can be made much longer than a ruler, of course, and its rigidity makes it handier than a tape measure for extending across open spaces or for vertical measurements.

There are numerous versions of the measuring stick. Some carpenters make or buy layout sticks, which are essentially horizontal story poles used for laying out things like wall plates. The rodman in a surveying crew holds another version of the measuring stick. Bricklayers use a marked corner pole, while siders often use a story pole. In addition to being stiff and easy to use, a measuring stick is really helpful for visualizing how small units—like tile, for example—will fit into a given space. Another nice feature of the measuring stick is that it can be customized by adding critical dimensions for the task it will be used for, like establishing the tops and bottoms of windows or lower and upper cabinets.

Tape measures

Manufactured tape measures, made first of fabric and later of steel, appeared late in the 19th century. It was only about 75 years ago that manufacturers began producing a "cross-curve" steel tape. The slight curve in the cross section of this type of tape measure gives it some rigidity when it's extended, yet it is still flexible enough to be rolled back into its case. Try to imagine a modern job site without any of these steel tape measures around.

There are good reasons for the tape measure's popularity. It's accurate, can measure long distances (some tapes measure an amazing 500 ft.), and can be quickly rolled up into a compact container. To lay out a foundation, I like to use a 100-ft. flat tape laid out in the decimalized feet of an engineer's scale. As you'll see in the next chapter, calculations used to square up a foundation frequently end up in a decimalized foot, and without a tape laid out in this scale, these numbers would have to be converted into feet and inches. For most other applications, though, a standard tape measure laid out in feet and inches is the most popular and versatile tool (three ways to measure distance are shown in the left drawings on p. 26).

Three Ways to Measure Distance

Traditional ruler

The traditional U.S. measuring system divides feet into twelfths, or inches, and divides inches into sixteenths.

Engineer's scale

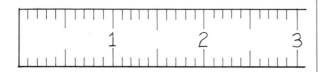

The engineer's scale divides feet into hundredths in an effort to bring the inch-foot measuring system in line with decimally organized arithmetic.

International system (metric)

Metric units are integrated in a decimal format (see the sidebar on the facing page).

A Hook That Adjusts

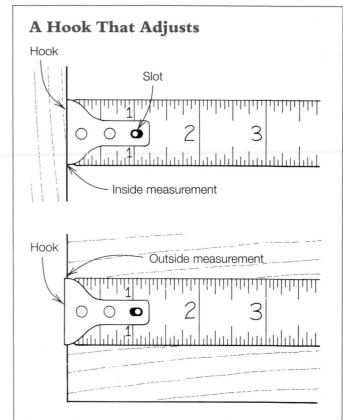

The hooks of most cross-curve steel tape measures are attached with rivets through slots instead of holes. This feature allows the hook to slide in or out to compensate for the thickness of the hook when taking either inside or outside measurements.

A 1-in.-wide, 25-ft. or 30-ft. steel cross-curve tape measure can be seen on just about every toolbelt. The length-measuring workhorse of construction sites, this type of tape measure has a hooked end that makes it easy for one person to pull a measurement. The hook is also designed to slide in slightly so that you can take an inside measurement (see the right drawings above). Simply butt the tape into a corner, then transfer the measurement by hooking the tape over the material.

The units on most cross-curve tape measures fit the needs of today's construction sites. Inches are listed con- tinuously (1 to 300 on a 25-ft. tape) so you can work in inches only. And 16-in. and 24-in. increments are high- lighted for the 16-in. and 24-in. on-center (o.c.) layout of studs, joists, and rafters. Foot and inch designations are typically included as well but are designed to recede slightly from the continuous-inch and 16-in. groupings. Some tape measures also have diamond-shaped marks at intervals of about 19¾₁₆ in., which are used to lay out trusses in heavy snow areas. Instead of the standard four trusses per 8 ft., this layout provides for five trusses per 8 ft. Some tape measures even have metric units, called the international system (for more on the metric sys- tem, see the sidebar on the facing page).

Although the cross-curve tape measure is the best over- all tool for taking and transferring linear measurements,

Inching Toward the Metric System

In the 1860s, there were about 150 different measuring systems used in the world. The two largest were the French metric system and the English imperial system, which (with a few minor differences) is the system the United States uses today. Now it is often called the U.S. Customary System.

Since that time, the rest of the world has overwhelmingly adopted the metric system (officially called the International System of Units). Today, the United States is the only large country to use the imperial system (the British jumped ship in 1965 and were followed soon after by the Canadians and Australians). U.S. scientists, doctors, and engineers have used metric measurements for decades, and in many industries, including the mammoth auto industry, conversion to metric is an accomplished fact. As of 1992, the single largest consumer in the United States, the federal government, has insisted that nearly everything it buys must come in metric units or containers.

Why has the world, including a large portion of the United States, moved relentlessly away from the customary measuring system? The honest answer is that it is replete with difficulties. There are two different tons, three ounces, two pints, and two quarts. The acre is an awkward 43,560 ft., the mile a forgettable 5,280 ft. In basic linear measurements, there are three incompatible systems at work. Arithmetic is decimally organized: Numbers are arranged in groups of ten and divided, using decimals, by tens. The primary unit of measurement, on the other hand, is grouped by twelves into feet but divided, by halving, into halves, eighths, quarters, sixteenths, and so forth. In contrast to the hodgepodge of our customary units, the metric system is the essence of simplicity and organization: All units and divisions of units are organized decimally (based on ten).

In 1866, when Great Britain was at the zenith of its power and influence, John Rabone, Jr., an English rule manufacturer, recognized the advantages of the metric system and predicted its approaching ascendancy. "Many nations," he observed, "now have a large proportion of their rules marked with the French metre, in addition to their own standard; thus, doubtless, gradually tending to the general adoption of so convenient and perfect a measure as the French metre is admitted to be." Will the meter ever rule U.S. construction sites? If past history is any indication, we can assume that sooner or later it will, for as Abraham Lincoln once said, "We cannot escape history." It is, perhaps, telling that history itself is organized decimally, by decades and centuries.

---

it does have a few liabilities. The hook and the curved cross section of the tape don't allow it to lie flat, which makes taking short, precise measurements awkward. Designed primarily to be hooked or held by another person and then pulled, this type of tape measure can be a nuisance when working alone. My tape invariably collapses when I try to extend it more than 7 ft. or 8 ft. over an open space. And when I'm working on a flat surface like a roof deck, the hook is useless and the case usually flops over whenever I let it go. There have been times when the floppy and flexible tape measure has driven earnest craftsmen to reach for a good, stiff ruler.

MEASURING AND MARKING TECHNIQUES

Builders are often faced with measuring and marking problems that involve more than simply finding the distance between point A and point B. For example, bricklayers and siders often need to expand or compress their brick or clapboard courses to work out evenly at the bottoms and tops of windows. In fact, dividing a predetermined distance—between the top and bottom of a window, say—into equal increments is a common problem in the building trades, and avoiding awkward layouts and making increments shrink or swell to their advantage are the marks of an experienced craftsman.

The way bricklayers lay out their courses is a good example of this principle at work. A mason who lays 24 courses of brick that are 2.67 in. thick, including the brick and the bed joint, will go up a total of 64 in. If he thickens his bed joints slightly and lays 24 courses that are each 2.75 in. thick, he will go up 66 in. While both of these course sizes would be visually acceptable—the difference in joint size is a little over ¹⁄₁₆ in.—one of these totals could be far more desirable than the other. Indeed, that extra 2 in. could mean the difference between a professional-looking job and a botched bit of masonry (see the drawing below). A good mason can control the height of his courses.

Dividing a distance into equal increments

There are a number of ways to divide a distance into equal increments. Bricklayers use brick spacing rules to control the size of their courses and to fit a given number of masonry units into a specific space. I have three brick spacing rules: one for standard bricks; another for oversized bricks; and a third for modular coordination between bricks, blocks, and several special modular masonry units used mainly in commercial work (I'll talk more about these rules in Chapter 8).

For most trades, a spacing rule isn't practical because the size of the units or courses varies too much from application to application. In these situations, you have to find the spacing yourself. Fortunately, there are three simple ways to divide a space into equal increments (see the drawings on the facing page). The first is to use the slant-rule trick. Let's say you have a space that is 58 in. high and you want to divide it into equal increments that are close to (but don't exceed) 5 in. Start by marking parallel lines at the top and bottom of the space. Now, place the end of the ruler on the bottom line and slant it in the space until the 60-in. mark (which represents the closest number to 58 that is evenly divisible by 5) is even with the top line. Mark at each multiple of five along the length of the ruler to divide the space evenly. If you go back to measure the increments, you'll find that each one measures approximately 4¹³⁄₁₆ in.

A different approach to this problem would be to use a calculator with an "add-on" feature (which is now pretty much standard). First, divide 58 by 5 to determine how many increments will be used. This comes to 11.6, so you'll actually need 12 increments. Now, divide 58 by 12 to find the size of the increments, which equals 4.8333333 in. Add this to itself to get 9.6666666, and from this point forward, pressing the "sum" button will add 4.8333333 each time to the preceding total. Don't be intimidated by the long decimals; they can be quickly converted by glancing at the conversion table in Appendix B (p. 210). As you convert the totals, round to the nearest sixteenth, but remember to keep the numbers on the calculator full so that you don't end up with cumulative error. You can either set up a ruler and mark these increments as you add them or jot them down and mark them off later.

Known to both the Greeks and the Romans, the divider is another of the many useful tools bequeathed to us by the ancient world. It too can be used to divide a space into equal increments. There are many sizes and styles of dividers used by carpenters. I have four, ranging in

Controlling the Size of Brick Courses

The brick courses on the left side of the window are only slightly thicker—about ¹⁄₁₆ in.—than those on the right. Yet this almost imperceptible difference multiplied 24 times (the number of courses) could result in a 2-in. gap above the window.

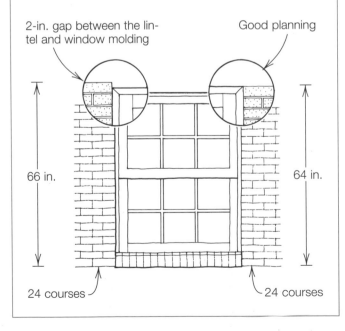

2-in. gap between the lintel and window molding

Good planning

66 in.

64 in.

24 courses

24 courses

Dividing a Distance into Equal Segments

How do you divide a 58-in. space into 12 equal increments?

Use the slant-rule trick

1. Mark parallel lines at the top and bottom of the space.
2. Slant the ruler so that the 60-in. mark (the closest number to 58 evenly divisible by 5) lines up with the top of the space.
3. Mark at each multiple of five along the length ot the ruler. Each one will measure approximately $4^{13}/_{16}$ in.

Use a calculator with an add-on feature

1. Divide 58 by 12 to get 4.8333333 ($4^{13}/_{16}$ in.), the initial increment.
2. Press the "sum" button to add 4.8333333 each time to the preceding total.

Use a divider

1. Calculate the approximate increment ($4^{13}/_{16}$ in.) and set the divider to this distance.
2. Walk the divider up the space. Adjust the divider until it lands evenly at the top of the space.

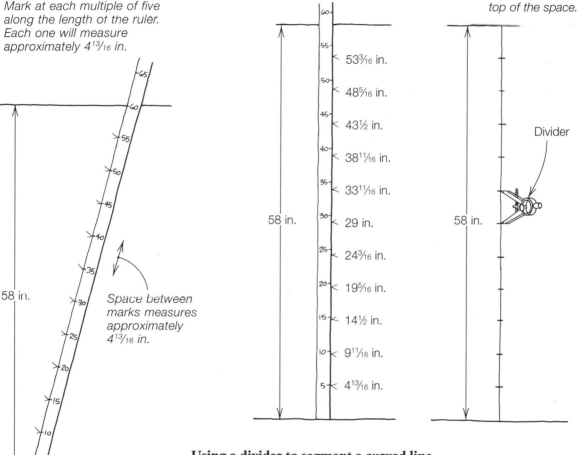

58 in.

Space between marks measures approximately $4^{13}/_{16}$ in.

53³⁄₁₆ in. → $53^3/_{16}$ in.
48⁵⁄₁₆ in. → $48^5/_{16}$ in.
43½ in. → $43^1/_2$ in.
38¹¹⁄₁₆ in. → $38^{11}/_{16}$ in.
33¹¹⁄₁₆ in. → $33^{11}/_{16}$ in.
29 in.
24³⁄₁₆ in. → $24^3/_{16}$ in.
19⁵⁄₁₆ in. → $19^5/_{16}$ in.
14½ in. → $14^1/_2$ in.
9¹¹⁄₁₆ in. → $9^{11}/_{16}$ in.
4¹³⁄₁₆ in. → $4^{13}/_{16}$ in.

58 in.

Divider

58 in.

Using a divider to segment a curved line

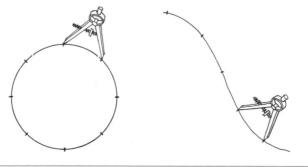

A divider is the best tool to use to make equal increments along a line that isn't straight, such as a curved or serpentine line. A circle can be divided equally by first finding the circumference, then dividing by the number of desired increments.

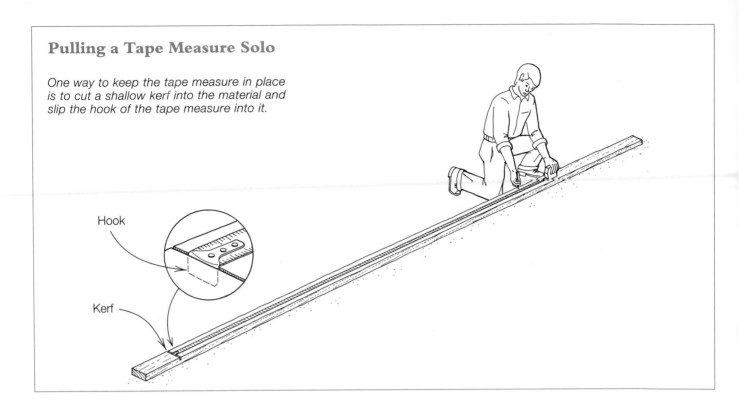

Pulling a Tape Measure Solo

One way to keep the tape measure in place is to cut a shallow kerf into the material and slip the hook of the tape measure into it.

Hook

Kerf

size from 6 in. to 18 in. One of my favorite tools, the divider can also be used to scribe irregular shapes and to draw geometric shapes and polygons, as you'll see later.

To divide 58 in. into equal increments with a divider, begin by calculating the increment, which we already know to be 4.8333333 in. (or $4^{13}/_{16}$ in.). Next, set the divider to that measurement and march it, end over end, up the 58-in. space. If it runs short or long over the 58-in. total, turn the adjustment screw to change the distance between the legs minutely, then repeat this process until the divider lands perfectly at the 58-in. mark. When it does, march the divider up once more, marking each equal increment. The divider, a versatile tool that will be revisited several times in this book, is especially effective for dividing circles and serpentine lines into equal parts (see the bottom drawing on p. 29).

Measuring and marking alone

Craftsmen frequently work alone, which complicates the tasks of measuring and marking. To a certain extent, the problems of measuring solo can be solved by using a ruler or a measuring stick. For distances beyond the range of a measuring stick (over 16 ft.), you usually use

a tape measure, which isn't a problem if the tape measure can be hooked and if it's supported the whole way.

A lead carpenter, working ahead of his crew, often lays out a wall plate 30 ft. or 40 ft. long simply by hooking the tape measure on the end of the plate and pulling with one hand while marking with the other. The problems start, however, when the tape can't be hooked or when it sags and falls off the material being measured.

One of the things you can do when working alone is to clamp or nail your Speed Square at the beginning of the layout and hook the tape over the square. (I've drilled two holes through my square specifically for nailing.) In some circumstances, you can clamp the tape directly to the workpiece or drive a 4d finish nail through the slot in the end of the hook to keep the tape in place. Another technique is to make a shallow cut in the material and hook the tape into the kerf, as shown in the drawing above.

As with pulling a tape measure, snapping chalklines doesn't necessarily involve two people. There are several quick ways to affix the line at one end. To strike a line

Snapping Chalklines Solo

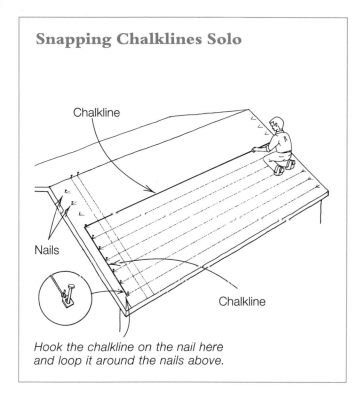

Chalkline

Nails

Chalkline

Hook the chalkline on the nail here and loop it around the nails above.

Leveling Solo

Using a spirit level and a straightedge

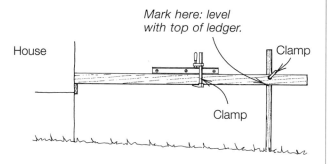

Mark here: level with top of ledger.

House

Clamp

Clamp

Using a water level

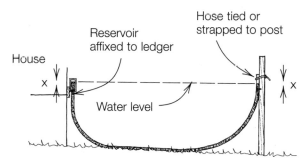

Hose tied or strapped to post

Reservoir affixed to ledger

House

x

x

Water level

1. Mark the water level.
2. Measure down to the top of the ledger.
3. Measure down an equal amount at the post.

Using a laser level

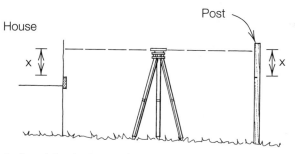

Post

House

x

x

1. Level the instrument.
2. Mark where the laser beam hits the house; rotate the instrument and mark where the laser beam hits the post.
3. Measure down from the mark to the top of the ledger.
4. Measure down an equal amount at the post.

on the rake of a shingle roof, for example, you can make a small cut with a utility knife in the shingle and slip the line into the slit. For marking wood, you can use a nail or cut a short kerf to hold the line. To secure a chalkline in the middle of a concrete floor, loop it around something heavy like a toolbox or a concrete block. To mark layout lines for roofs or for siding, drive nails halfway into the sheathing and hook the line on them. To speed things up, don't unhook the string after snapping each line; instead, simply loop it around the next nail and pull it across (see the drawing above).

Leveling a distance alone can be tricky, too (see the drawings at right). As I've shown, it's possible to extend a spirit level to about 16 ft. with a straightedge. When you're working alone, it's often necessary to provide support at the ends of the straightedge and to clamp the level to the straightedge. To level distances over 16 ft. solo, you can use either a water level or a laser level. The water level costs a lot less but, in my experience, is not nearly as easy to use as a laser level.

Chapter 3

SQUARING UP THE JOB

TOOLS FOR SQUARING UP THE JOB

SQUARING UP LARGE PROJECTS

MEASURING AND TRANSFERRING ANGLES

MEASURING AND TRANSFERRING CURVES AND SHAPES

LAYING OUT LARGE ANGLES AND SHAPES

In the previous chapter, I talked about the tools and techniques craftsmen use to make the job plumb and level, as well as those for taking and transferring linear measurements. In this chapter, I'll focus on tools and techniques you can use to square up the job. I'll also show you how to measure and transfer angles, curves, and other shapes.

TOOLS FOR SQUARING UP THE JOB

The straight line and right angle predominate the world of building. As I've noted already, this isn't due to a lack of imagination on the part of designers and builders but rather to an overriding concern for cost and quality. For scores of centuries, builders have seen the practical advantage of building with square materials. Rectangular bricks, found beneath the ancient city of Jericho, predate the Babylonians by thousands of years. The Egyptians, as you have seen, used chalklines to snap straight lines. They also had planes equipped with bronze cutting edges for truing boards. And, for making accurate 90° angles, they had squares.

The basic function of the square, which hasn't changed in over 5,000 years, is to scribe a line that runs perpendicular to another. Because the plain, sturdy 90° angle often has to be divided in half, squares have also been equipped for centuries with a way to scribe a 45° angle. Until the 19th century, squares were generally made of wood. In 1835, however, the first factory-made metal squares appeared. In a few short years, a steel square

Measuring and Marking without Numbers

Measuring and marking need not include numbers. Very often the best way to measure a given material is to hold it in place and mark it directly, without using a tape measure or any tool other than a pencil. Avoiding numbers does not necessarily mean avoiding measuring tools, though. A lot of tools have no numbers yet do a beautiful job of transferring measurements. The greatest virtue of these tools is their simplicity. Because they bypass the language of measurement—numbers—nothing is lost in translation. As a result, they can be extremely accurate and easy to use, yet their unsophisticated design often means they are inexpensive and durable.

Three uncomplicated marking tools are the butt gauge, divider, and mortise gauge. The butt gauge is about as simple and cheap as a tool gets. To use it, slide it against the edge of a door or door jamb and smack it with a hammer, which will imprint the outline of a butt hinge onto either the jamb or edge of the door. As you've seen in Chapter 2, the divider can quickly divide a straight line or a circle into even increments, often with no numbers cluttering up the process. The mortise gauge is little more than a post with an adjustable fence mounted on it. The fence rides along the edge of the workpiece, while a sharp pin in the post scores a parallel line anywhere from ⅛ in. to 6 in. from the edge.

Some numberless measuring devices are attached to tools that are primarily devoted to nonmeasuring tasks. One of these is the gauged roofing hammer. Simply hook the gauge, which is exactly 5 in. from the head of the hammer, onto the bottom of the shingle that has just been installed and line up the next shingle by resting it on the head of the hammer. A roofer can maintain the recommended 5-in. course exposure between chalked layout lines without having to fumble around with a tape measure.

Frequently, the numberless tools I use are odds and ends I pick up around the job. Plywood manufacturers recommend leaving a ⅛-in. space between sheets to allow for expansion. I use 8d nails driven partway into the framing to create this gap. I also use scraps of plywood, lumber, and trim to make test cuts, measuring sticks, stop blocks, and so forth. In fact, most of the special-purpose jigs and templates that I fabricate on site are made up of bits and pieces found on the job. While some of them are nameless and perhaps only used once, each is a measuring or marking tool created out of a specific need.

much like the one you are familiar with became the standard squaring tool on construction sites. Today, there are many types of squares on the job site; they can do a lot more than scribe a square line, though.

Rafter square

The classic rafter square, which is now available in steel or nonrusting aluminum alloy, has a 24-in. by 2-in. body and a 16-in. by 1½-in. tongue. It has a graduated scale on each edge (eight scales in all), with each divided into inches and fractions of inches. On five of these scales, the inches are divided according to the commonly used halving method (halves, quarters, eighths, and sixteenths). Two of the scales, however, have inches divided into twelfths, while the last scale is divided into tenths (see the left drawing on p. 34).

The twelfths scale provides an easy way to make accurate drawings using a 1-in. scale (1 in. = 1 ft.). With this scale, each inch represents a foot, and each fractional division represents an inch. A distance of 14 ft. 9 in., in other words, would be represented by measuring 14⁹⁄₁₂ in. along the square. In a similar way, the tenths scale can be used to render drawings in a decimalized foot. By squaring across from the tenths scale to the

Inch Scales on the Rafter Square

Each edge of the traditional rafter square is divided into inches and scaled in different ways.

Tenths scale

Eighths scale

Sixteenths scale

Sixteenths scale

Twelfths scale

Using the Scales on a Rafter Square

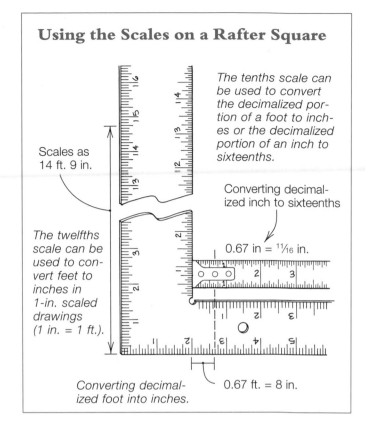

The tenths scale can be used to convert the decimalized portion of a foot to inches or the decimalized portion of an inch to sixteenths.

Scales as 14 ft. 9 in.

The twelfths scale can be used to convert feet to inches in 1-in. scaled drawings (1 in. = 1 ft.).

Converting decimalized inch to sixteenths

0.67 in. = ¹¹⁄₁₆ in.

Converting decimalized foot into inches.

0.67 ft. = 8 in.

In addition to providing a precise 90° angle, the rafter square can be used to lay out any obtuse or acute angle. To lay out the angled cuts for a 5-in-12 roof, for example, hold the square so that the marks representing 5 in. and 12 in. line up with the edge of the board and then scribe the angle, as shown in the drawing on the facing page. Both sides of the square are covered with tables and scales (see the drawings on p. 36), many of which have fallen into disuse and often baffle even seasoned builders. Here are brief descriptions of those tables and scales.

Hundredths scale Following tradition, some squares have a hundredths (of an inch) scale, the purpose of which is to help convert a decimalized inch into a fraction of an inch. This method is usually accurate within ¹⁄₁₆ in., but I rarely use this scale because I'm usually holding a calculator in my hand when I'm dealing with

twelfths scale, furthermore, you can convert a decimalized foot into inches and fractions of inches with surprising accuracy, usually within ⅛ in. It's also possible to convert a decimalized inch into sixteenths. For this you need either a rafter square with a hundredths scale or another ruler, which is placed next to the rafter square and even with the tenths scale. The transferred measurement should be accurate within ¹⁄₁₆ in. Transferring measurements by comparing different scales isn't a task for people who are farsighted, however, since it involves comparing a single inch from one scale to a single inch from the other (see the right drawing above).

Using the Rafter Square to Lay Out Angle Cuts

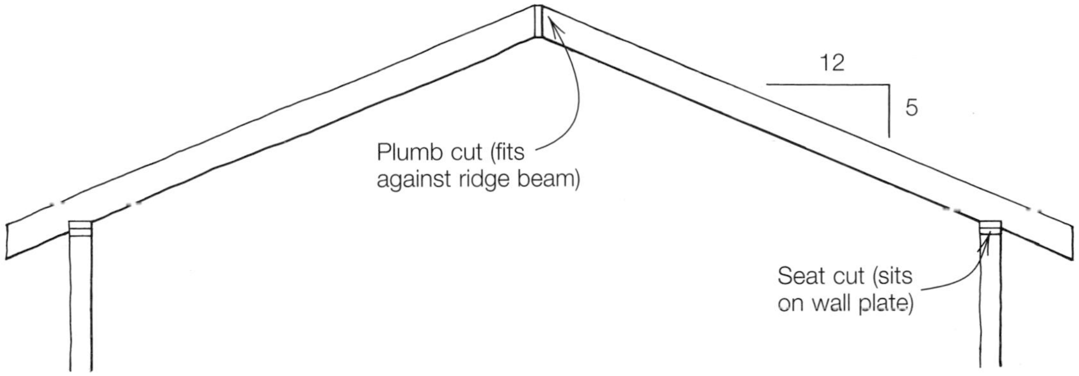

Plumb cut (fits
against ridge beam)

12

5

Seat cut (sits
on wall plate)

Rafter square

*To mark the seat and plumb cuts of a 5-in-12
pitched rafter, line up the marks at 5 in. and
12 in. (as shown) and scribe the appropriate
edge of the square.*

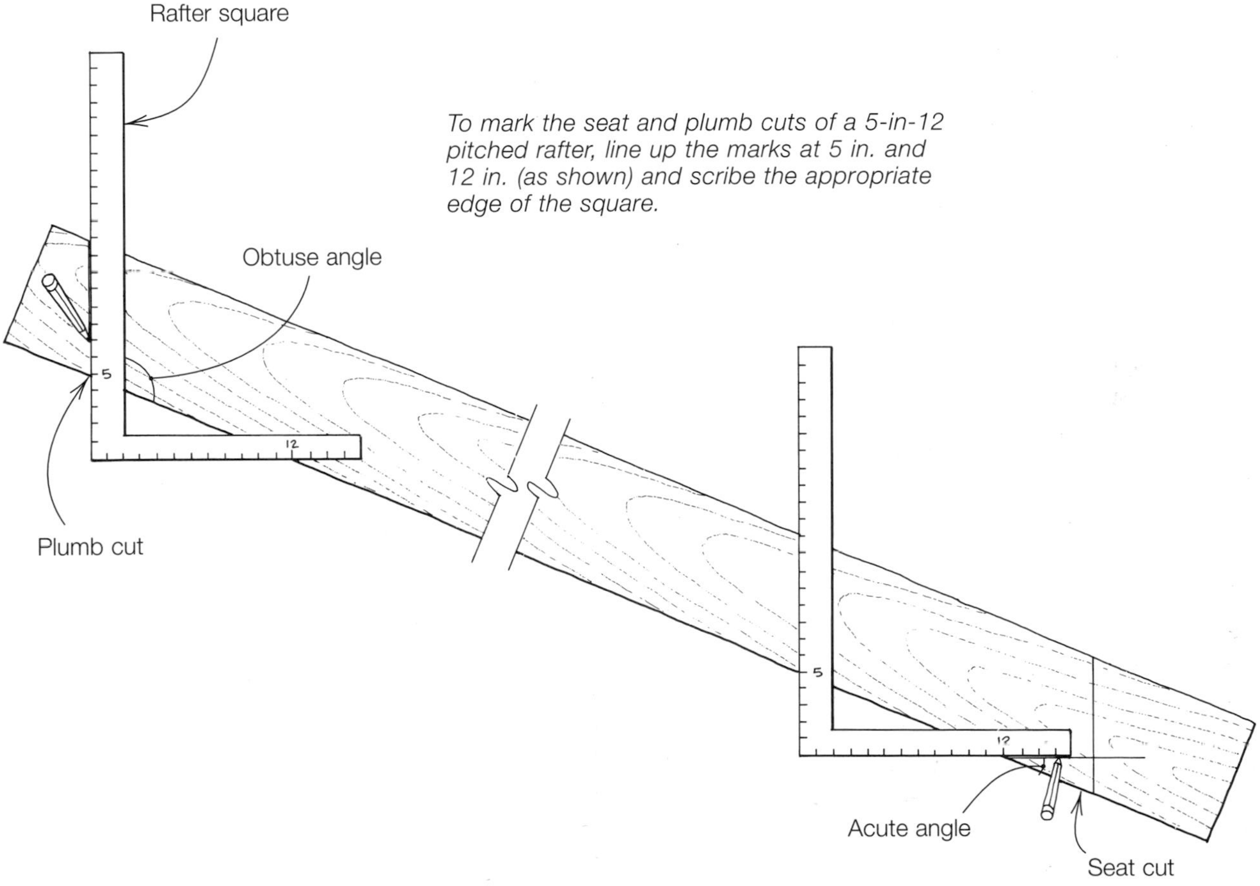

Obtuse angle

5

12

Plumb cut

5

12

Acute angle

Seat cut

Tables and Scales on a Rafter Square

Hundredths scale

Designed to convert inches from decimals to sixteenths, this scale is hard to read and rarely used. Nowadays it is omitted from many rafter squares.

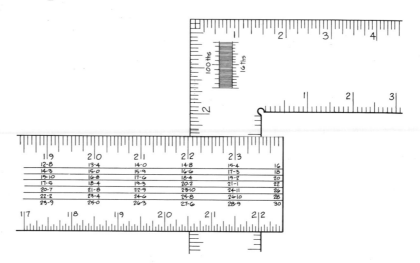

Essex board measure table

A rarely used table that calculates board feet in a piece of lumber.

Brace table

This table provides the hypotenuse (or brace) of a series of right triangles with two equal sides. For example, the first entry indicates that a right triangle with sides of 24 has a hypotenuse of 33.94.

Octagon scale

Provides a proportion (half the length of a side) for octagons up to 67 in. wide. To find this length for a 15-in.-wide octagon, for example, lay a ruler or divider against the scale and measure the distance between 0 and 15.

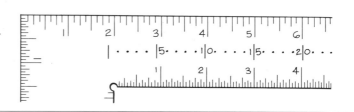

decimals. A mathematical conversion takes just a few seconds and is more precise.

Essex board measure table Very few modern carpenters have the faintest idea of how to use this arcane table. For that matter, very few carpenters have any reason to use it. The Essex board measure table is supposed to help builders calculate the number of board feet in a given piece of lumber, a simple mathematical calculation that builders need to do once in a blue moon: multiply the width by the thickness by the length (in inches), then divide by 144. The Essex board measure table, however, manages to make it confusing, and some of the newer rafter squares have replaced this table with a

more intelligible version. But the new one doesn't get very much use, either.

Brace table Another traditional table is the brace table, which provides the hypotenuse (or brace) for a series of right triangles. Few carpenters are able to divine the purpose of this table just by looking at it. Who would recognize, for instance, that $\frac{30}{30}42\frac{43}{}$ means that a right triangle with two 30-in. sides will have a hypotenuse of 42.43 in.? Because the relationship between the three sides remains the same no matter whether the units are feet or inches, the brace table can be a handy tool for squaring up both large and small jobs. It's rarely used, however, because most people don't realize what the numbers mean. I'll return to it in the section on squaring up large projects.

Octagon scale Perhaps the most esoteric feature of the rafter square is the octagon scale, which can be used to lay out octagons from 1 in. to 67 in. in width. Most people who own a rafter square couldn't begin to explain what these dots and numbers represent. Once in a while, however, it's necessary to lay out an octagon, and this scale can be helpful. I'll talk more about it later in this chapter.

Rafter tables As might be expected, the most important tables on the rafter square are the rafter tables. The first table—"length common rafter per foot run"—enables you to find the rafter length for various roof pitches. To use this table, first find the exact run of a rafter, which is typically close to half the width of the building or addition. Next, convert this sum into a decimalized-foot number. Finally, multiply this number by the number listed in the table for the given roof pitch to arrive at the length (in inches) of the rafter. This process, which I'll discuss in more detail in Chapter 6, is a basic algebraic operation.

The "length common rafter per foot run" table actually indicates the hypotenuses of a series of right triangles (17 in all). The base of all of the triangles is 12 (indicated by the phrase "per foot run"), while the altitude (vertical side) of each triangle is indicated by the even number in the 24-in. scale above the table along the outer edge of the square. And directly under that number in the table is the hypotenuse. Under the 7-in. mark in the 24-in. scale, for example, appears the number 13.89, which indicates that a right triangle with a base of 12 and a vertical side of 7 has a hypotenuse of 13.89 (see the drawing at right).

As in the brace scale, the relationships between the units remains constant, regardless of whether feet, yards, furlongs, cubits, or li (a Chinese unit of measurement that comes in handy during games of Scrabble) are used. For example, a right triangle that has sides of 7 meters and 12 meters has a hypotenuse of 13.89 meters, while a right triangle with sides of 7 in. and 12 in. has a hy-

Using the Rafter Square to Determine Rafter Length

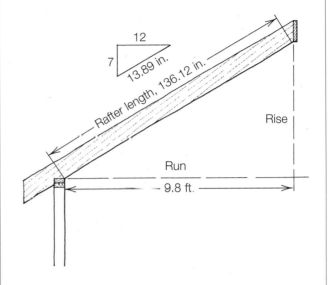

The "length common rafter per foot run" table (see p. 38) gives the length (in inches) of a rafter for every foot of run in a given roof pitch. To use the table:

1. *Convert the run into decimalized feet (9.8 ft.).*
2. *Find the "length common rafter per foot run" for the roof pitch. For a 7-in-12 roof, this is the first entry under the number 7, or 13.89.*
3. *Multiply the run by the number in the table (9.8 × 13.89) to find the length of the rafter (136.12 in.).*

potenuse of 13.89 in. This information is useful not only for calculating the length of rafters but also for squaring up large jobs and for laying out many angles that aren't 90°. I'll refer to the "length common rafter per foot run" table several times in succeeding chapters and I'll discuss it in detail in Chapter 6.

The next three rafter tables are quite useful for laying out roofs with hips and valleys. I will discuss these tables—"length hip or valley per foot run" and both "difference in length of jack" tables—in detail in Chapter 6 (for a look at the rafter tables, see the drawing on p. 38).

Reading the Rafter Tables on a Rafter Square

The numbers in the "length common rafter per foot run" table of a rafter square correspond to the hypotenuse of a right triangle with sides that equal a given pitch.

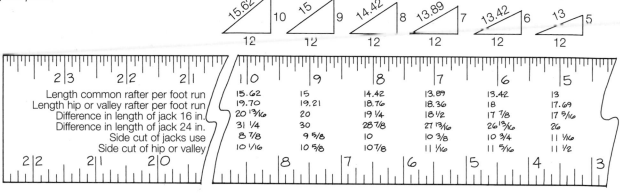

Length common rafter per foot run	15.62	15	14.42	13.89	13.42	13
Length hip or valley rafter per foot run	19.70	19.21	18.76	18.36	18	17.69
Difference in length of jack 16 in.	20 13/16	20	19 1/4	18 1/2	17 7/8	17 5/16
Difference in length of jack 24 in.	31 1/4	30	28 7/8	27 13/16	26 13/16	26
Side cut of jacks use	8 7/8	9 5/8	10	10 3/8	10 3/4	11 1/16
Side cut of hip or valley	10 1/16	10 5/8	10 7/8	11 1/16	11 5/16	11 1/2

The last two rafter tables are just about worthless nowadays, however. These two "side-cut" tables provide information for laying out the bevel on the top edges of regular hip and valley jack rafters. Normally a 45° angle, this bevel is made more acute when combined with the angled cut that conforms to the pitch of the roof. In the days when carpenters cut roof rafters with a handsaw, this side-cut layout information was essential because it indicated the angle along the top edge of the board. Today, of course, the bevel is laid out by setting a circular saw at 45°. The side-cut tables, then, have been rendered obsolete by the circular saw and should be ignored, unless you still cut rafters with a handsaw.

As you can see, the tables on the rafter square, which were developed in the mid-19th century, sometimes have little to do with the construction problems carpenters face today. Much of the work once done using the rafter square, furthermore, can now be done with a handheld calculator. Like other tools that have survived alongside new and more sophisticated instruments, however, the rafter square still has a place on modern construction sites. I'll return to it many times in the course of this book.

Speed Square

For all of its tradition and versatility, the rafter square no longer reigns supreme on construction sites. That honor now belongs to the Swanson Speed Square and its many imitators (see the drawing on the facing page). Invented in 1925 by Albert J. Swanson, a carpenter, the first squares were made by hand and peddled in small quantities, usually directly to other tradesmen. In 1945, however, Swanson started the Swanson Tool Co., Inc., and began to produce and distribute his square on a much larger scale. The triangle-shaped aluminum-alloy Speed Square comes in two sizes: the original 7¼-in. by 7¼-in. by 10¼-in. size and the Big 12, which is 12¼ in. by 12¼ in. by 17¼ in.

There are a number of reasons why the Speed Square has become the framing square of choice among modern builders. The first advantage is its size. It is small enough to fit into a tool apron (unlike a bulky rafter square) yet has the capacity to square across two 2x4s laid side by side. This means that carpenters can use it to lay out the top and bottom plates of a wall simultaneously or to scribe a line across a 2x8.

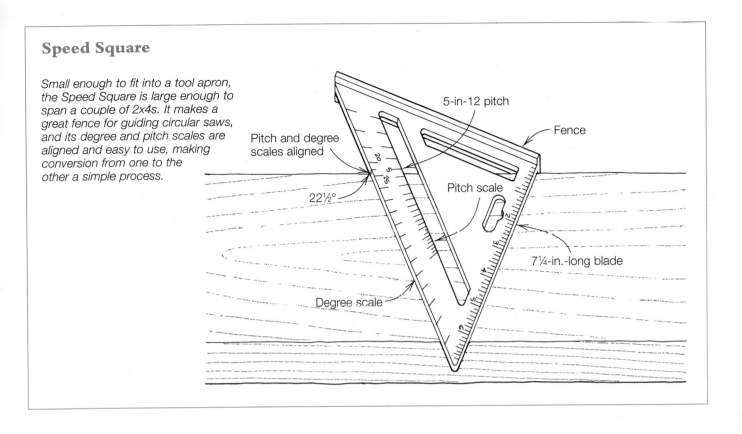

Speed Square

Small enough to fit into a tool apron, the Speed Square is large enough to span a couple of 2x4s. It makes a great fence for guiding circular saws, and its degree and pitch scales are aligned and easy to use, making conversion from one to the other a simple process.

Pitch and degree scales aligned

5-in-12 pitch

Fence

22½°

Pitch scale

7¼-in.-long blade

Degree scale

Another feature is the shoulder, or fence, which engages the edge of a board to align the square for either a 90° or 45° angle. By rotating the square on the corner pivot point of the fence, any angle between 0° and 180° can be quickly laid out. And because the Speed Square is a generous 3/16 in. thick, it makes a fast and accurate fence for guiding power tools through square cuts.

The real stroke of genius in the design, however, is that the Speed Square carries aligned scales for both roof pitch and degrees, making it easy to convert a roof pitch or any unknown angle into degrees without using trigonometry. This is an important bridge between a carpenter's layouts, which are usually described in terms of rise and run, and his circular saw, which has scales divided into degrees.

Combination square

Not too long ago, carpenters routinely carried a combination square in their toolbelts (a few loyal adherents still do). In the 1970s, however, the Speed Square abruptly replaced the combination square as the tool of choice for squaring boards and for marking 45° miters. Today, the combination square is not used nearly as often for those tasks, but it is still quite useful.

The combination square consists of a fence and a perpendicular straightedge that is usually 12 in. long and marked off in inches and fractions of inches. The most important feature of the combination square these days is the fact that the length of the straightedge can be adjusted. This makes it an excellent tool for tasks like measuring the depth of a mortise or marking a line parallel to the edge of a board.

Miter saws

Some of the best squaring tools I own have motors. About 25 years ago, precise, lightweight electric miter saws started appearing on construction sites. At first, they were treated with reverence and used only for trim, but carpenters soon figured out that they were also great for cutting 2x4s and bought these precise little workhorses by the thousands. Manufacturers responded by producing better miter saws with blades up to 15 in. in diameter, compound-miter saws, compound-miter-crosscut saws, and a whole slew of stands, extension tables, and other accessories.

One big advantage to these saws is that they eliminate the need to mark a square cutting line. The material just needs to be marked for length. Also, these saws can be set up quickly to make precise, repetitive cuts at any angle from 45° to 90°. And compound-miter-crosscut saws can easily make the compound cuts needed for jack rafters without a cutting line. As a result of these precise saws, carpenters are increasingly leaving their Speed Squares (or other squares of choice) parked in their aprons.

Working with a Basic Calculator

As with any tool, the level of proficiency you have with a calculator increases the more you use it. Here are a few of the techniques I've learned over the years.

Working with the Pythagorean theorem

Finding the hypotenuse of a right triangle with sides of, say, 28 ft. and 54 ft. requires several operations on the calculator. This is where the tool's memory capacity comes in handy.

Begin by squaring 28: enter 28, press × (the multiplication sign), then press = (the equal sign). The product of 28^2, 784, will now be displayed on the screen. Store this number by pressing M+ (memory plus) and then clear the screen by pressing C.

Next, square 54: enter 54, press ×, press =. The screen will display 2916. Again, store this by pressing M+. Now clear the screen again (C) and retrieve the product of 784 and 2916 by pressing MR (memory recall). With this sum—3700—on the screen, find the hypotenuse by entering √ (the square-root sign). The hypotenuse, 60.827625, will appear on the screen.

Converting from decimals to fractions
With 60.827625 ft. displayed on the screen, enter − (the minus sign), 60, then =. This leaves the decimalized portion of the final foot—0.827625—on the screen.

To convert this to inches, press ×, 12 , then =. This comes to 9.9315 in. To find the decimalized portion of this number, first remove the 9 whole inches by pressing -, 9, then =. This leaves the decimalized portion of the final inch—0.9315—displayed on the screen.

To convert this to sixteenths, press ×, 16, then =. The result —14.904—can be rounded up to 15, which is the number of sixteenths in 0.9315. Putting this all together, 60.827625 ft. = 60 ft. 9^{15}/$_{16}$ in.

Finding the hypotenuse of a right triangle with equal sides
The formula for finding the hypotenuse of a right triangle with equal sides (or for finding the diagonal of a square) is 1.41421 multiplied by the length of one of the sides. This is a long number that can be difficult to remember and tedious to punch into the calculator. Fortunately, there is a nice shortcut that is not only faster but also more precise (because it yields a decimal with more digits).

The number 1.41421 is the hypotenuse, rounded to hundred thousandths, of a right triangle with a base and altitude of 1. The first step in finding the hypotenuse is to square both sides and add the products. For this triangle, the sum of the two sides squared is 2. The hypotenuse, then is $\sqrt{2}$, which comes to 1.4142135 in my basic calculator.

The easiest and most precise way to find the hypotenuse of a right triangle with equal sides (or the diagonal of a square), then, is to multiply $\sqrt{2}$ by the length of a side. To determine the hypotenuse of a right triangle with equal sides of 19.625, for example, enter 2, √ , ×, 19.625, then =. This equals 27.753939, give or take a millionth.

Other squares

There are many other kinds and sizes of squares on the market. In addition to the squares mentioned here, I have a 2-in. engineer's square for checking the squareness of my chisels and plane irons as I sharpen them, as well as a 4-ft. T-square for marking plywood and drywall. In between these, I have over a dozen other squares of various sizes and designs, many of which will be mentioned as I describe specific techniques later on in the book.

SQUARING UP LARGE PROJECTS

So far, I've talked primarily about tools for squaring up materials. Builders, of course, also have to square up very large areas that are well beyond the reach of these hand tools. There are four basic approaches to the task of squaring up large jobs: The first method uses precise instruments, like the transit and the laser level; the second method uses the Pythagorean theorem; the third uses the rafter square; and the fourth uses accurate scale drawings.

Using transits and lasers

In Chapter 2, I explained how craftsmen can extend the spirit level by using a transit or a laser level. Both of these classes of instruments can extend the square as well. The transit uses the 360° scale at its swiveling base, while the laser uses a precisely positioned mirror to split its beam into a right angle.

Though I've often admired the precise machining of both my transit and laser level, I never use either of these instruments for turning a right angle. The problem is that it's necessary to reference the precise point at which that 90° turn takes place. This is hard to do with an instrument. For a freestanding structure, you can carefully set the instrument up over a fixed point on the ground using a plumb bob. But what do you do when the point of reference is a mark on the side of a wall? For laying out a large right angle, my tools of choice are geometry and a steel tape measure, because they are faster and easier than trying to set up an instrument over a point.

Using the Pythagorean theorem

The Greek philosopher and mathematician Pythagoras (born ca. 582 B.C.) observed that when the base and altitude of a right triangle are squared (multiplied by themselves) and then added together, they always equal the square of the hypotenuse, or the diagonal side opposite the 90° angle. Pythagoras reduced this observation into the simple formula $a^2 + b^2 = c^2$. This formula for calculating the hypotenuse of a right triangle is probably the single, most important mathematical equation in construction. By calculating and then carefully measuring the hypotenuse, you can ensure that the other two sides of any size triangle are exactly perpendicular to each other. This is an effective way to square up both large- and small-scale projects and is used in all stages of building construction. Everyone engaged in construction layout should know and understand this simple formula: the Pythagorean theorem.

Finding the hypotenuse Finding the hypotenuse (or c) of an abc right triangle is simple (see the top drawing on p. 42). In a right triangle with sides of 4 and 3, you just multiply 4 × 4, which is 16, and 3 × 3, which is 9, then add 16 to 9 to get c^2, or 25. The hypotenuse squared, however, doesn't do a builder much good; you need the plain old hypotenuse, or c. This means finding the square root, or the number that, when multiplied by itself, will yield 25. The square root in this particular example, 5 (5 × 5 = 25), is easy to figure out. But in most real-life building situations, finding the square root of c^2 is far more difficult. Very few college graduates can easily figure out the square root of a number like 549 without a calculator. With a basic calculator, however, it can be done instantly simply by entering the number and then pushing the square-root ($\sqrt{}$) function key (for more on using a basic calculator, see the sidebar on the facing page).

To demonstrate the usefulness of the Pythagorean theorem, let's tackle a real-life building problem: how to square up the foundation for a 15-ft. by 18-ft. addition (see the bottom drawing on p. 42). First, mark where the addition begins and ends on the house, which establishes the base of the triangle. Next, set up a parallel level line exactly 15 ft. from the house, which represents

The Pythagorean Theorem

An invaluable mathematical tool for builders, the Pythagorean theorem can be used to calculate the hypotenuse of any right triangle.

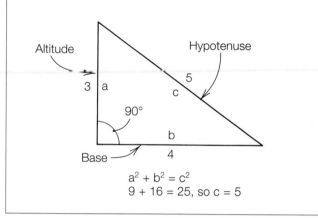

Altitude

Hypotenuse

3 a

5

c

90°

b

Base

4

$a^2 + b^2 = c^2$
$9 + 16 = 25$, so $c = 5$

Using the Pythagorean Theorem to Square Up a Foundation

Use the Pythagorean theorem ($a^2 + b^2 = c^2$) to square up the foundation for a 15-ft. by 18-ft. addition. Once the diagonals are equal, the foundation is square.

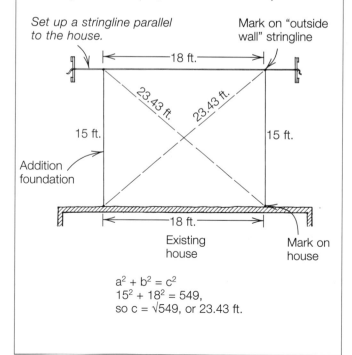

Set up a stringline parallel to the house.

Mark on "outside wall" stringline

18 ft.

23.43 ft.   23.43 ft.

15 ft.

15 ft.

Addition foundation

18 ft.

Existing house

Mark on house

$a^2 + b^2 = c^2$
$15^2 + 18^2 = 549$,
so $c = \sqrt{549}$, or 23.43 ft.

the outside wall of the addition and establishes the length of the altitude of the triangle. Then determine the hypotenuse of this right triangle to square up the 15-ft. side with the 18-ft side. Here are the three steps of the calculation:

1. Find c^2: $a^2 + b^2 = c^2$

$15^2 + 18^2 = c^2$

$225 + 324 = 549$

2. Find c: $c^2 = 549$

$\sqrt{549} = 23.43$

3. Convert decimalized foot to feet and inches (see the sidebar on p. 44):

23.43 ft. = 23 ft. 5.17 in. = 23 ft. 5³⁄₁₆ in.

After determining that the hypotenuse equals 23 ft. 5³⁄₁₆ in., pull this measurement diagonally across the future foundation and mark the "outside wall" stringline with a felt-tip pen. To check your work, measure diagonally across the other way and mark the stringline again. Finally, measure from mark to mark along the stringline. It should come to an even 18 ft.

Using a rafter square

Before the introduction of handheld calculators in the 1970s, carpenters relied on the geometry etched on the faces of their rafter squares. This information can still be very helpful. Let's take a look at how a rafter square might be used to square up a 15-ft. by 18-ft. foundation for an addition.

The brace table Earlier I mentioned that the brace table on a rafter square indicates the hypotenuse for a series of equal-sided right triangles. The brace table starts at ²⁴⁄₂₄33⁹⁴ and goes up by threes to ⁶⁰⁄₆₀84⁸⁵. Then there is an odd entry that reads ¹⁸⁄₂₄30.

In this particular example, let's use the third entry on the table, ³⁰⁄₃₀42⁴³, which indicates that a right triangle with two 30-ft. sides will have a hypotenuse of 42.43 ft.

Squaring Up a Foundation Using a Rafter Square

Use your rafter square to make sure the corners of the foundation for a 15-ft. by 18-ft. addition are square.

Using the brace table

Use the $\frac{30}{30}42\frac{43}{}$ entry on the brace table and divide that figure—42.43—in half to get the hypotenuse of a right triangle with two sides 15 ft. long.

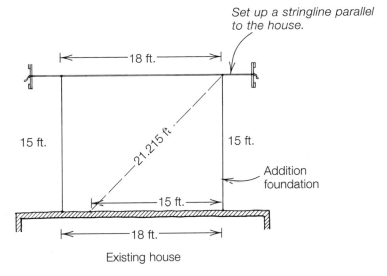

Set up a stringline parallel to the house.

18 ft.

15 ft. 21.215 ft. 15 ft.

Addition foundation

15 ft.

18 ft.

Existing house

Using the 3-4-5 method

Multiply all three sides of a 3-4-5 triangle by 5 to create a 15-20-25 triangle. Measure 20 ft. from one of the corners marked on the house, pull the 25-ft. diagonal from that point, and mark the stringline.

Using the common rafter table

The entry for the diagonal of a triangle with sides of 15 and 12 (a 15-in-12 pitch) is 19.21. This 12-15-19.21 right triangle can be used to locate both outside corners of the addition foundation.

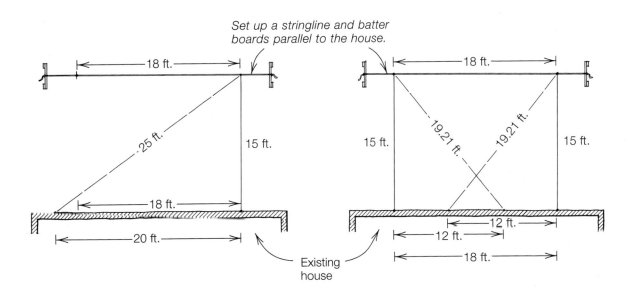

Set up a stringline and batter boards parallel to the house.

18 ft. 25 ft. 15 ft. 18 ft. 20 ft.

18 ft. 19.21 ft. 19.21 ft. 15 ft. 15 ft. 12 ft. 12 ft. 18 ft.

Existing house

Converting Decimalized Feet to Fractions

One big selling point for a $75 construction calculator is that it can work in feet, inches, and fractions of an inch, as well as convert decimals to fractions. While these features make it well suited for calculating the diagonals of buildings and the length of roof rafters, a construction calculator doesn't do anything that my $6 calculator can't do, except convert pitch into degrees.

But computing in feet and inches doesn't require a special calculator. To begin with, you don't have to convert decimalized feet into feet and inches. A tape measure laid out in decimalized feet (or an engineer's scale) can be used to measure the hypotenuse of the actual layout in the exact form that it was calculated. (This type of tape measure can be found anywhere surveying equipment is sold.)

If you choose to convert to feet and inches, you can do it by looking at a tape laid out in both inches and decimalized feet or by looking at the combination inch/engineer's foot, a scale that combines both decimals and fractions. (This type of scale is also available where surveying equipment is sold.)

If you want to convert a decimalized foot to inches mathematically, however, the process takes less than 30 seconds with a basic calculator (for more on using a basic calculator, see the sidebar on p. 40). Take, for example, the 23.43-ft. hypotenuse that you calculated on p. 42. To convert 0.43 ft. to inches, multiply 0.43 × 12. This comes to 5.16 in. To convert 0.16 to sixteenths of an inch, multiply by 16. This comes to 2.56, which can be rounded to three, or ³⁄₁₆, which means the hypotenuse is 23 ft. 5³⁄₁₆ in. (The algebra behind these conversions is discussed on p. 46.)

Divide these numbers in half to find the hypotenuse of a right triangle with two 15-ft. sides: 21.215 ft. Apply this information to a 15-ft. by 18-ft. foundation by measuring 15 ft. in from one of the corners marked on the house, then pulling the 21.215-ft. (or 21-ft. 2⁹⁄₁₆-in.) diagonal, or hypotenuse, and marking the string (see the top drawing on p. 43).

Incidentally, there is an important relationship between the numbers in the brace scale: If you divide any of the hypotenuses listed by the length of the corresponding side, you always come up with a number close to 1.41421. The first entry, for example, provides a hypotenuse of 33.94. Dividing this by the length of the sides, 24, gives you the number 1.41416. Therefore, the formula for finding the diagonal of any square can be written as: (the diagonal of a square) = 1.41421 × (the length of one side).

The last entry in the brace table, $\frac{18}{24}30$, describes the relationship between the sides of a triangle with a base of 24, an altitude of 18, and a hypotenuse of 30. If you use this triangle to square up the foundation, you will be using the time-honored 3-4-5 method of squaring (see the bottom left drawing on p. 43). Earlier, in the section on the Pythagorean theorem, I used the example of a triangle with sides of 3 and 4 and a hypotenuse of 5, but you can multiply these three numbers by any number and still come up with the three sides of a right triangle. If, for example, you multiply 3, 4, and 5 by 6, you get a right triangle with sides of 18 and 24 and a hypotenuse of 30. The $\frac{18}{24}30$ entry, then, is placed prominently at the end of the brace table as a reminder of this extremely useful geometric relationship.

In this example, the width of the addition (15 ft.) divided by 3 equals 5 ft. Multiply this number by 4 to get the other side of the triangle, and multiply by 5 to get the hypotenuse. Thus, to lay out this foundation, measure 20 ft. (4 × 5) in from one of the corners marked on the house, then pull the 25-ft. (5 × 5) hypotenuse from that point. It's not necessary to have nice, even numbers like 15 to use this method. If, for example, the foundation is going to be 13 ft. wide, you can divide that number by 3, then multiply that total, which is

4.333, by 4 and 5. In this case, you'd end up with a triangle with a 13-ft. side, a 17.33-ft. side, and a hypotenuse of 21.665 ft.

In all three previous examples, a proportion supplied by the brace table was either divided or multiplied. Once a proportion is proven correct, you can enlarge or reduce it by multiplying or dividing all the parts by the same number. By knowing this simple technique and being aware of the right triangles listed on the face of your rafter square, you can square up any large layout without doing geometry. It's already done; you need only to enlarge or reduce it.

The common rafter table There is yet another handy right triangle, complete with a hypotenuse, on the rafter square that could be used for this foundation example. If you look under the number 15, in the "length common rafter per foot run" table, you'll see the number 19.21. This table actually indicates the hypotenuses of a series of right triangles with a base of 12 and with altitudes indicated by each even number in the 24-in. scale above the table and along the outer edge of the square. This means that a right triangle with one side that is 12 ft. and another that is 15 ft. will have a hypotenuse of 19.21 ft. To lay this out, measure 12 ft. in from the corner marked on the house and then pull the 19.21-ft. hypotenuse from that point (see the bottom right drawing on p. 43).

Using a scale drawing
The least complicated method of squaring up a 15-ft. by 18-ft. foundation would be to make a scale drawing with a rafter square. Professional-grade rafter squares are both precisely square and exactly scaled.

To square up this foundation, simply draw a right angle with your rafter square on a flat surface, such as a piece of plywood, and mark carefully at the 15-in. mark on one side and at the 18-in. mark on the other. Now, using the twelfths scale, measure the hypotenuse, remembering that each inch on the scale represents 1 ft. and that each twelfth represents 1 in. This scaled measurement should get you to within ½ in. of the actual hypotenuse of the full-size layout. Using this measurement as a starting point, you can get precisely even diagonals in the layout through trial and error.

MEASURING AND TRANSFERRING ANGLES
The straight line and right angle may be the rule on construction sites, but there are many exceptions to this rule. The two most common exceptions are roofs and staircases. These sloping structures are essentially functional (although they can be quite beautiful, as well). Many other violations of the right-angle rule, however, are entirely decorative in nature. Molding, curves, nonstructural arches, and diagonal or irregular surface treatments are often included in the design because they break up the monotony of the square and rectangle.

Sometimes designers go deeper than the surface and have the structure itself deviate from the straight line and right angle. Curved walls, structural arches, and out-of-square floor plans are but a few examples of how they might do this. Along with these deliberate departures from the straight and square, builders often encounter materials that are not quite square or were imperfectly installed. In these situations, things that were supposed to be square somehow didn't end up that way.

All of these exceptions to the right-angle rule present interesting challenges for a builder. They have also inspired some of the most clever tools and techniques to be found in a craftsman's bag of tricks.

Describing an angle
There are two basic ways angles are described and laid out (see the drawing on p. 46). The first is to describe them in terms of pitch, or units of rise per 12 units of run. A 7-in-12 roof pitch means that there are 7 in. of rise for every 12 in. of run. The second way to describe angles is in terms of degrees, so that a 7-in-12 pitch can also be called a 30.26° angle. Pitch can easily be converted to degrees using either the Swanson Speed Square or Stanley's Quick Square, both of which measure angles in pitch *and* degrees. Another way to convert pitch to degrees is with a scientific or construction calculator, while a third is with the help of a conversion table (see Appendix C on p. 211).

Two Ways of Describing an Angle

An angle—which is a portion of a circle—can also be described by the slope, or pitch, that it creates when it is part of a right triangle. A triangle with a base of 12 and altitude of 7 has an angle of 30.26° and a pitch of 7-in-12. This means that for every 12 units of run, the diagonal rises 7 units.

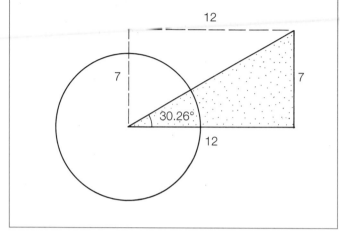

Determining the fourth proportional

Unfortunately, pitch is not always described in terms of rise per 12 units of run. A staircase with a unit run of 10 in. and a unit rise of 7.5 in. would be one such example. How could you convert this 7.5-in-10 pitch into degrees? While either a scientific or a construction calculator could do this in seconds, the pitch can also be easily converted by using a basic algebraic process called "determining the fourth proportional." This is a very useful tool and, like the Pythagorean theorem, should be familiar to any builder engaged in layout. Here's how it works:

The problem can be stated as "7.5 is to 10 as *what* is to 12" and written as:

$$\frac{7.5}{10} = \frac{x}{12} .$$

The object here is to isolate (and find) x, which can be done by multiplying both sides of the equation by 12.

$$\frac{12}{1} \times \frac{7.5}{10} = \frac{90}{10} = 9 .$$

So, a 7.5-in-10 pitch is also a 9-in-12 pitch. A Speed Square or a conversion table can be used to convert this 9-in-12 pitch into 37°. There's a shortcut in working this equation. You can also "cross multiply" like this:

$$\frac{7.5}{10} = \frac{x}{12} .$$

After cross multiplying 12×7.5, divide the result, 90, by 10. Thus, x = 9.

Before moving on to another simple method to convert a 7.5-in-10 pitch into degrees, let's go a step further with this rather awkwardly named process. Determining the fourth proportional can also be used to convert decimals into fractions. For example, 0.57 can also be written as $^{57}/_{100}$. To convert that fraction to sixteenths, first state the problem as "57 is to 100 as *what* is to 16," which can be written as:

$$\frac{0.57}{100} = \frac{x}{16} .$$

After cross multiplying 16×57, divide the result, 912, by 100. This comes to 9.12, which can be rounded to 9. Thus, $0.57 = ^{9}/_{16}$.

Sometimes it's necessary to go in the opposite direction and convert fractions into decimals. To convert $^{9}/_{16}$ into a decimal, simply divide 9 by 16 to get 0.5625.

Determining the fourth proportional is a process that can also be used for figuring out the length of a rafter, the height of a ridge, the dimensions of an out-of-square foundation, and many other thorny layout problems. It's particularly useful in conjunction with the tables on the rafter square, and I'll return to it many times in the course of this book.

Determining Pitch and Degrees without Using Math

The Speed Square can be used to measure the angle of any straight line drawn across a board, providing this measurement in both degrees and roof pitch.

1. Lay out the pitch with a rafter square, or transfer an unknown angle with a bevel square.

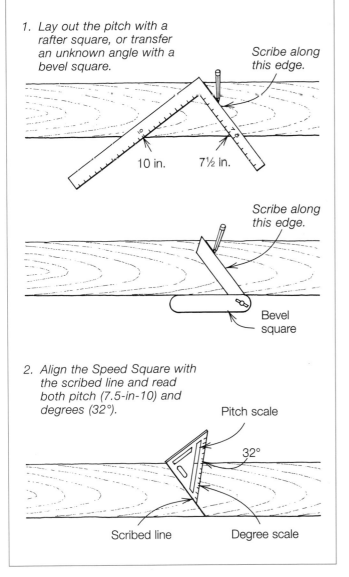

Scribe along this edge.

10 in.   7½ in.

Scribe along this edge.

Bevel square

2. Align the Speed Square with the scribed line and read both pitch (7.5-in-10) and degrees (32°).

Pitch scale

32°

Scribed line   Degree scale

Finding pitch and degrees without using math

Let's return to the problem of converting a 7.5-in-10 pitch into degrees. Instead of using math or a calculator, you can do this with a rafter square and a Speed Square. Begin by laying out the 7.5-in-10 pitch on a board with the rafter square. Hold the rafter square so that the marks at 7½ in. and 10 in. line up with the edge of the board and scribe a line. Then line up the Speed Square with the scribed line and read the degrees (see the drawing at left).

Slightly modified, this technique can be used to find the degrees of any unknown angle. First, use a bevel square (a particularly useful square that can be adjusted to angles other than 90°) to find and transfer the unknown

Splitting an Angle

It isn't always necessary to measure an angle to split it. To find the correct miter angle for the trim of a staircase, for example, draw lines parallel to the skirt and landing, then mark from the corner to the intersection of the parallel lines.

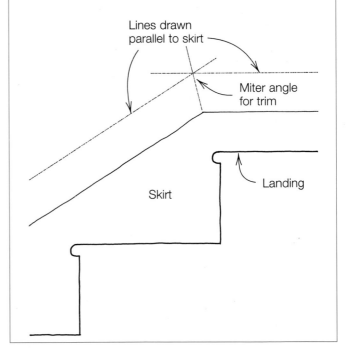

Lines drawn parallel to skirt

Miter angle for trim

Skirt   Landing

angle onto a board. Then line up the Speed Square and read the degrees or pitch. Whether scribed with a bevel square, dividers, or a block of wood, any straight line on a board can be quickly described in degrees or pitch using the Speed Square.

Measuring angles with a saw

The reason why it's important to be able to convert a pitch or an unknown angle into degrees is because saws have scales that are divided into degrees. A motorized miter or compound-miter saw, however, is a precise measuring instrument in its own right. If you're casing an opening that is slightly out of square, for instance, you can cut a test piece from a scrap of the trim you're using, check for fit, and adjust the saw one way or the other. In many situations, there's no need to measure the angle prior to using the saw. Or you can set a preexisting (but unknown) angle on a workpiece against the fence of a miter saw, set the blade to the angle, and read the degree of the cut right off the scale.

Splitting an angle

Sometimes, in the course of running trim or laying out wall plates, it's necessary to split an odd (other than 90°) angle by mitering the material. To figure out the miter of the trim that rides on the skirt of a staircase, for example, first scribe parallel lines a couple of inches above the skirt using a rafter square, a level, or anything that has parallel edges (see the right drawing on p. 47). Next, draw a line from the corner of the skirt through the intersection of those lines. Then hold a scrap of trim in place and mark it at the corner of the skirt and where the angle-splitting line is. Line up the miter saw with these marks, cut the scrap at this angle and see if it fits. Adjust the angle of the saw, if necessary, until you get a good fit.

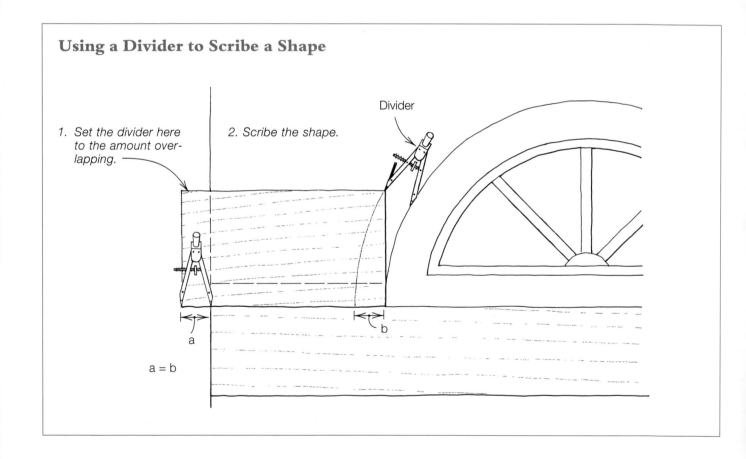

Using a Divider to Scribe a Shape

1. Set the divider here to the amount over-lapping.

2. Scribe the shape.

Divider

a

b

a = b

MEASURING AND TRANSFERRING CURVES AND SHAPES

So far, this discussion has been limited to taking and transferring straight angles, but occasionally carpenters have to measure and transfer curves and shapes. The primary tool for this is the divider.

The most common divider on construction sites is the loose-leg wing divider. The loose leg can be removed and replaced with a pencil, while the term "wing" describes how the divider is clamped into position. When fitted with a pencil, a divider can scribe curves, irregular edges, or imperfections from one material to another. Because an accurate scribe requires that the divider be held at a constant angle as close to 90° to the scribed surface as possible, some dividers have built-in spirit levels. The divider not only duplicates curves and irregular shapes, but it can also do this at a predetermined distance (limited, of course, by the size of the divider). A properly adjusted divider can transfer both the right shape and the correct height or length at the same time (see the drawing on the facing page).

Laying out circles, octagons, and other shapes with a divider

The divider is essentially a hefty compass that can be used to make circles and arches on the job site. The divider can also be used to lay out an octagon. The simplest way to do this is first to draw a circle, then adjust the divider to about one-eighth of its circumference. March the divider around the circle, adjusting as necessary by trial and error, until it is divided into eight equal parts. After marking these points, connect them with straight lines, and you'll have an octagon (see the drawing below). This technique can be used to divide a circle evenly into other multiple-sided shapes as well, such as pentagons or hexagons.

You can save a lot of time when you want to divide a circle evenly by first determining the circumference of

---

Using a Divider to Lay Out Shapes and Patterns

A divider can be helpful for tasks like laying out octagons or sunburst patterns.

Octagon

1. Adjust the divider to about one-eighth of the circle's circumference.
2. March the divider around, adjusting as necessary, until the circle is divided into eight equal parts.
3. Mark these points and connect them with straight lines to lay out an octagon.

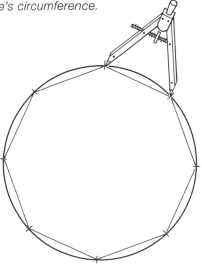

Sunburst

1. Divide a semicircle into equal parts.
2. Extend lines from the center of the base through the marks to make the sunburst pattern.

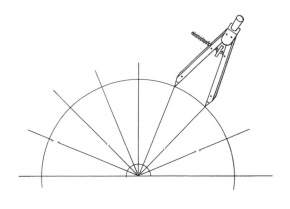

Using the Octagon Scale on the Rafter Square

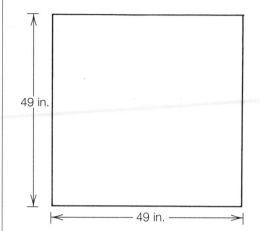

49 in.

49 in.

1. Lay out a 49-in. square.

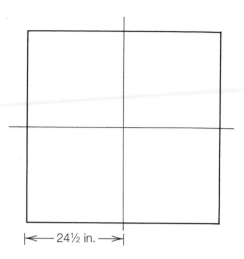

24½ in.

2. Divide each side of square in half.

Octagon scale (full size)

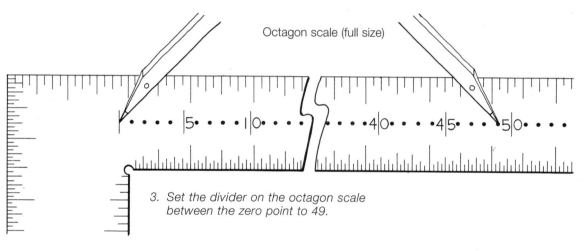

3. Set the divider on the octagon scale between the zero point to 49.

4. Step that distance out from center mark on each side. Then connect the marks to get the inside of the octagon.

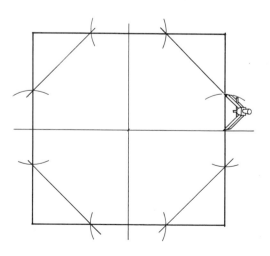

the circle. The formula for this is 2πR, where π = 3.1416. To calculate the circumference of a circle with a 7-in. radius, for example, multiply 2 × 3.1416 × 7, which equals 43.98 in. To get the initial divider measurement for an octagon, divide 43.98 by 8.

Using a divider in conjunction with the octagon scale

When it comes to laying out octagons, there are two shortcomings to the technique I just described. The first is that the size of the octagon is limited by the size of the divider that is available. My largest divider (the largest one I've ever seen) is 18 in. tall and opens up to almost 19 in. The second shortcoming is that it's difficult to lay out an octagon of a predetermined width (measured from opposite sides) using this method.

To lay out octagons to exact widths, it's necessary to start with a square rather than with a circle. A handy way to lay out octagons up to 67 in. wide is to use the octagon scale on the rafter square. Here's how it works. Let's say you determine that a 49-in.-wide rough opening will be needed for a 48-in.-wide octagonal window. First, lay out a 49-in. square, then lay out the center of each side (see the drawings on the facing page). After marking the centers, set the divider on the rafter square's octagon scale so that it spans the distance between the zero point to the dot representing 49.

Now, use the divider to transfer that distance to the layout, stepping out from the center mark toward the corner of each side and marking. The divider isn't absolutely necessary for this operation, because the measurement can also be transferred with a ruler, but it is more convenient. These marks represent the eight corners of the 49-in.-wide octagon. Connect them with a straightedge, and the layout will be complete.

Like many of the tables on the rafter square, the octagon scale is a compilation of geometric calculations. In the next section, I'll explain the geometry that is stored on the octagon scale as we examine how to lay out large angles and shapes.

LAYING OUT LARGE ANGLES AND SHAPES

You've already seen how builders extend the level and the square to lay out the large surfaces that make up a house. For the most part, you can use the same tools and techniques, slightly modified, to extend large acute and obtuse angles, circles, octagons, and other shapes.

Using the Hypotenuse to Lay Out Large Angles

You can use the hypotenuse of a right triangle to lay out an oblique angle, such as when an addition veers off at an angle other than 90°.

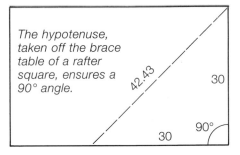

The hypotenuse, taken off the brace table of a rafter square, ensures a 90° angle.

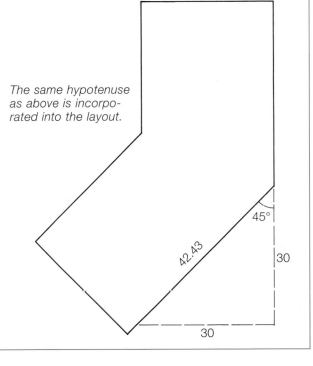

The same hypotenuse as above is incorporated into the layout.

To lay out a foundation at an out-of-square angle, for example, you have the same options as you have when you lay out a square foundation: a transit, the Pythagorean theorem, or the tables on your rafter square. Often, the difference between laying out a square corner and an obliquely angled corner is, literally, just a matter of degrees. If you're using a transit to lay out a foundation with a 45° turn, for example, you can set the instrument over a point that represents the corner. Instead of rotating the instrument 90°, as you would if you were laying out a square foundation, you simply rotate the transit 45°.

The very same right triangle that you used earlier to ensure that a foundation is square can also be used to lay out an oblique angle, such as you might find when an addition to a house veers off at an angle other than 90°. The only difference is that in the latter case, the hypotenuse becomes part of the final layout (see the drawing on p. 51). Of course, the geometry stored in the tables on the rafter square can also be used to achieve this same purpose.

Using the proportions of right triangles

As you've seen, right triangles have precise proportions that can be enlarged by multiplying all three sides by the same number, which is what you do when you use the geometry stored on a rafter square. There is a limited amount of space on the rafter square, however, and the proportions of just 17 right triangles are supplied. Furthermore, the angles of all of these triangles are described solely in roof pitch (x-in-12). Angles aren't always described in terms of rise and run, however; often, they're specified in degrees. And as you've already seen, it's sometimes necessary to convert from pitch to degrees, and vice versa.

The degrees to roof pitch conversion table (Appendix C) on p. 211 addresses both of these shortcomings. First, it provides the proportions for different right triangles. Second, it gives the angle formed by the 12-in. base and the hypotenuse of all these triangles in both degrees and roof pitch.

It should be noted that using a base of 12 when providing the proportions of right triangles is a tradition that's tied into our 12-in. foot. Mathematicians—and builders in other countries—use 1 as their base. Since this system is often easier to use, I've also listed the proportions of 46 right triangles in Appendix D (p. 212), using 1 as the base. If you take any of these proportions and multiply all three numbers by 12, of course, you end up with the proportions listed for the same angle in Appendix C. In Chapter 4, you'll see how to use these proportions to lay out foundations that turn at angles other than 90°.

As extensive as both Appendix C and D are, they do not cover every conceivable problem that you might encounter. In the rare case where you might need to determine the angle or the proportions of a right triangle that isn't described in roof pitch or whole degrees, you would have to use trigonometry, the branch of mathematics that deals with triangles and their properties. A construction or scientific calculator would be very helpful for this once-in-a blue-moon situation.

Laying out large circles and curves

The largest divider I've seen can scribe a circle that is only about 3 ft. in diameter. To make a larger circle, you can rig up a radius with a fixed pivot point and swing a large arc. For the radius, use a strip of wood, and for the pivot point use a nail or screw. After measuring the appropriate distance, drill through the wooden radius and insert a pencil in the hole. On very large layouts that are beyond the reach of a wooden or solid steel radius, use a light chain or steel tape measure to pull the radius. For some masonry projects, you may need to set up a batter board to support the radius (see the top drawing on the facing page). And to keep the face of the work plumb, you can attach a square directly to the radius.

Sometimes curves are called for that are not a segment of a circle and thus cannot be laid out by rigging up a radius. One such case would be a winding brick walkway. To avoid the flat spots that mar a job like this, some sort of guide needs to be used. Strips of plastic molding or 1-in. plastic pipe attached to stakes driven in the ground serve this purpose well.

Radius Setup for a Circular Brick Wall

Masons use this setup to build evenly curved and level brick walls and walkways.

Rafter square

This arm of the square is plumb.

Pivot

Radius arm is level.

Batter board holds radius arm level.

For organic curves, use a flexible material like plastic molding or flexible plastic pipe attached to stakes as a guide.

Stakes

Flexible material

Making a Large Octagon Out of Two Squares

Placing one square on top of another equally sized square and then rotating the first one 45° lays out an octagon. Here the eight corners of the octagon correspond to the points where the sides of the square intersect.

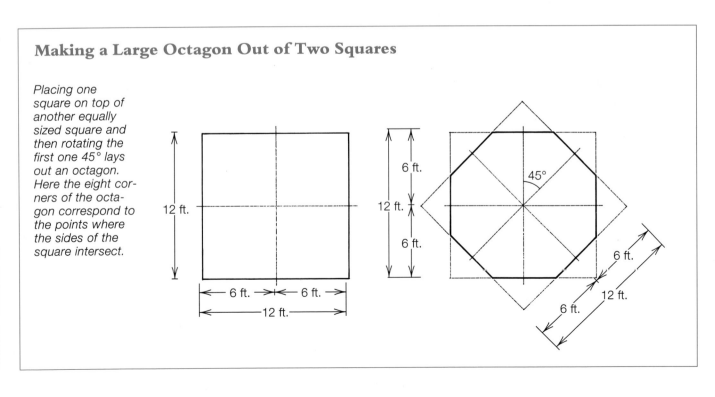

12 ft.

6 ft.

6 ft.

12 ft.

6 ft.

6 ft.

12 ft.

12 ft.

45°

6 ft.

6 ft.

12 ft.

A Geometric Puzzle

The sides of an octagon exist in a measurable geometric relationship to one another.

x = y

y = d – s

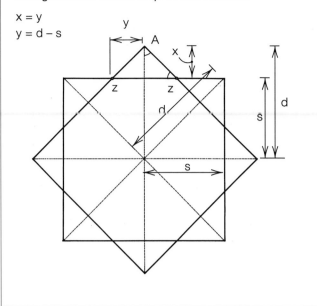

Laying out large octagons

The Pythagorean theorem not only helps to lay out large squares, rectangles, and oblique angles, but it can also be used to lay out a large octagon. To see how this works, let's use the layout of a 12-ft.-wide gazebo as an example. Begin this job by drawing a scaled 12-ft. square and dividing it into four equal squares. Drawing the exact same square, rotating it 45°, and superimposing it on the first square will quickly and easily form the eight corners of the octagon (see the bottom drawing on p. 53).

While this is all very tidy, it would be a lot easier to lay out a single square and know how far to measure over from the center of each side, just as you did when using the rafter square's octagon scale. As the drawing at left indicates, the distance (x) to the apex of the small triangle (A) equals the distance (y) from the center of each side of the large square to the intersection point of the octagon (z). This distance is the diagonal (d) of any of

Finding the Length of the Sides of an Octagon

To find x,

1. Calculate d (equal to the hypotenuse, A, of the shaded triangle).
You can use:
 • Pythagorean theorem ($a^2 + b^2 = c^2$)
 • Formula for finding diagonal of a square: 6 × 1.414 = 8.484
 • Next-to-last entry on the brace table, $^{60}_{60}84^{85}$, divided by 10.
2. Subtract s from d: 8.484 – 6.
3. x = 2.484.

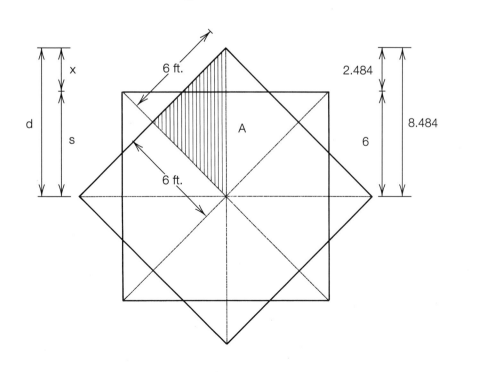

Laying Out a 12-ft. Octagon

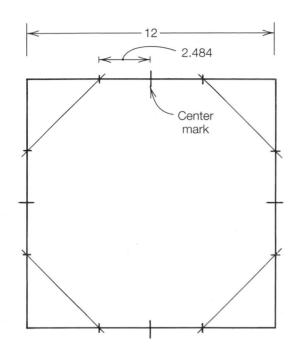

1. Lay out a 12-ft. square.
2. Mark the center of each side.
3. Multiply the length of the sides by 0.207 (12 × 0.207 = 2.484).
4. Measure 2.484 ft. (or 2 ft. 5³⁄₁₆ in.) from the center of each side and mark.
5. Connect the marks.

the small squares *minus* the length of the side of that square (s).

In the bottom drawing on the facing page, $x = d - s$. You know already that $s = 6$, and to find side d you need to find the hypotenuse of a right triangle with two sides of 6. You can get this figure from the brace table by dividing the last entry, $^{60}_{60}84^{85}$, by 10. Therefore, $d = 8.484$. Subtracting 6 from 8.484 will give you x, which is also the distance from the center of one of the sides of the large square to one of the corners of the octagon, which is 2.484 (see the top drawing on the facing page). This is

the same distance, provided in inches, that is on the octagon scale of the rafter square.

You have now determined the same proportion, $^{2.484}/_{12}$, that is provided on the octagon scale. Just for fun, let's see how it would work out for a 67-in. octagon, the largest entry on the octagon scale. The problem can be stated as: "2.484 is to 12 as x is to 67," and written as:

$$\frac{2.484}{12} = \frac{x}{67}.$$

Determining the fourth proportional gives you 13.87 (or 13⁷⁄₈), which is exactly the distance provided by the octagon scale for a 67-in. octagon. This proportion can be reduced to a simple decimal by dividing 2.484 by 12, which comes to 0.207. With this decimal, you have the number needed to reduce this whole process to a simple formula. The formula for finding the distance from the center of one side of the large square to the corner of

Laying Out a Large Pentagon with a Transit

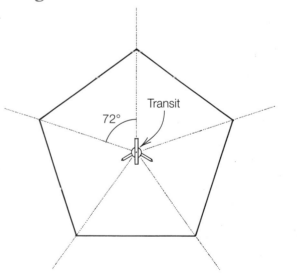

1. Set up the transit over a point representing the center of the building.
2. Turn the transit 72° at a time to lay out the angles.
3. Measure from the center to lay out five corners.

Enlarging a Pentagon Proportionally

While the actual dimensions of figures like octagons and pentagons may vary, the proportions of the triangles that make up their sides remain constant.

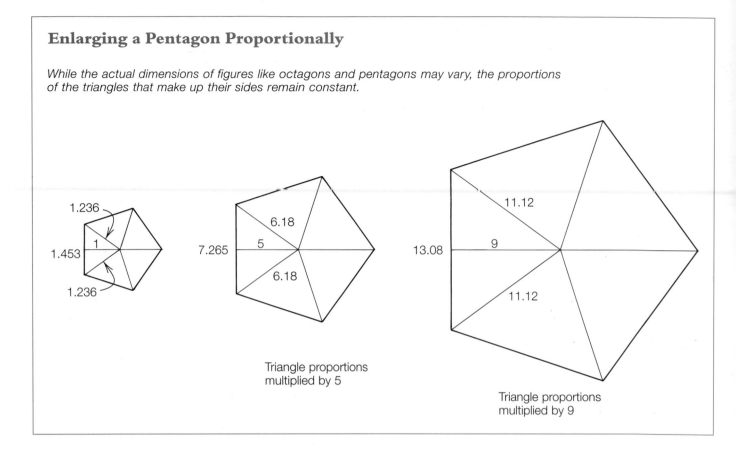

Triangle proportions multiplied by 5

Triangle proportions multiplied by 9

an octagon, then, is 0.207 times the length of the side of the large square. Let's see how it works on a 12-ft. gazebo (see the left drawing on p. 55): 0.207 × 12 = 2.484. Not bad!

Laying out other large polygons

Let's say you're hired by a retired general to build his dream house, which he has designed in the shape of a pentagon. How do you lay out the foundation? The easiest way to lay out a pentagon, hexagon, or other multisided shape is to set up a high-quality transit over the center point of the building. The angles of the building can be laid out by turning the instrument the proper number of degrees (determined by dividing 360 by the number of sides) at a time. To lay out a pentagon, for example, turn the instrument 72° at a time (360° ÷ 5 = 72). Once the angles have been laid out, measure from

the center point to lay out the five corners of the pentagon (see the right drawing on p. 55).

Another approach to laying out polygons can be used in lieu of (or in combination with) the technique just described. In the drawing above, notice how the pentagon can be divided into five equal triangles. It's easy for anyone familiar with trigonometry to compute the precise proportions of these triangles. And with these proportions in hand, you can enlarge the pentagon to any size you want by multiplying all of the proportions by the same number, just as you were able to do with the triangles on the rafter square. To show how this works, I've taken the proportions of the triangles that make up a pentagon and multiplied them by 5 and 9.

Laying Out a Pentagon by Triangulation

Once the base dimensions of a pentagon or other polygon have been determined, the basic proportions of its major triangles can be used to lay out its sides.

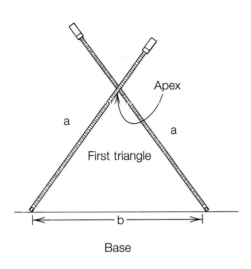

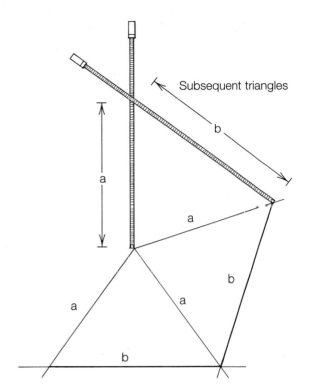

1. *Use two tape measures to mark the intersection, or apex.*

2. *Continue to lay out the remaining sides until the pentagon is completed.*

Once you have determined the exact dimensions of the major triangles of a pentagon, you can lay it out by triangulating the dimensions. Begin this process by marking the beginning and end of the base of the first triangle (see the drawing above). Next, pull two tape measures, one from each of the marks, and mark the apex of the triangle where the tapes intersect at the correct dimension. For the next four triangles, pull one tape measure from the corner of the base and the other from the apex of the triangle (which is also the center of the pentagon).

With the correct proportions in hand, this process can be repeated for any regular polygon. I'm not particularly a whiz at trigonometry, so to get the proportions for numerous regular polygons, I conferred with one of my customers, who just happens to be a professor of mathematics at Duke University. After a few minutes at his computer, the good professor produced the proportions for polygons with up to 25 sides (these are compiled in Appendix F on p. 213). If you ever need the proportions for a polygon with more than 25 sides, I'm afraid you'll have to find your own professor of math.

Chapter 4

LAYING OUT FOUNDATIONS

The foundation of a house has two basic functions. First, it provides a rugged structural base for the building. Second, and more important for the purpose of this book, the foundation serves as the transition from the irregular surface of the land to the straight lines, right angles, and plumb and level planes that make up the house. The top of the foundation is usually the primary reference for the layout of the rest of the house. In this chapter, you'll see how builders bring a square and level structure out of the ground.

Strange as it may seem, we won't be working "from the ground up," as the saying goes. The layout of a foundation actually starts from the top, when the builder establishes the top line of the foundation. From there, he measures down to determine the correct depth of the excavation, the elevation of the footing, and the correct height of block courses.

SITING THE HOUSE

The annals of building lore are filled with stories of houses that were built in the wrong place. Unlike many of the tales and anecdotes that are told and retold on building sites, a lot of these stories are true and are entertaining only to those who were not involved.

The financial consequences of building in violation of property rights or zoning ordinances can be devastating. So when a house has to be built close to the building line (the property line or the required offset from the property line), it's prudent to hire a professional surveyor to stake out its corners. Some builders do this as a matter of course, if only to spread out their liability if any errors are made.

It isn't always necessary to hire a surveyor to lay out the corners of a house, however. Where there is a wide margin of error between the planned house or addition and the building line, the builder, designer, and homeowner can site the house themselves without anxiety—as long as they stay well clear of the building line. Keeping off the building line not only helps builders sleep at night but also leaves room within the building line to add on to the house in the future.

On any new construction project, I like to get out onto the land with the owner and the architect (if there is one) after the boundary of the property has been surveyed and marked and the building line established. Together, we can make some preliminary decisions about the building site. If a septic system is planned, for example, the location of the tank and leach field must be established in relation to the house. The site's topography, road location, the driveway, neighbors, prized trees, the sun, the best view, and, on some sites, the position of rock outcroppings, streams, and ponds are all typical parts of the equation.

For this task, I bring a 100-ft. tape measure, stakes, string, flagging tape, and a transit with a measuring stick or surveyor's rod. The homeowner should bring a plan of the house, the plot plan, and (most importantly) his or her spouse. After setting up stringlines that represent the boundary of the land and the building line, a process of give-and-take begins. Out of this process, it's usually possible to decide tentatively on the location and orientation of the house.

Oftentimes, final siting decisions hinge on the feasibility of the septic-system plan. In my area, a septic plan must be presented to town or county officials who require an on-site "perc" (percolation) test to see if the soil is suitable in the proposed location for the system. Sometimes a driveway plan must be submitted as well, and only after these required plans pass inspection can the house be more definitely sited.

At this point, I usually arrange to meet the homeowner at the land again and set up stringlines indicating the outline and elevation of the top of the foundation. The building code in my area requires foundation walls to extend at least 8 in. above the finished grade, and I use these stringlines to show how high the foundation will project from the existing grade. Of course, because the finished grade can be adjusted with heavy equipment, there is some flexibility in how high the foundation can be made (see the drawing below).

Before settling on a final elevation, however, it's prudent to think about the plumbing, particularly if you're planning a basement bathroom. To more delicately paraphrase my plumber, wastewater doesn't flow uphill. If a

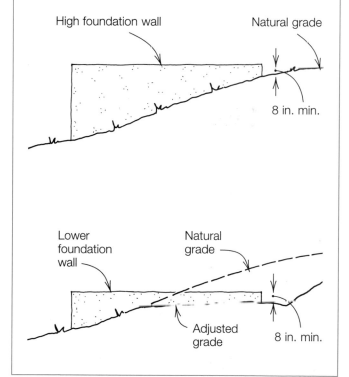

Adjusting the Grade

A high foundation wall for a building on a sloped site is obtrusive. Lowering the natural grade at the high end of the site will lower the overall height of the foundation.

High foundation wall

Natural grade

8 in. min.

Lower foundation wall

Natural grade

Adjusted grade

8 in. min.

septic system is planned, it's a good idea to meet the septic contractor at the site and make sure the foundation height you're planning will not be too low for the septic tank. If the house will be hooked up to a municipal or county sewer system, wastewater flow is usually not a concern because sewer lines are usually buried deeper than basements. On a house that will sit well below street level, however, it would be wise to check with the plumber and make sure the foundation will be high enough for plumbing that will accommodate a basement bathroom. Sometimes, however, a basement bathroom just isn't feasible without a wasteline pump.

LAYING OUT A SIMPLE FOUNDATION

After you've settled on the location and elevation of the house and procured all the necessary permits, you're ready to set things up for the excavator. After he's done, there will be a large, crudely leveled, oversized hole in the ground. Within this opening, you need to lay out a level and square structure at a predetermined height and location (I've included some layout pointers in the sidebar at left).

Foundations are massive, three-dimensional structures that must be built within close tolerances on or in the irregular surface of the earth. In addition to this, some foundations are quite complex in design. While laying out a foundation would appear to be a daunting challenge, in actual practice each stage in the process is fairly easy. As you'll see, the important thing is to break the layout down into simple elements, and each layout begins as a single stringline with a dot on it. From this reference point, a square and level plane representing all (or a major section) of the foundation can be laid out.

Here I'll describe how I proceed when I'm planning a concrete-block foundation 27 ft. wide by 48 ft. long. The same basic principles can be used to lay out a formed concrete foundation or, for that matter, a foundation made out of just about any material.

Preparing for the excavation

If you're building a foundation with a full basement, the length and width of the excavation should be about 5 ft. beyond the length and width of the planned foundation. If there are stringlines already set up indicating the site of the foundation, you can mark the ground about 5 ft. outside of the stringlines with dry cement, lime, or spray paint and have the excavator dig to your marks. Since digging to this chalked line will wipe out the house corners that you've so painstakingly established, you'll need to set up a series of reference stakes outside of the excavation that can be used to reestablish the foundation perimeter (see the drawing on the facing page).

Practical Layout Pointers

I recommend devising a plan of action and arriving on site with completed calculations and sketches. Calculating the hypotenuse of a right triangle while crew members are standing by is a waste of money. Worse than that, the pressure to hurry and the distractions of trying to do several things at once can lead to errors. It's far better to do calculations and make sketches at home on a desk or table than to do these things on the hood of your truck.

Along the same lines, I recommend making up a checklist of things that have to go in or through the footing or foundation. Think about all the ancillary things that you intend to install or allow for. Then write them down, because they're easy to forget. Some of these items include pipes or sleeves, keyways, and reinforcing steel. To these I would add all openings (doors, windows, and vents), beam pockets, footings for piers, and, at the top of the foundation, anchor bolts or straps.

Finally, keep in mind that there will be tons and tons of dirt and material moved around your job site. As you drive reference stakes and set up batter boards, you need to think about the routes of loaders, backhoes, and concrete trucks. Sometimes, despite your best planning, a batter board has to be removed to let equipment in. When this happens, don't fret. It's a normal part of the job and usually only takes a few minutes to reinstall the board.

Using Stakes to Establish Foundation Lines

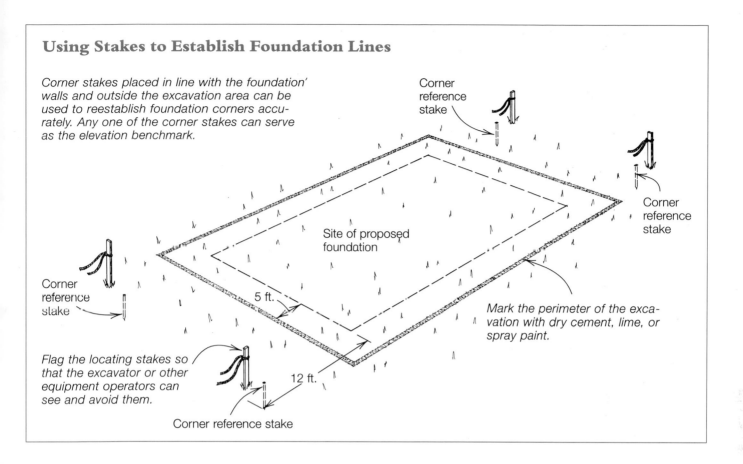

Corner stakes placed in line with the foundation' walls and outside the excavation area can be used to reestablish foundation corners accurately. Any one of the corner stakes can serve as the elevation benchmark.

Corner reference stake

Corner reference stake

Site of proposed foundation

Corner reference stake

5 ft.

Mark the perimeter of the excavation with dry cement, lime, or spray paint.

Flag the locating stakes so that the excavator or other equipment operators can see and avoid them.

12 ft.

Corner reference stake

Drive the stakes just about flush with the ground and in line with both of the long walls of the foundation but about 12 ft. beyond the corners. Next, drive locating stakes—so they protrude about 2 ft. from the ground—next to these corner reference stakes. Note the distance from each reference stake to the actual house corner both on the nearest locating stake and in a logbook of some sort. Then tie red flagging tape to the locating stakes so that the excavator can see them and avoid disturbing them.

In contrast to the relatively rough measurements required for the length and width of the house, the depth of the excavation needs to be accurate within a few inches. To achieve this degree of accuracy, you need to use a point of reference outside the excavation and measure against that reference as the cellar hole is being dug. One of the corner stakes will make a good reference point. So, before taking down the stringlines representing the top of the foundation, set up a transit and shoot the elevations of both the top-of-foundation stringline

and the reference stake. Then, by subtracting the elevation of the reference stake from the elevation of the top-of-foundation stringline, you can determine what I call the "difference in elevation." Since it's essential to remember this dimension, write it down in a logbook.

Next, determine the height of the top of the basement floor in relation to the height of the top of the foundation (see the top drawing on p. 62). In this example the height is 96 in. With this information, which can be taken off the blueprints, you can easily figure out exactly how far down from the top-of-foundation stringline to dig. Since the bottom of the excavation in the example is 8 in. below the top of the basement floor, you must excavate to a depth 104 in. below the top-of-foundation stringline. Comparing the difference in the elevations of the top-of-foundation stringline and the stake tells you how far down to dig from the top of the stake. Here, the difference in elevation between the top-of-foundation stringline and the reference stake is 33 in., while the difference in elevation between the ref-

Determining Basement Elevation

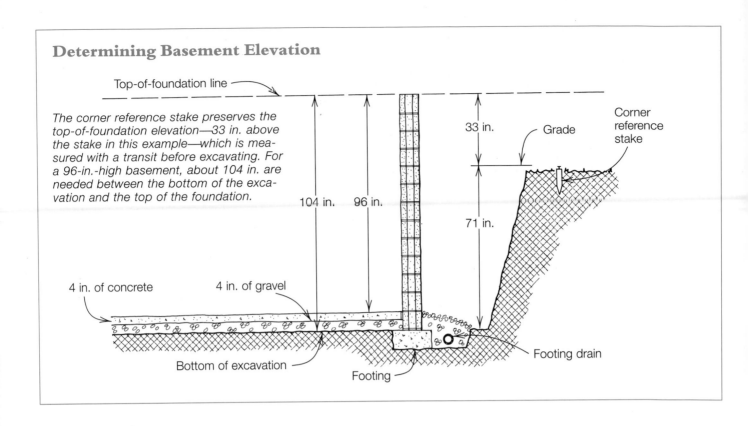

Top-of-foundation line

The corner reference stake preserves the top-of-foundation elevation—33 in. above the stake in this example—which is measured with a transit before excavating. For a 96-in.-high basement, about 104 in. are needed between the bottom of the excavation and the top of the foundation.

33 in.

Grade

Corner reference stake

104 in.   96 in.

71 in.

4 in. of concrete

4 in. of gravel

Bottom of excavation

Footing

Footing drain

Digging the Basement to the Correct Depth

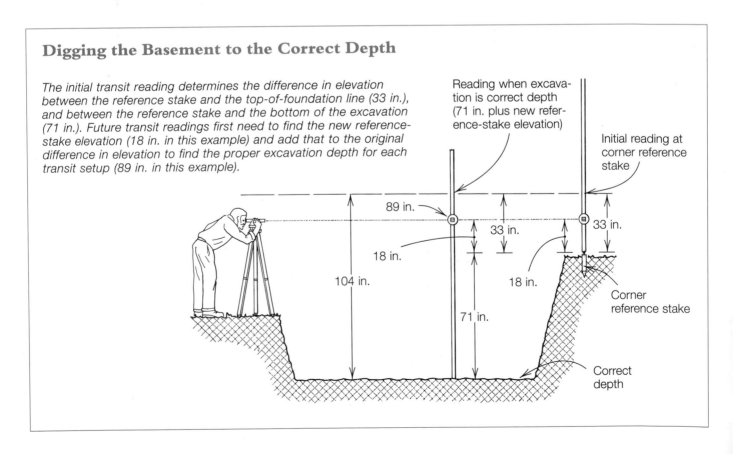

The initial transit reading determines the difference in elevation between the reference stake and the top-of-foundation line (33 in.), and between the reference stake and the bottom of the excavation (71 in.). Future transit readings first need to find the new reference-stake elevation (18 in. in this example) and add that to the original difference in elevation to find the proper excavation depth for each transit setup (89 in. in this example).

Reading when excavation is correct depth (71 in. plus new reference-stake elevation)

Initial reading at corner reference stake

89 in.

33 in.

33 in.

18 in.

104 in.

18 in.

71 in.

Corner reference stake

Correct depth

erence stake and the bottom of the excavation is 71 in. (104 – 33 = 71). Note all of these elevations in a log, then take down the stringlines representing the top of the foundation and put the transit away. Now you're ready to begin digging.

After the excavator has roughed out about three quarters of the basement opening, set up a transit outside the excavation (and away from his dirt-removal path) and begin periodically checking the depth of the opening (you'll need a helper with this job). The first thing to do is shoot the height of the reference stake in relation to the new position of the transit. Since you already know how far down to dig from this elevation (71 in.), usually all you'll need to do is add that distance to the reading you've just taken at the reference stake (see the bottom drawing on the facing page).

Every so often, the excavator should stop so that you and your helper can check against the level plane projected by the transit to see how much farther he should dig. It's a good idea to check in several locations to see where the high points are. By doing this, the excavator can get the bottom of the hole increasingly level as he approaches the correct depth. At the end of this process, check with increasing frequency—you may have to tell the excavator to remove as little as 3 in. or 4 in. in specific spots in the hole. The degree of precision here depends on the type of soil you're digging in, the equipment you're using, and the skill level of the excavator.

Laying out the top of the foundation

After the excavator is finished, reestablish the top-of-foundation line and the location of the corners, which were wiped out by the excavation but preserved by the

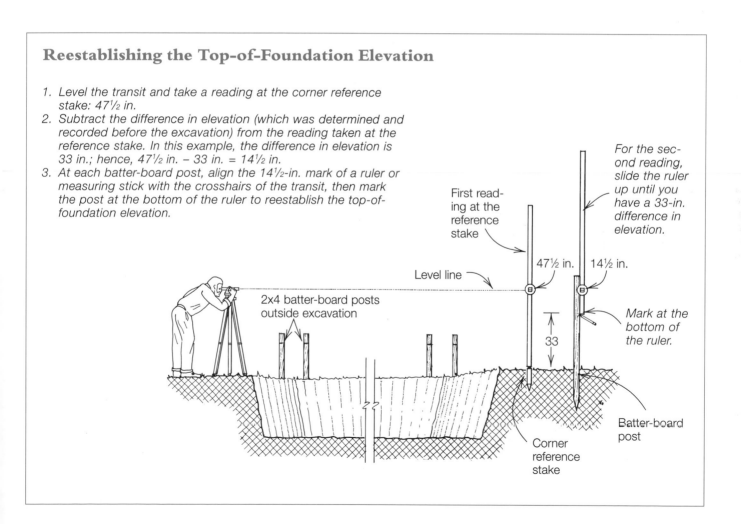

Reestablishing the Top-of-Foundation Elevation

1. Level the transit and take a reading at the corner reference stake: 47½ in.
2. Subtract the difference in elevation (which was determined and recorded before the excavation) from the reading taken at the reference stake. In this example, the difference in elevation is 33 in.; hence, 47½ in. – 33 in. = 14½ in.
3. At each batter-board post, align the 14½-in. mark of a ruler or measuring stick with the crosshairs of the transit, then mark the post at the bottom of the ruler to reestablish the top-of-foundation elevation.

For the second reading, slide the ruler up until you have a 33-in. difference in elevation.

First reading at the reference stake

Level line

2x4 batter-board posts outside excavation

47½ in.   14½ in.

33

Mark at the bottom of the ruler.

Corner reference stake

Batter-board post

Using a Leveling Instrument

There are two things that can be a little confusing when you first use a transit, builder's level, or laser level. The first occurs when the instrument is placed in its most common position, which is at a higher elevation than the elevations being measured. Usually in this position, the higher the number you read, the lower the elevation (see the top drawing at right). Unfortunately, this isn't always the case.

Since the level plane is usually set up above both the elevations being shot, you usually just subtract one reading from the other to ascertain the difference in elevation. This can't be taken as an ironclad rule, however. Once in a while, the level plane you're measuring against falls between the two elevations being shot. In such a circumstance, you'd have to add the two readings together to ascertain the difference in elevation. If the level plane is below both elevations being shot, you're back to subtracting the one reading from the other to determine the difference in elevation. But here, the higher reading indicates a higher elevation (see the bottom drawings at right).

The second confusing thing about using a leveling instrument is that the amount of the initial referencing measurement doesn't really matter. It can be any number, and it can be a certain number one day and a

completely different number the next. This slippery state of affairs occurs because what you are measuring is the *difference in elevation* between two or more positions, not an absolute height. That difference is measured against the level plane projected by the instrument, and the height of the level plane

changes every time you set the instrument up.

This is not as confusing as it sounds. If you know where the projected level plane is in relation to the elevations being shot, the rest is common sense. If there's any confusion, make a quick sketch to clear it up.

Reading the instrument

Usually, the higher the number, the lower the elevation.

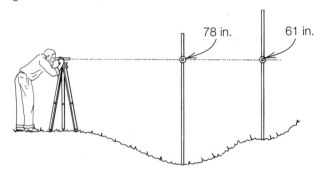

Measuring differences in elevation

When the level plane is between elevations, add the two differences together to get the total difference in elevation between A and B.

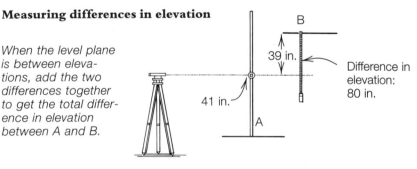

When the level plane is below both elevations, subtract the lower number (B) from the higher one (A) to find the difference in elevation.

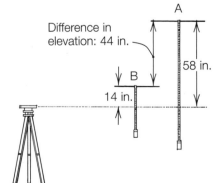

corner reference stakes. Begin by setting up batter boards to hold a stringline directly over the reference stakes. First, drive 2x4 batter-board posts into the ground, two for each of reference stake, leaving them higher than the planned top of the foundation and set perpendicular to the foundation line and about 3 ft. apart. Then shoot the height of the reference stake again, which in this example is 47½ in. below the level plane projected by the transit (see the drawing on p. 63).

Have your helper move a ruler or measuring stick over to one of the 2x4 batter-board posts and (holding the ruler vertically) go up the appropriate amount to get the top-of-foundation elevation. Usually this amount is the difference between the reading at the reference stake (47½ in.) minus the original difference in elevation (33 in.), or 14½ in. in this example. When you can see the 14½-in. mark in the crosshairs of the transit, have your helper mark the post at the bottom of the ruler.

It's important to note that each time you set up a transit, you establish a new level plane (for more on using a leveling instrument, see the sidebar on the facing page). Therefore, the actual elevation numbers are relative, while the difference in elevation between the reference stake and the top-of-foundation line—again, 33 in. in this example—remains the same throughout. It is this constant (the difference in elevation) that must be referred to and accounted for every time you set up the transit and establish a new level plane when determining the top-of-foundation height on the batter boards.

After your helper has marked the top-of-foundation height on all four posts, attach horizontal batter boards between each pair of posts and aligned with the marks on the posts (for help in setting up batter boards, see Tricks of the Trade at right). The batter boards reestablish the top elevation of the foundation wall, but now you also need to restore the original top-of-foundation line. To do this, run a stringline from one batter board to the other and directly over the reference stakes. Reestablish the corners along that stringline simply by plumbing up from the reference stake, marking the string with a felt-tip pen, and then measuring in the appropriate distance (12 ft. in this example). After establishing this first corner, you can find the second one by

Tricks of the Trade
Setting Up Batter Boards

There are a couple of simple things you can do to simplify setting batter boards. The first is to use screws instead of nails to attach the batter boards to the posts. Driving nails in with a hammer often knocks the post loose and makes the assembly wobbly and inaccurate. Using a drill and drywall screws reduces the chance that the posts will be jarred loose. For small jobs that I expect to knock out in three or four days, I forego fasteners altogether and hold the batter boards in place with C-clamps.

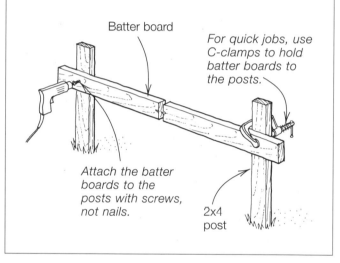

Batter board

For quick jobs, use C-clamps to hold batter boards to the posts.

Attach the batter boards to the posts with screws, not nails.

2x4 post

measuring out from the first mark the length of the foundation specified in the blueprints. In this example, that distance is 48 ft.

At this point, you have the option of either laying out the entire top of the foundation or transferring the building corners you've just reestablished to the bottom of the excavation. When laying out a concrete-block foundation, I generally prefer to work from the top, setting up batter boards outside the excavation with stringlines representing the top outside edge of the foundation (see the drawing on p. 66). To lay out a poured concrete foundation, on the other hand, I normally use

Establishing the Top Line and Corners of the First Wall

Set up batter boards at the correct elevation and stretch a stringline representing the top of the foundation between them. Then reestablish the corners by measuring in the appropriate distance from the corner reference stake. After marking the corners on the top line of the foundation, transfer them to the bottom of the excavation with a plumb bob.

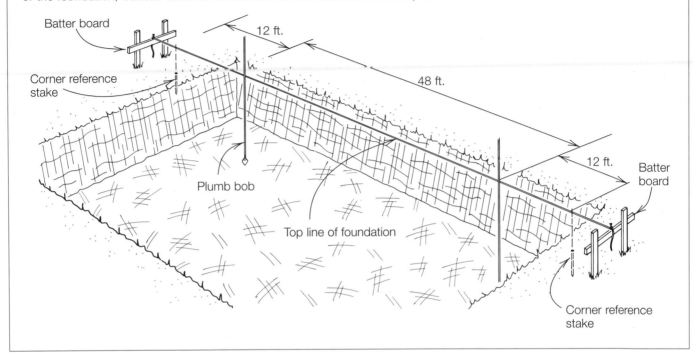

Batter board

Corner reference stake

12 ft.

48 ft.

12 ft.

Batter board

Plumb bob

Top line of foundation

Corner reference stake

a plumb bob to transfer the corners to the bottom of the excavation and complete the layout at that lower level, totally within the excavation. Since I'm describing a concrete-block foundation here, I'll continue with the batter boards at the top-of-foundation level.

After establishing the top line and corners of the first long wall, install a second pair of batter boards to hold the stringline representing the long wall that runs parallel to it (see the bottom drawing on the facing page). First, drive four 2x4 posts into the ground, making sure that their tops remain above the top-of-foundation level and that they will straddle the second top-of-foundation line. Next, use a transit to mark these posts level with the top-of-foundation stringline you've just set up and attach horizontal batter boards. Finally, set up a stringline exactly parallel to and the specified distance from—27 ft. in this example—the first line (for help in

setting up parallel stringlines, see Tricks of the Trade at the top of the facing page).

Now that you've established the two long walls, you need to lay out the two sidewalls. On the first stringline, you've already marked two of the corners of the foundation. Square across from those marks to the other stringlines, thus laying out the two sidewalls. To do this, calculate the hypotenuse of the right triangle formed by sides of 27 ft. and 48 ft. Using the Pythagorean theorem ($a^2 + b^2 = c^2$), plug in the numbers:

$$27^2 + 48^2 = c^2$$

$$729 + 2304 = 3033$$

$$\sqrt{3033} = 55.07 \text{ ft., or 55 ft. } {}^{13}\!/_{16} \text{ in.}$$

Tricks of the Trade
Setting Up Parallel Stringlines

When you're trying to get one stringline precisely parallel to another, it's important to make sure that your tape measure is perpendicular to the line being measured from. An easy way to do this is to swing the tape in an arc and slide the line to the high point in the arc. The shortest distance—20 ft. in the drawing at right—indicates that the tape measure is perpendicular and thus in the right position for an accurate reading.

Mason's line blocks (usually free for the asking from your block supplier) are great for initially setting stringlines on batter boards. These blocks are held in place by string tension and can be slid along the batter board as the string location is adjusted. Once the stringline is exactly right, clearly mark that location, later installing a screw to hold the line more securely in place. Some builders use a saw kerf, which allows a knotted string to be easily and accurately lifted out and replaced. And it's a good idea to have two or three different-color felt-tip pens on hand when marking stringlines and batter boards. When you have to make corrections or adjustments, you can switch colors to avoid confusion.

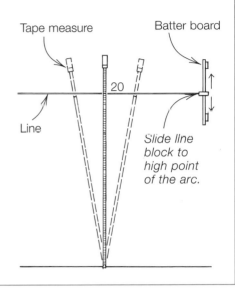

Tape measure

Batter board

20

Line

Slide line block to high point of the arc.

Laying Out the Top of a Foundation

Establish the two long walls and one set of corners, then use the Pythagorean theorem ($a^2 + b^2 = c^2$) to calculate the length of the diagonals, which can then be used to establish the second set of corners. Then install batter boards and stretch stringlines between them for the two sidewalls.

This example is for a 27-ft. by 48-ft. foundation.

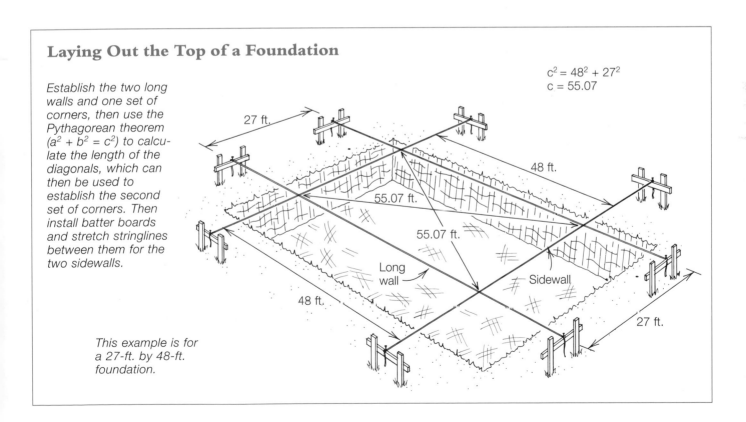

$$c^2 = 48^2 + 27^2$$
$$c = 55.07$$

27 ft.

48 ft.

55.07 ft.

55.07 ft.

Long wall

Sidewall

48 ft.

27 ft.

To lay this out, pull a 100-ft. tape measure (laid out in the decimalized feet of the engineer's scale) diagonally across from the "corner dot" on the first stringline to the second stringline, marking it where it intersects at 55.07 ft. This dot represents the third corner. To lay out the fourth, pull 55.07 ft. diagonally across from the second corner on the first stringline and mark again. To check your work, measure from dot to dot along the second stringline, which should come out to an even 48 ft.

Let's say that when you picked up your helper this morning, he sat on your calculator and broke it. How could you square up this foundation without a calculator. In this case, you could use the $\frac{27}{27}38^{18}$ entry on your rafter square, which tells you that the diagonal of a right triangle with 27-ft. sides is 38.18 ft. Measure 27 ft. down from one of the corner dots on the first stringline, mark, and then pull the 38.18-ft. diagonal (38 ft. 2³⁄₁₆ in.) from that mark to the second stringline (see the left drawing on the facing page).

Now, what would you do if you left your rafter square at home? You could use the 3-4-5 method, dividing the width—27 ft.—by 3, then multiplying that sum—9—by 4 and 5 to get the other side and the hypotenuse of the triangle. These come to 36 and 45, respectively. To lay this out, measure 36 ft. from a corner, make a dot on the line, and then pull a 45-ft. diagonal (see the right drawing on the facing page). No matter which technique you use, be sure to check the layout by pulling diagonals across both directions to make sure they're equal. Then set up batter boards and stringlines to cross the corners at a perpendicular, thereby representing the sidewalls of the foundation (to learn how to lay out a foundation without batter boards, see the sidebar on p. 70).

Laying out the footing

After the top of the foundation has been laid out, measure down from the stringlines to establish the top of the footing. It's important to get this measurement right, even though it will ultimately be buried and out of sight. If you're using concrete block, you're normally locked into a distance divisible by 8 in., but occasionally (when a 4-in. course is planned at the top of the wall, for example) the distance is divisible by 4 in.

In any case, it's foolish not to get the footing level and an even number of block courses down from the top-of-foundation line. When the footing isn't installed at the right elevation, the masons either have to "hog up" the first course with bricks or break or cut the bottom of the first course of blocks. This is hard, slow, and unnecessary work that can result in a sloppy job in which structural integrity is compromised by excessively fat joints. I find working on an uneven footing or a footing poured at the wrong height to be extremely aggravating, mainly because I know the problems could have been avoided with a little planning.

The foundation in this example has 13 full block courses planned (see the top drawing on p. 62). To get the footing at the right elevation, then, you need to lay out the top of it 104 in. down from the top-of-foundation line, since each block course, including the bed joint, is 8 in. high ($8 \times 13 = 104$). In addition to being placed at the right elevation, the footing has to be located accurately, with the foundation above it resting in the center rather than at its edge. To locate the footing accurately, transfer the corners formed by the top-of-foundation stringlines with a plumb bob, marking the ground with small stakes (see the drawing on p. 66). From these stakes, which represent the outside corners of the foundation, you can measure and lay out the footing trench.

According to the building code in my area, the footing must project 4 in. beyond the thickness of the foundation wall. In this example, a 12-in.-thick block foundation is planned. If you were building in my area, the footing would need to be 20 in. wide. To center the footing under the foundation wall layout, measure 4 in. out from the stakes and 16 in. toward the inside of the foundation. I usually lay out the trench an additional 8 in. toward the outside, however, which would make this trench 28 in. wide. The wider footing trench gives me room to use a form board along the outside of the footing, which provides an excellent guide during the concrete pour for getting the top of the footing level and at precisely the right height. Then, after the concrete sets up, I strip the form boards, and I'm left with an 8-in.-wide channel where I can install the footing drain.

It's essential to get the form boards right. Dig the trench, plumb down from the top-of-foundation lines, measure out 4 in., and set up a stringline (see the left drawing on

Laying Out Rebar in a Block Wall

Rebar ties a block foundation wall to the footing and should be placed during the footing pour so that it is centered on the block cores. Establish a centerline for the foundation wall, then place the rebar every 32 in., beginning 4 in. in from the end of the wall.

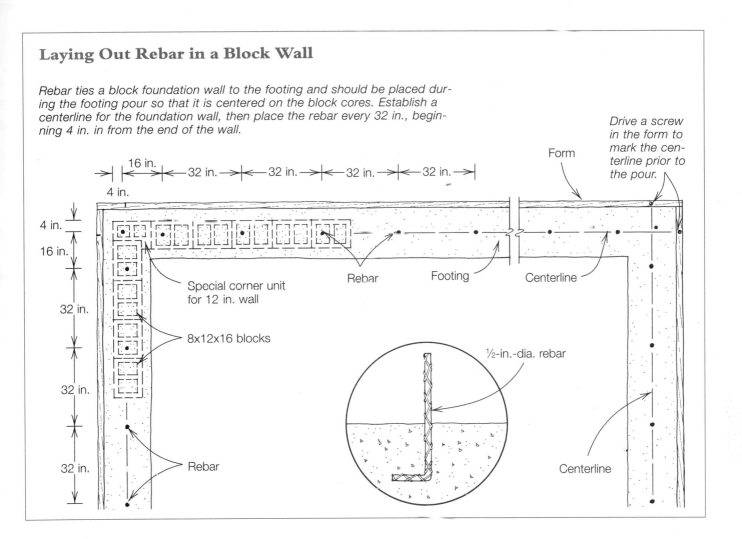

Drive a screw in the form to mark the centerline prior to the pour.

Form

16 in.

32 in.

32 in.

32 in.

32 in.

4 in.

4 in.

16 in.

32 in.

32 in.

32 in.

Special corner unit for 12 in. wall

8x12x16 blocks

Rebar

Rebar

Footing

Centerline

½-in.-dia. rebar

Centerline

Another way to proceed (and the way I prefer to work) is to set up story poles (see the right drawing on p. 74). Begin this process by marking the four outside corners of the foundation with a plumb bob lowered from each intersection of the top-of-foundation lines. After marking the corners on the footing, nail a 2-in. steel story pole (I weld L-brackets to the bottom of the poles specifically for this purpose) directly to the concrete with case-hardened nails at each corner. Set the story poles plumb and hold them firmly in place with two braces. Use C-clamps to attach the braces to the poles and to anchor them firmly either to stakes or to 12-in. blocks set squarely on the ground outside the footing.

Then mark off the block courses, starting at the top-of-foundation line and measuring down in 8-in. increments. At the lowest mark, pull a stringline from pole to pole; then you're ready to start laying the first course of blocks. To hold the stringline to the pole, use mason's line blocks (available from your masonry supplier). Using this technique, there is no need to build a corner first. You can lay the whole foundation directly off the story poles, if you desire.

Laying out a poured concrete foundation

When poured concrete walls are used instead of concrete blocks, it's easiest to begin the layout by transferring the house corners to the inside of the excavation.

Forming a Keyway in a Foundation Footing

A keyway helps tie a poured foundation wall to a footing and can be made by embedding a 2x2 in the top of the footing while it is being poured. The keyway should be centered on the foundation wall, which should be centered over the footing.

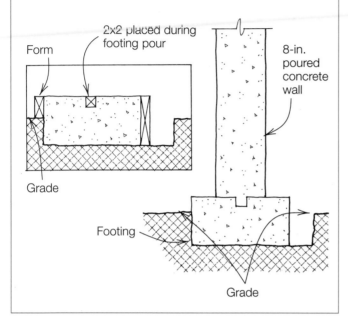

Form

2x2 placed during footing pour

8-in. poured concrete wall

Grade

Footing

Grade

Laying Out Block Courses with Story Poles

Story poles set up at each outside corner speed up the laying of block. After establishing the top-of-foundation line on the pole, mark from the top down in 8-in. increments.

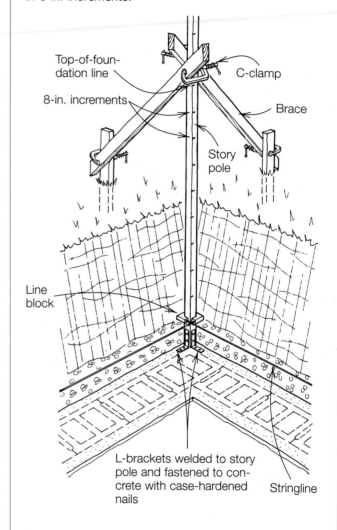

Top-of-foundation line

8-in. increments

C-clamp

Brace

Story pole

Line block

L-brackets welded to story pole and fastened to concrete with case-hardened nails

Stringline

Plan view of setup

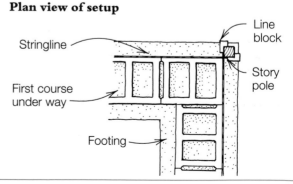

Stringline

First course under way

Footing

Line block

Story pole

There you can execute the entire layout at the footing level. Normally I set up batter boards at the level of the top of the footing (usually 96 in. down from the top-of-foundation line). I use the same approach that I just described for a concrete-block wall, only here I start about 8 ft. lower.

First, establish the outside dimensions of the walls, then measure out 4 in. and in 12 in. (assuming you're using 8-in. forms) from these to establish the dimensions of the footing (see the drawing on the facing page). A lot of builders forego batter boards altogether, however, and square up the foundation before the footing is poured by setting up a transit over one of the corners. Once they get the corners of the foundation staked, they measure out the appropriate amount to lay out the footing.

After the footing has been poured, you can carefully lay out the placement of the walls on the footing with a

Laying Out a Poured Concrete Foundation

Layout of a poured foundation wall takes place at the footing level, rather than above grade. After the footings have been installed and the outside corners transferred to the footings (see the drawing on p. 66), lay out the concrete forms directly on the footings.

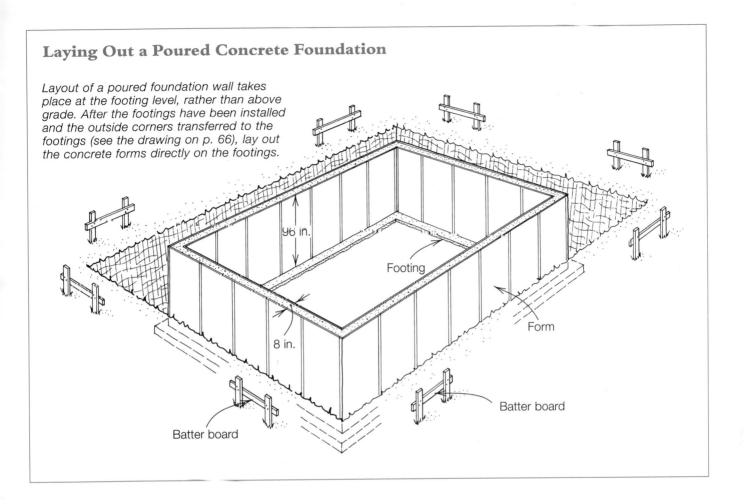

96 in.

8 in.

Footing

Form

Batter board

Batter board

Batter board

chalkline. You can set up the foundation wall forms plumb along these lines. Then the concrete is poured to a consistent height above the footing, usually to the top of the forms.

Establishing the top of a foundation for an addition

Unlike the foundation for a freestanding building, where a difference of an inch or two in the final height is usually not too important, the final height of the foundation for an addition usually has to be right on the money. This is because you want to arrive at a finished floor height in the addition that is flush with the existing floor. To begin, start where you want to end up: at the very top of the finished floor.

First mark the height of the existing finished floor right on the outside of the house where it is clearly visible. One way to do this is to set up a transit, shoot the elevation of the floor through an open door or window, and transfer that elevation to the outside wall of the house (see the drawing on p. 76).

Next, find out (usually from the blueprints) the precise dimensions of the addition's floor covering, subfloor, joists, and sills. On a typical addition, this might mean a carpet and pad (¾ in.), tongue-and-groove plywood (¾ in.), 2x10 joists (9¼ in.), and 2x8 mudsills (1½ in.), or 12¼ in. total. Measuring down from the existing finished floor 12¼ in. gives you the correct height for the top of the addition's foundation. With your transit, mark this elevation at both ends of the planned addition and chalk a line representing the top of the foun-

Laying Out the Top of a Foundation for an Addition

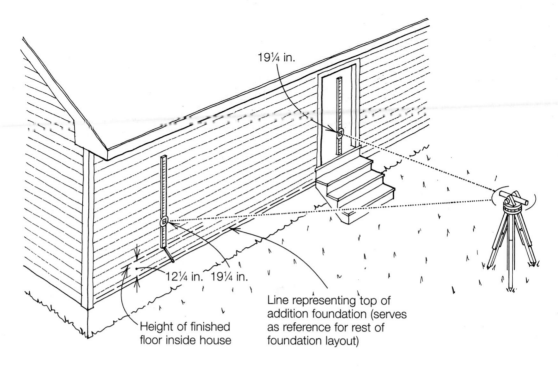

19¼ in.

12¼ in. 19¼ in.

Height of finished
floor inside house

Line representing top of
addition foundation (serves
as reference for rest of
foundation layout)

1. Shoot the floor elevation (19¼ in.) through an open door (or window).
2. Hold a ruler against the outside wall so that 19¼ in. appears in the crosshairs of the transit.

3. Mark the bottom of the ruler.
4. Measure down the exact thickness of the new floor system (see the drawing on the facing page) and mark the top-of-foundation height.

dation directly on the house. This chalkline serves as the baseline for the layout. After measuring and marking the first two corners of the addition on the chalked line, set up batter boards to lay out the outside (parallel) wall and lay out the rest of the foundation in the usual way.

Don't try to determine the height of the existing foundation. This is just about impossible to do with any degree of certainty on many houses and, in any event, the height of the existing foundation is often immaterial. Especially in older houses, the combined thickness of the existing mudsill, floor joists, subfloor, and finished floor rarely matches the total of those that will be installed in an addition. It would be silly, then, to make the foundations the same height when the materials

that rest on them are different and add up to unequal thicknesses (see the drawing on the facing page).

In most cases, the difference in the final height of the foundations disappears under the exterior carpentry. And when masonry units are used, the eye often forgives brick or block courses that don't line up perfectly. If there is a misalignment, it can often be blocked from view by a strategically placed shrub. There are times, however, when matching the existing brick or block courses is an important visual concern. When this is the case, you can build the new foundation even with the old one and then make adjustments to the floor system (adding a mudsill or using larger or smaller floor joists, for example). Alternatively, you can finagle a masonry

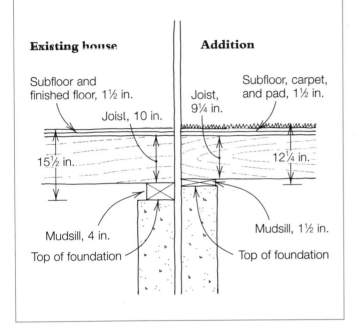

**Leveling a New Floor
with an Existing One**

*Different floor systems can vary in thickness by several
inches, depending on their age and type of construction.
Addition foundations should be planned to bring the new
floor system level with the existing floor system, rather
than to match the existing foundation.*

Existing house

Subfloor and
finished floor, 1½ in.

Joist, 10 in.

15½ in.

Mudsill, 4 in.

Top of foundation

Addition

Joist,
9¼ in.

Subfloor, carpet,
and pad, 1½ in.

12¼ in.

Mudsill, 1½ in.

Top of foundation

foundation (by pouring a concrete cap, for instance),
making the elevation the correct height for the addition
while matching the courses of the existing foundation
(see the top drawings on p. 78).

LAYING OUT
COMPLEX FOUNDATIONS

Not all foundations are simple rectangles. Houses are
often L- or T-shaped, or they might have insets, projec-
tions, curves, or angles. One part of the foundation
might be higher or lower than another part. One part
might be built as a full basement, while another might
be a slab or crawl space. The possible configurations of
foundations are just about as varied as the houses that
sit on them. And yet, the layout of even the most complex of foundations nearly always starts with a simple,
level, and carefully squared rectangle.

I use a basic rectangle to serve as a reference for any type
of foundation layout. Once a primary rectangle has
been laid out, it's simply a matter of adding or subtracting the other geometric forms that make up the rest of
the design. In Chapter 3 you saw how these complex
shapes are laid out on paper. Now let's take a look at
how they are laid out over freshly dug earth.

Adding rectangular elements

For most houses, elements that are added or subtracted
from the primary rectangle are themselves simple rectangles. In some cases, these are small insets or projec-
tions, such as the foundation of a chimney or small
porch. These can be simply measured from the primary
rectangle at the footing level without adding additional
layout stringlines. In other instances, another rectangle
will have to be laid out with additional batter boards
and stringlines (see the bottom drawing on p. 78).

This secondary rectangle is laid out just like the simple
foundation described previously, except that, in this
case, the reference line is already set up and is one of the
stringlines that makes up the primary rectangle. To locate the corners of the secondary rectangle, just measure
the distance that is specified in the plan from one corner of the primary rectangle and mark the stringline
with a felt-tip pen. Once you have the corners of the
first wall established, again set up batter boards, stretch
a parallel stringline for the opposite wall, and pull the
hypotenuse (or diagonal) to lay out the sidewalls, just
like for the primary rectangle.

On very involved foundations, it might become necessary to install a number of pairs of batter boards and to
calculate several hypotenuses to square up the various
sections of the foundation. Yet each section that is
added is as simple as the original primary rectangle. It
should be noted that stringlines for different walls can
be combined on the same batter board. On very complex foundations, builders sometimes erect a continuous batter board around the entire planned foundation.

Making a change in the foundation level

Houses are often built with some sections lower than
others. A common example of this is when an attached
garage is built a foot or so below the level of the house.
To see how a lower section could be laid out, let's say
that the owner of the 48-ft. by 27-ft. house you've been

Two Ways to Match Block or Brick Foundations

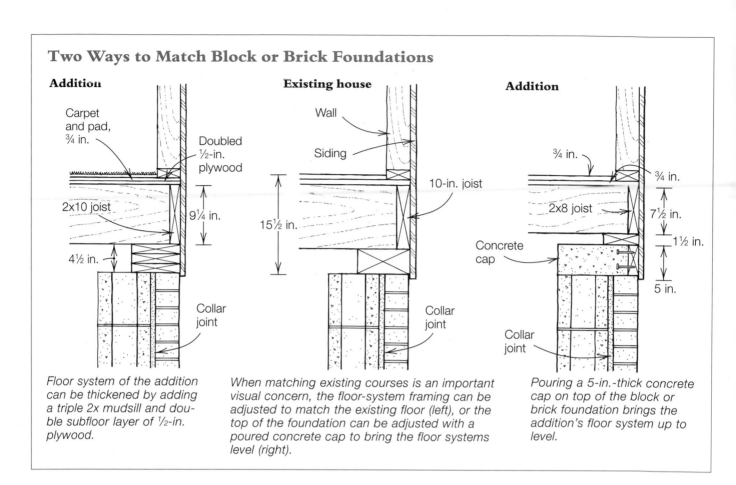

Addition

Carpet and pad, ¾ in.

Doubled ½-in. plywood

2x10 joist

9¼ in.

4½ in.

Collar joint

Floor system of the addition can be thickened by adding a triple 2x mudsill and double subfloor layer of ½-in. plywood.

Existing house

Wall

Siding

10-in. joist

15½ in.

Collar joint

When matching existing courses is an important visual concern, the floor-system framing can be adjusted to match the existing floor (left), or the top of the foundation can be adjusted with a poured concrete cap to bring the floor systems level (right).

Addition

¾ in.

¾ in.

2x8 joist

7½ in.

1½ in.

Concrete cap

5 in.

Collar joint

Pouring a 5-in.-thick concrete cap on top of the block or brick foundation brings the addition's floor system up to level.

Adding Rectangular Elements to a Basic Foundation

Once the primary foundation rectangle has been squared, smaller rectangular elements that extend off the foundation —for example, a garage or sunroom— can be located accurately. The string-lines used to mark the primary rectangle also serve to establish one side of each smaller rectangle, while corners are established according to blueprint dimensions. Each rectangle is then squared according to the same technique used for the primary rectangle.

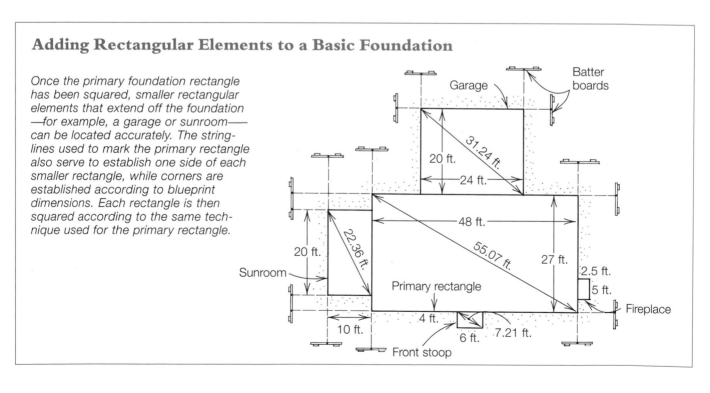

Garage

Batter boards

31.24 ft.

20 ft.

24 ft.

48 ft.

55.07 ft.

27 ft.

22.36 ft.

20 ft.

Sunroom

Primary rectangle

2.5 ft.

5 ft.

Fireplace

10 ft.

4 ft.

6 ft.

7.21 ft.

Front stoop

working on opted to include a 24-ft. by 24-ft. garage attached to the rear of the house. The garage foundation is designed to be 15-in. lower than the rest of the house. How can this be laid out?

In this situation, combine the batter boards that represent both the back wall of the house and the adjoining wall of the garage. After laying out the primary rectangle, set up a second pair of batter boards exactly 15 in. below the batter boards used to hold the stringline representing the back wall of the house foundation (see the drawing at right). Then plumb down with a 2-ft. level from the upper batter board and mark the lower one. Stretch a stringline between the marks on these lower batter boards to establish the first top-of-foundation line of the garage. Next, transfer the location of the corner of the house to the lower stringline, measure in the appropriate distance (as specified in the plan), and mark the first two corners of the garage. From this reference, you can lay out the rest of the garage foundation in the usual manner.

Adding oblique angles

When the foundation turns at an angle other than 90°, start with the primary rectangle and add or subtract a right triangle. The hypotenuse of this right triangle then represents the baseline for the second rectangle, which joins the first at an oblique angle. After you've established this new reference line, you can lay out the rest of the intersecting rectangle in the usual way.

For example, let's say that this 27-ft.-wide foundation turns 45° at the 36-ft. mark along its long side. Begin by laying out a 27-ft. by 36-ft. rectangle. Now, to get the 45° turn, you need to lay out the hypotenuse of a right triangle with both sides 27 ft. long. If the primary rectangle has been laid out precisely square, all you need to do is measure back 27 ft. from the appropriate corner.

To double-check this layout, calculate the hypotenuse of a triangle with two sides of 27. This sum, 38.18 ft., is conveniently etched on the brace table of your rafter square. But if your square is still at home beside the bookshelves you didn't quite finish over the weekend, you can also use the formula for finding the diagonal of a square (see p. 44): $\sqrt{2} \times 27$ (or 1.41421).

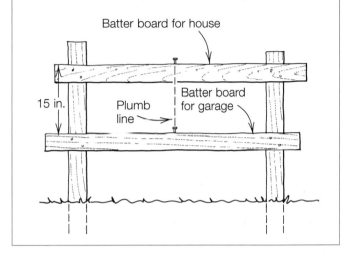

Using Batter Boards to Indicate a Change in Foundation Level

When a foundation changes level (for example, when a garage is attached to a house), a second set of batter boards can be added below the first at the new elevation. A second stringline stretched directly below the first one represents the change in level.

Batter board for house

15 in.

Plumb line

Batter board for garage

After marking the hypotenuse along the primary rectangle, set up batter boards and stretch a stringline that represents both this hypotenuse and the baseline of the secondary rectangle. Then set up batter boards to hold a stringline that represents the wall that runs parallel to the new baseline. Let's say, though, that this intersecting rectangle is quite a bit smaller than the primary rectangle. The wall that runs parallel to the new baseline is just 22 ft. away, and the angled wing of the house is only 20 ft. wide. To lay this out, measure 20 ft. along the baseline (from the point at which the foundation will turn) and mark the stringline. Next, calculate the hypotenuse formed by a right triangle with sides of 20 and 22, which comes to 29.73 ft., and pull this distance, marking the second stringline where this measurement intersects with it to establish the third corner. Then pull the same dimension from the other point along the baseline and mark again. The measurement from dot to dot, of course, should be 20 ft. (see the drawing on p. 80).

Adding a Rectangle that Intersects at 45°

When a foundation turns 45° from the primary rectangle (indicated by the dark line), first find the baseline (x) of the new intersecting rectangle (shaded area), set up batter boards and parallel stringlines for the first set of walls (a and d) of the new rectangle, then square up the corners by finding the diagonal (c).

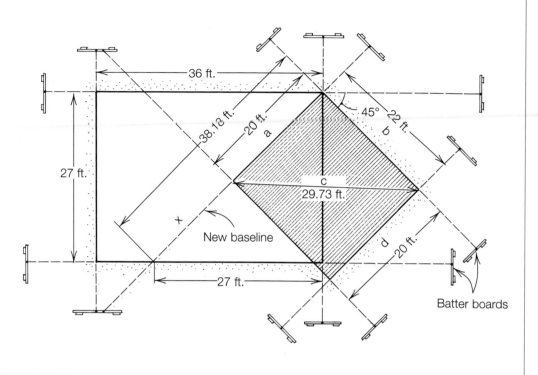

As angles go, 45° is pretty easy to work with, so let's try one that's a little more challenging. For the sake of simplicity, I'll use the same foundation but change the angle that the addition veers off from 45° to 30°. To establish the baseline of the secondary rectangle in this situation, turn to Appendix D on p. 212. According to the appendix, the hypotenuse of a right triangle with a 30° angle and a base of 1 is 1.1547, and the altitude is 0.57735. Here, the base of the triangle you're dealing with is 27 ft. To find both the hypotenuse and the altitude of that triangle, then, just multiply 1.1547 and 0.57735 by 27, which comes to 31.18 ft. and 15.59 ft., respectively. Now, all you have to do is pull 15.59 ft. in from the corner of the 36-ft. by 27-ft. rectangle and mark the line.

To check your work, pull the 31.18-ft. hypotenuse diagonally. It should engage the line of the primary rectangle where you marked the 15.59-ft. measurement. This mark establishes the baseline for the second rectangle.

From this line, you can proceed exactly as described previously to lay out the rest of the foundation.

Another way to establish the new baseline would be to use the figure for 30° in Appendix C (see p. 211). According to the appendix, a 30° angle has a 6.9298-in-12 pitch. Therefore, for every 12-in. of run, there are 6.9298 in. of rise. The run here is 27 ft., so $27 \times 6.9298 = 187.06$ in. (or 15.59 ft.). This is the amount you need to measure in from the corner along the second stringline. Set up a line from the corner to this point to establish the baseline of the secondary rectangle (see the drawing on the facing page).

This angle could also be laid out using a transit or builder's level with a high-quality horizontal scale (sometimes called an azimuth circle or a vernier scale). To use this technique, set the instrument precisely over a point—typically a nail driven into a stake set nearly flush to grade—representing one of the corners of the primary rectangle. This, of course, has to be done at

Two Ways of Adding a Rectangle that Intersects at 30°

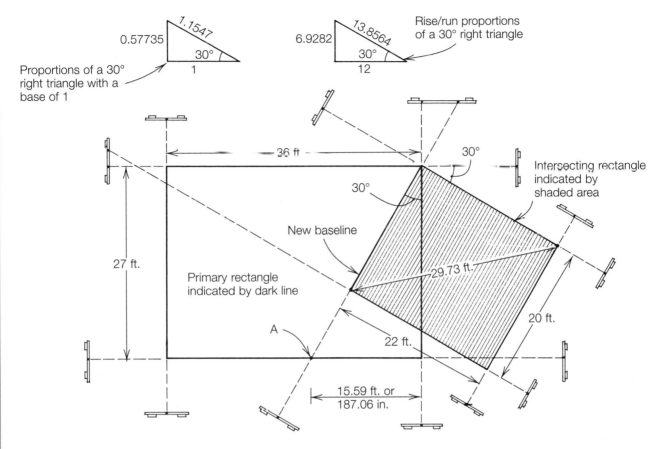

Proportions of a 30° right triangle with a base of 1

1.1547 · 0.57735 · 30° · 1

Rise/run proportions of a 30° right triangle

13.8564 · 6.9282 · 30° · 12

36 ft

30°

30°

30°

Intersecting rectangle indicated by shaded area

New baseline

27 ft.

Primary rectangle indicated by dark line

29.73 ft.

A

22 ft.

20 ft.

15.59 ft. or 187.06 in.

Method 1
1. Look up proportions for a 30° triangle in Appendix D.
2. Multiply the proportion for the altitude—0.57735—by 27 to get 15.59.
3. Measure 15.59 ft. from the corner and mark the stringline at A.
4. Set up batter boards for the new baseline and lay out the remaining intersecting rectangle.

Method 2
1. Look up rise/run proportions for a 30° triangle in Appendix C.
2. Multiply rise per foot (6.9282) by 27 to get 187.06 in. (or 15.59 ft.).
3. Measure 187.06 in. along the stringline and mark at A.
4. Set up batter boards for the new baseline and lay out the remaining intersecting rectangle.

ground level within the excavation. From the loop centered under the pivot point, suspend a plumb bob and carefully coax the instrument into position so that the plumb bob is directly over the nail. When it is, the pivot of the instrument is centered over the corner. After leveling the instrument, shoot the other corner of the primary rectangle. A transit can be tilted to see the other corner stake, while a builder's level will require a second person to hold a plumb bob or spirit level over the

corner while you aim the instrument. Once the instrument is aimed precisely at the second corner, the scale can be set to zero. Now, to make a 30° turn in the other direction, rotate the instrument 150° (see the left drawing on p. 82).

Laying out circles and polygons
As you saw in the previous chapter, circles, semicircles, and polygons are often laid out with reference to a cen-

Using a Transit to Turn a 30° Angle

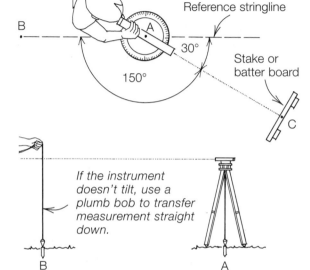

Reference stringline

B

A

30°

150°

Stake or
batter board

C

*If the instrument
doesn't tilt, use a
plumb bob to transfer
measurement straight
down.*

B   A

1. Set up the instrument (transit or builder's level)
   directly over corner point A.
2. Aim instrument at the second corner point (B)
   along the reference stringline.
3. Set the horizontal scale to zero.
4. Rotate the instrument 150° and have a coworker
   mark location C.

Laying Out a Curved Portion of a Foundation

*The center point that establishes the curved portion
of this foundation is measured from the outside walls
of the primary rectangle. Both the length of the radius
and the exact position of the pivot point should be
specified in the plan. A radius board can be used to
lay out the curved portion of the footing.*

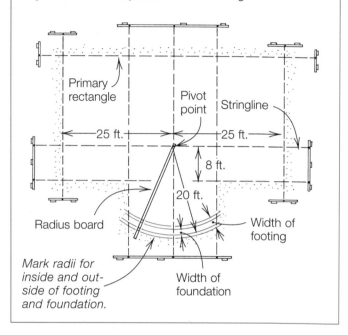

Primary
rectangle

Pivot
point

Stringline

25 ft.   25 ft.

8 ft.

20 ft.

Radius board

Width of
footing

*Mark radii for
inside and out-
side of footing
and foundation.*

Width of
foundation

ter point. When these forms are part of a larger foundation, the center point must be established in reference
to the primary rectangle.

I generally set up a batter board or use a firmly anchored
stake to hold the pivot point when I swing the radius
for a circular foundation, and I swing both the inside
and the outside of the footing from the same pivot
point. Later, I use the same pivot point to swing the radius of the foundation as well. The easiest way to do this
is at the footing level (see the right drawing above).

To lay out an octagonal foundation, start with four pairs
of batter boards and lay out a square. Measure and mark
the center of each side, then calculate the distance needed from these center points to get the eight points of the
octagon. As you discovered in Chapter 3, you can calculate that distance by multiplying the length of one
side of the square by 0.207 (see p. 55). For example, the
points of an octagon 8 ft. across are located 1 ft. 7⅞ in.
from the center points of the sides of an 8-ft. square
($8 \times 0.207 = 1.656$ ft., or 1 ft. 7⅞ in.). Measure and mark
the eight points of the octagon on the stringline marking the perimeter of the 8-ft. square, then set up four
more stringlines to lay out the rest of the foundation
(see the top drawing on the facing page).

Laying Out an 8-ft.-wide Octagon

1. Lay out an 8-ft. square, being sure to check that the diagonals are equal.
2. Find and mark the center of each side.
3. Multiply the length of a side by 0.207 (8 ft. × 0.207 = 1.656 ft.).
4. Measure 1.656 ft. out from the center marks and mark the eight corners of the octagon on the stringlines.
5. Set up batter boards to hold four new stringlines.

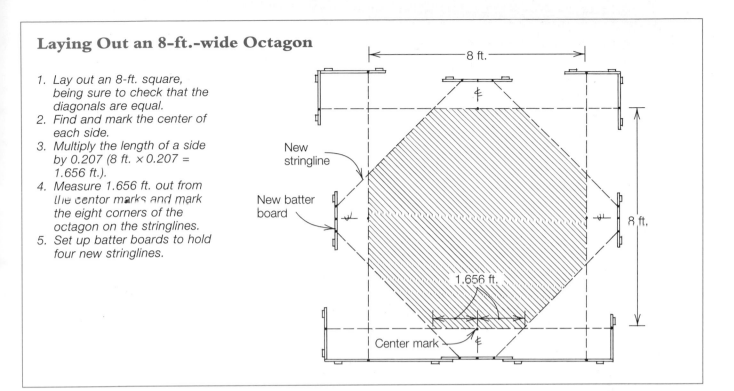

New stringline

New batter board

8 ft.

8 ft.

1.656 ft.

Center mark

Organically shaped foundations are rare but not unheard of. Although it's necessary to draw these out freehand, this doesn't mean that measurement and layout should be left to chance. Unless you're willing to rely on serendipity, an organic layout should begin with a scale drawing. Over the scale drawing, you can superimpose a rectangle and scale important points in the shape. Later, on the job site, you can lay out the full-size rectangle and use it as a reference to lay out the points you have scaled. There is often a lot of creative license granted to the craftsman on these kinds of jobs. Where great fidelity to the drawing is required, however, you can set up a grid of strings within the rectangle and transfer more points, thus achieving a higher degree of precision (see the drawing at left). This is essentially the technique archaeologists use to map out the position of items found on archaeological sites.

LAYING OUT SLAB-ON-GRADE AND CRAWL-SPACE FOUNDATIONS

There are two main differences between laying out a full basement foundation and laying out a slab-on-grade or crawl-space foundation. The first is the distance measured down from the top-of-foundation line. The sec-

Laying Out an Organically Shaped Foundation

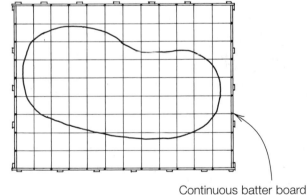

Continuous batter board

1. Begin with a scale drawing of the foundation.
2. Superimpose a rectangle on the drawing. For greater fidelity, divide the rectangle into a grid and map the shape onto the grid.
3. Lay out the full-scale rectangle on site.
4. Measure points as scaled from the drawing.
5. A continuous batter board (as shown in the drawing) can be used to reproduce the grid. The finer the grid, the higher the degree of accuracy.

An Example Crawl-Space Foundation

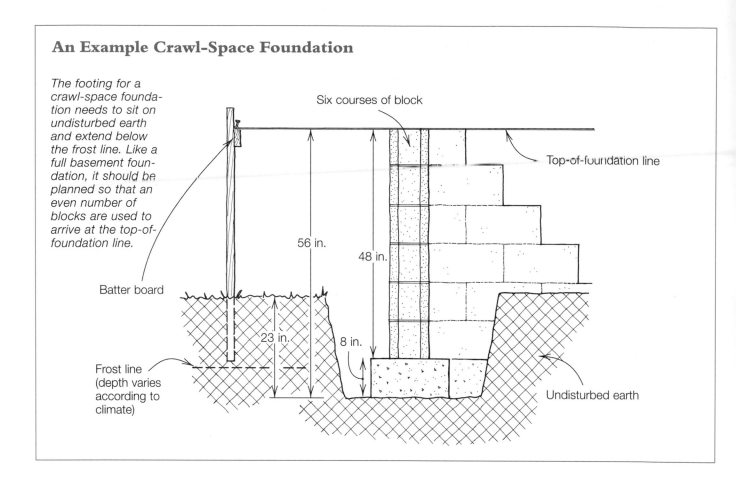

The footing for a crawl-space foundation needs to sit on undisturbed earth and extend below the frost line. Like a full basement foundation, it should be planned so that an even number of blocks are used to arrive at the top-of-foundation line.

Batter board

Frost line (depth varies according to climate)

Six courses of block

Top-of-foundation line

56 in.

48 in.

23 in.

8 in.

Undisturbed earth

ond is the degree to which the surface of the ground is level when the footing is laid out and installed. When you're building a basement, the footing and foundation layout begins after a level opening has been carved into the earth. When no basement is planned, however, the land is simply cleared of trees, brush, grass, and topsoil and left close to its natural grade.

You can lay out the top of a slab-on-grade or crawl-space foundation the same way you lay out the top of a full basement foundation. Then you lay out the footing centered on the lines representing the top of the foundation. After the footing has been marked on the ground, however, the similarities in laying out these different types of foundations become less apparent. The footing for a slab-on-grade or crawl-space foundation must be dug into the uneven surface of the ground. In addition

to making the trench the proper width and getting it correctly centered beneath the foundation wall, the trench has to be dug to the right elevation.

Laying out the footing

There are three important considerations when laying out and digging the footing for one of these foundations. First of all, the bottom of the footing should sit on suitable load-bearing soil. In most cases, this simply means getting down to undisturbed soil. Second, unless special measures are taken to protect the footing from freezing, the footing trench should extend below the frost line, which varies according to climate. Third, the bottom of the footing trench should be at an elevation that works out with the final elevation of the foundation. A foundation built with 8-in. blocks, for example, should be planned so that the distance between the top of the footing and the top of the foundation wall is

Stepping a Footing Up a Sloping Grade

Where a foundation steps up to follow a sloping grade, the footing should be stepped in 8-in. increments so that block courses won't need to be cut. A transit can be used to keep the footing trench at the right depth as it steps up the grade.

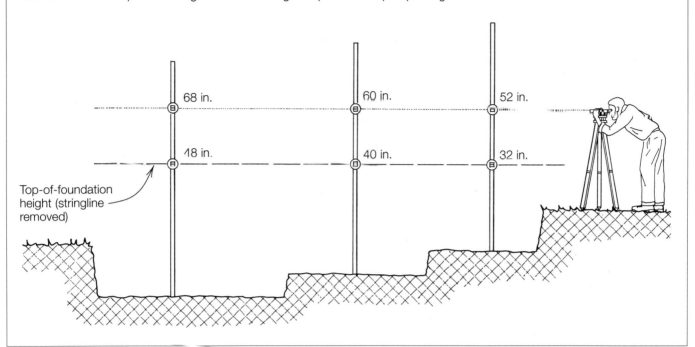

68 in.   60 in.   52 in.

18 in.   40 in.   32 in.

Top-of-foundation height (stringline removed)

evenly divisible by 8 in. (see the drawing on the facing page). So if an 8-in.-thick footing is planned, the bottom of the trench should also be a distance that is divisible by 8 in. from the top-of-foundation line.

To get the footing the right depth, you have to measure against the top-of-foundation line as you dig. Unfortunately, the stringline often gets in the way, particularly if a backhoe is used to dig the trench. I've found that it's usually easier to remove the stringline and set up a transit, using a measuring stick or surveyor's rod to measure the elevation of the bottom of the trench periodically. First, though, you need to shoot the top-of-foundation

height and then add to this the distance that the footing sits below the top-of-foundation line. After calculating the proper depth for the footing, check the elevation of the bottom of the footing regularly as the backhoe operator works toward the bottom.

Footings for slab-on-grade and crawl-space foundations sometimes have to step down to follow the slope of the land. These steps should be made in 8-in. increments to maintain even block courses below the top-of-foundation line (see the drawing above).

Chapter 5

LAYING OUT FLOORS, WALLS, AND CEILINGS

Most houses in the United States today are built according to the platform framing system (see the drawing on the facing page). In this type of framing, the floor system serves as a platform upon which the walls are built. If a second floor is added, it serves as a second platform upon which the second-story walls are built. At the uppermost story, the ceiling and roof structures take the place of the floor platform to complete the frame. This "layered" arrangement makes it easy to divide the layout process into neat compartments. In this chapter, I'll describe techniques for laying out and building floors, walls, and ceilings. In Chapter 6, I'll examine methods for laying out basic roof structures. (Before beginning, please read the sidebar on structure and design on the facing page.)

PREPARING THE FOUNDATION

In the last chapter, I noted that the top of the foundation is the primary reference for the layout of the rest of the house. Because of the important role that it plays, you should carefully check the foundation before beginning any floor system.

First, measure both the diagonals and the top of the foundation with a 100-ft. tape to make sure the foundation is square and accurately reflects the dimensions on the plans. If the foundation differs less than 1 in. from the plans, this error can easily be eliminated by adjusting the position of the mudsill, typically a pressure-treated 2x6 or 2x8 that sits on top of the foundation wall. To do this, measure in the width of the mudsill stock from the outside edge of each of the walls and

Anatomy of a Platform-Framed House

Platform frames are built in layers, with each layer bearing structurally on the preceding layer.

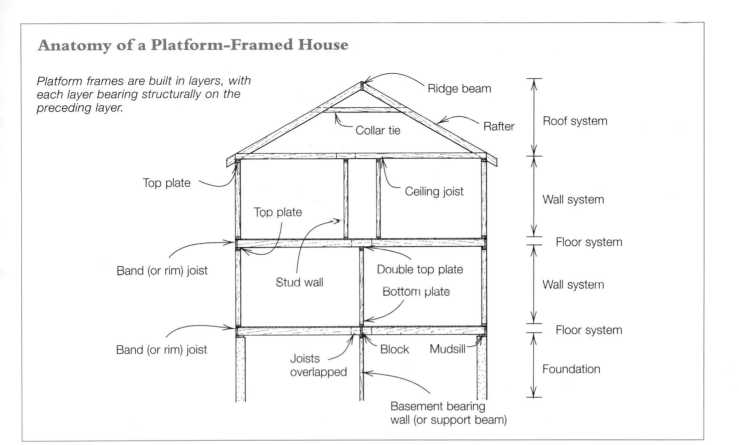

Ridge beam

Collar tie

Rafter

Roof system

Top plate

Ceiling joist

Wall system

Top plate

Floor system

Band (or rim) joist

Double top plate

Wall system

Stud wall

Bottom plate

Band (or rim) joist

Floor system

Joists overlapped

Block

Mudsill

Foundation

Basement bearing wall (or support beam)

Some Notes on Structure and Design

The first responsibility of frame carpenters is to build safe, sound structures. By and large, they do this simply by understanding and following standard building practices, adhering to the specifications on the plans, and conforming to the building code. This chapter doesn't go into structural design. Any attempt to provide a general structural guide would be futile, both because the topic is too complex to cover in the few pages allotted here and because local conditions vary so much. I can offer some general advice, however.

First of all, get a copy of your local building code. It's packed with useful information and will pay for itself many times over. Second, take the span tables and nailing schedules in the code book seriously. These items have been worked out by structural engineers and are based on the accumulated experience of generations of builders. Third, don't be afraid to overbuild. Keep in mind that you're building for the 100-year storm or earthquake. The nailing schedule required by the code may seem excessive, and indeed it may be on the mild day that

you're working. It's designed, however, to help the structure survive the fury of Mother Nature, as well as her daily abuse. Finally, don't design by the seat of your pants. Structural innovation is the purview of structural engineers who have been trained to calculate loads, stresses, and the strengths and weaknesses of materials. When a design requires methods that are outside standard building practices not covered by the building code, insist on bringing in an engineer.

Fixing an Out-of-Square Foundation

Minor flaws in the foundation can be corrected when the mudsill is laid out and installed. Here the 2x6 mudsill will overhang an out-of-square foundation by ¾ in. at the upper right-hand corner to get the floor system square.

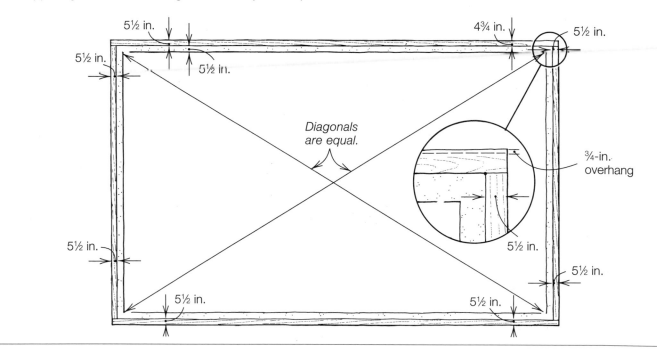

5½ in. 5½ in. 4¾ in. 5½ in.

5½ in. 5½ in.

Diagonals are equal.

¾-in. overhang

5½ in. 5½ in. 5½ in.

5½ in. 5½ in. 5½ in.

mark the top of the foundation near each corner. Then make the minor adjustments necessary to get the mud-sills parallel and square and snap chalklines on top of the foundation. In the drawing above, for example, the mudsill at the upper right-hand corner overhangs the foundation by ¾ in. to compensate for a slightly out-of-square foundation. If the foundation differs more than 1 in. from the plans, you can adjust the floor system further in the next stage, when the floor and band joists (also called rim joists) are installed.

After making any necessary corrections and verifying that the foundation layout is square and accurate, set up a transit and check the height of all the corners. While I've never heard a definitive answer as to what should be considered acceptably level, on most houses I would accept a difference in level of ¾ in. from one end to the other and ½ in. across the width. In the case of the 48-ft. by 27-ft. foundation described in the previous chapter, this would work out to about ¼ in. for

every 12 ft. This is less than the average crown in a 12-ft. long floor joist and is about half the acceptable deflection of a joist that length, according to the building code in my area.

If the corners are acceptably level, pull a stringline from corner to corner to check for dips and humps along the length of the wall. Place two 2x4 blocks on each end of the stringline so that it stays clear of the work surface and doesn't give a false reading. Set up the stringline and pull it taut, then slide another 2x4 block along the top edge of the foundation wall right next to the stringline to check for irregularities (see the drawing on the facing page). Because the thickness of 2x4s can differ by as much as ⅛ in., take all three of these blocks from the same scrap of wood.

Correcting foundation flaws
Now, what can you do if the wall has humps and dips? The first matter to address is the question of what is an

Using a Stringline to Check the Top of the Foundation

You can find dips and humps in the top of a foundation wall by stretching a stringline along the top.
Offsetting the stringline with 2x4 blocks will keep the
stringline clear of the top of the wall, and another
2x4 scrap can be used as a gauge.

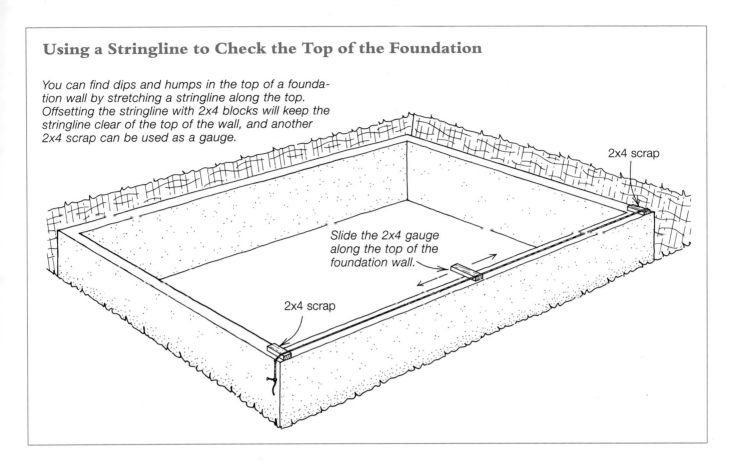

2x4 scrap

Slide the 2x4 gauge
along the top of the
foundation wall.

2x4 scrap

acceptable deviation from the ideal: a perfectly straight wall top. Because lumber thickness varies so much, it strikes me as ludicrous to worry about those less than ⅛ in. You can shim shallow dips (those less than ⅜ in.) with tapered wood shims or simply fill them with construction adhesive as you install the mudsill. High spots are more difficult to deal with. You can either grind them away, remove some of the wood on the underside of the mudsill, or just let the mudsill ride over it and make the adjustment later when you install the band and floor joists (my preferred approach).

Foundations that are grossly out of level or unacceptably uneven should be repaired by pouring a leveling bed of cement all the way around the top of the foundation. To put an even top on the foundation, use a transit to establish a level line a couple of inches down from the top of the foundation. Then clamp straight form boards to these lines and pour the cement (see the drawing on p. 90). Fortunately, the kinds of mistakes I've just described are rare, but they do occur. As a job

superintendent, I once had the displeasure of finding out that a foundation was poured 3½ in. out of level. That mistake cost the foundation company several hundred dollars and the foreman of the crew—who was a drinking man—his job.

Installing mudsills

After checking the foundation and making (or at least noting) any necessary adjustments, it's time to install the mudsills. Typically, anchor bolts or straps that tie the mudsill to the foundation will have been embedded in the top of the foundation by the foundation crew.

So, in addition to making any adjustments needed in the length, width, and elevation of the mudsill, you'll also have to lay out the location of the anchor bolts or straps on them. To do this, place the mudsill on top of the wall in the same position lengthwise that it will be when it's installed but offset laterally and pushed up against the bolts. Then mark the position of the bolts by sliding a Swanson Big 12 square along the mudsill until

Fixing an Out-of-Level Foundation

A foundation that is far out of level or unacceptably uneven can be repaired by pouring a leveling bed of cement on each wall.

1. *Use a transit to establish a level line.*
2. *Clamp form boards to the foundation at the level line (boards must be straight and all the same width).*
3. *Fill the form with concrete.*

Bar clamp

Form board

Level chalkline

---

it engages the side of each bolt. Mark both sides of each bolt with two parallel lines on the mudsill, which makes it easier to locate the center of each bolt hole. Then measure the distance between the chalkline (that marks the inside edge of the mudsill on the top of the foundation) and each anchor bolt and transfer these measurements to the mudsill. After marking both the inside measurement and the outside edge of the anchor bolt (I usually just do this by eye), you'll end up with a square about ½ in. wide. Later, when you drill the mudsill to accommodate the bolt, center the bit in this square (see the drawing on the facing page).

Installing center beams and bearing walls

After the mudsills have been securely bolted, it is often necessary to build a center beam or wall that is flush with the mudsill. This beam or wall will support the floor joists. The difficulty here is that the lower structure (basement floor, stemwall, or pier) is often uneven.

To end up with an even surface at the main floor level, then, stretch a taut stringline from mudsill to mudsill across the foundation and build to that line. If a beam is placed on masonry piers, as is often the case when a crawl-space foundation is used, you can shim it to line up with the string. If a beam will be supported by wood posts, position the posts where they will be permanently installed and then mark where they engage the stringline. To get an accurate reading, make sure each post is held plumb as you mark it. After deducting for the width of the beam, you can cut and install the posts. Then you can build and install the beam over the posts.

To build a center bearing partition with a double top plate, first lower a plumb bob from each end of the top line and mark where it engages the basement floor. Lay out the position of the bottom plate with a chalkline, then cut and fit pressure-treated 2x4s to serve as the bottom plate of the wall. Once these are in position along the chalkline, lay out the stud locations (I'll discuss techniques for laying out walls later in this chapter).

Now, because the floor is uneven, you must measure, mark, and cut each stud individually (see the drawing on p. 92). To do this, stand a stud on top of the bottom plate at each layout position, then mark the top of the stud at the stringline. Lay the marked stud down in place along the layout, get a new stud, and mark it at

Laying Out Anchor Bolts on the Mudsill

When laying out the mudsills, it's important to mark the locations of the anchor bolts on them.

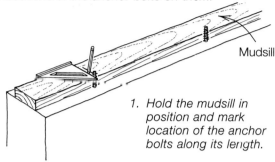

1. Hold the mudsill in position and mark location of the anchor bolts along its length.

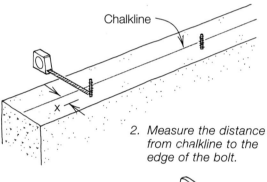

Chalkline

X

2. Measure the distance from chalkline to the edge of the bolt.

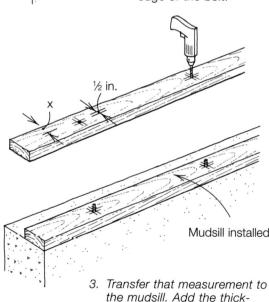

½ in.

X

Mudsill installed

3. Transfer that measurement to the mudsill. Add the thickness of the bolt by eye (about ½ in.). Drill through the center of the laid-out square.

Mudsill

the next location. This way each stud is custom-fit to its location along the high and low spots on the floor. Mark all of the studs, subtract the thickness of the two top plates (between 3 in. and 3¼ in.), then cut the studs in order and return them to their proper place along the layout. Now you can cut and lay out the top plates and build the wall. When you raise the wall, its top should be straight and flush with the mudsill.

There are two things you need to do to get accurate results when you use this method. First, put plenty of pressure straight down on the bottom plate when you're holding the stud in position for marking. I find that just standing on the plate near the layout mark usually removes any gaps between the plate and the concrete floor. Second, hold the stud plumb (clamp a level to it to make this easier) as you mark it.

LAYING OUT AND INSTALLING THE FLOOR SYSTEM

After checking the foundation, securing the mudsill, and installing the center beam or bearing wall, you're ready to build the frame of the floor. As noted earlier, this structure provides a second chance to compensate for mistakes made during construction of the foundation. Keeping this in mind, let's look at how the floor system might be laid out and built.

Installing the band joist

The first thing to do is lay out the location of the band (or rim) joist. If the mudsill is level and flat and accurately reflects the dimensions on the plans, just measure the thickness of the band joist (nominally 1½ in.) in from the outside edge of the mudsill, mark its position, and strike chalklines. Now you can either install the band joist or lay out and install the floor joists. It does not matter which you install first, but in either case, work to the line you've struck on top of the mudsill.

Although the sequence of this installation is not too important, the way the lumber is selected and used is very important. Always save the straightest boards for the band, and "crown" each and every floor joist by marking with an arrow the direction that the joist bows. Also, check the end of every timber with your square to make sure that it's cut at 90°. As you work, set aside the boards with the largest bows, twists, and cups. You can use these later for shorter elements, such as headers, bridg-

Installing a Level Bearing Wall

Because basement floors are typically uneven, the studs of a bearing wall that will support the first-floor joists should be individually cut to length. A stringline stretched between the mudsills provides a consistent reference point for length, and a level will help ensure that studs are held plumb when they're being marked.

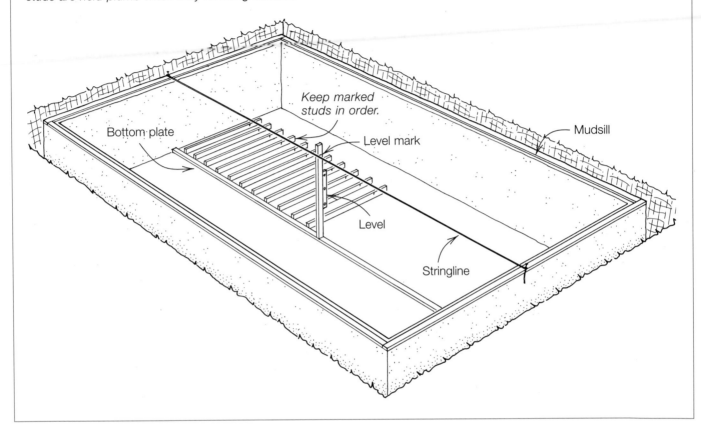

Keep marked studs in order.

Bottom plate

Level mark

Mudsill

Level

Stringline

ing, and blocking. (For more on this selection process, see the sidebar on the facing page.)

What if the foundation has flaws that you weren't able to get rid of when you installed the mudsill? Let's say, for instance, that the foundation and mudsill are nice and flat except for one nasty hump. To get rid of the high spot, first pick out a straight piece of lumber for the band joist and set this board in place along the layout line on the mudsill so that it runs over the high spot. Using shims and a 4-ft. level, adjust the board until it's level. Then set your wing dividers to the widest gap (usually at the end of the board) and scribe the bottom of the board (see the drawing on p. 94). Cut along the

scribe line, then install the board. Later, of course, as you fit floor joists to the band joist, you'll need to trim their bottoms to make the top of the joists even with the band joist.

What if the foundation is level, but the dimensions are off by several inches? One solution would be to cantilever the floor system out over the foundation. The amount that you can cantilever the joists is not always clearly spelled out in the code book, so it's a good idea to consult with both a structural engineer and the building inspector before making this change.

Whether the cantilever has been planned all along or is a midcourse remedy for poor workmanship, I install the

Taming Lumber

In books like this, framing is drawn with a straight edge and a pencil. All of the boards are perfectly straight, and the assembled frames are pictures of order. In the real world, however, lumber comes out of the forest and can be quite wild. It varies in thickness and width, and its imperfections and distortions have given rise to a number of adjectives—bowed, twisted, checked, and waney—that carpenters use to describe it.

To tame their wild wood, carpenters use two basic approaches. First of all, they constantly examine and sort through their lumber. A common sight wherever houses are being framed is the carpenter with a board tilted up to eye level, intently sighting down the board's edge. He might be looking for the straightest stock to use for a top plate, or he might be crowning the board.

In fact, most long pieces of lumber are slightly bowed. When a carpenter crowns a board, he looks for the high side—or crown—and marks it, usually with an arrow that indicates the direction of the crown. When these boards are used to build a roof, a floor, or any other sloped or horizontal structure, they are installed with the crown up. This gives the surface of the structure more uniformity than if a "crown-up" board were installed beside a "crown-down" board. More important, it resists and compensates for midspan deflection: As a crowned board sags, it straightens out (see the drawing below).

Along with this process of sorting and organizing lumber, carpenters also use a variety of tools and techniques to push or pull lumber around so that it is straight and accurately placed. Once they have it in the desired position, they pin it in place with nails, braces, and other boards. Sometimes these are temporary, while other times they become a permanent part of the structure. Frame carpenters are constantly straightening out and squaring up lumber as they work. For this reason, layout can't always be separated from the actual building process. In fact, the two processes are quite intertwined.

"Crowning" lumber

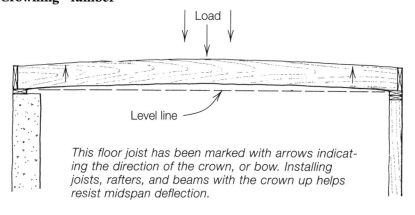

This floor joist has been marked with arrows indicating the direction of the crown, or bow. Installing joists, rafters, and beams with the crown up helps resist midspan deflection.

floor joists before the band joist, since without them there is nothing to hold it up. To get a straight edge on the floor system, nail the first and last joist in place and then set up a stringline from the top outside corner of the first joist to the top outside corner of the other joist. Then set each intervening joist just a hair short of the stringline. After all the joists have been set to the stringline, you can then install the band joist.

Laying out floor joists

There are several things to consider when laying out floor joists. First, to ensure that the plywood sheathing breaks evenly on the joists, you should lay the joists out in even increments (remember to think modularly). By far the most common increment is 16 in., but in some special circumstances the plans might specify 12-in. or 24-in. increments. To avoid cumulative error, it's best to use a steel tape and measure from a single point. It often

Scribing a Band Joist

When a foundation has a high spot, the band joist can be scribed and cut to fit so that the floor joists will remain level. First lay the band joist in place, shim it level, then scribe the contour of the foundation. Floor joists around the high spot will need to be trimmed at the end to sit flush with the top of the band joist.

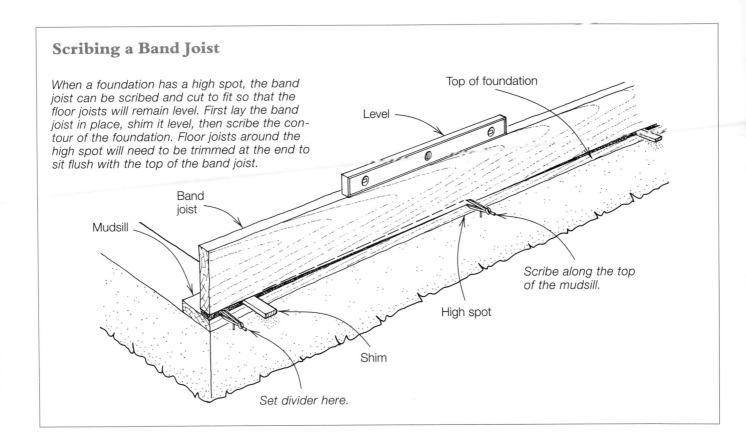

Top of foundation

Level

Band joist

Mudsill

Scribe along the top of the mudsill.

High spot

Shim

Set divider here.

happens that a carpenter's tape measure is shorter than the foundation (such as if a carpenter with a 25-ft. tape were laying out a 48-ft. foundation). If this is the case, you should measure from the fewest sources possible; a 48-ft. foundation, for example, should be laid out in two pulls using a 25-ft. tape measure.

After marking the entire length of the layout on the mudsill, go back over the marks with a pencil and a square and scribe straight layout lines. At the same time, indicate on which side of the line to place the floor joist. The traditional way to do this is to draw an X consistently either to the left or right of the line. Then install the joist on top of the X. If the X is placed just before the layout line (i.e., closest to the point from which the tape is pulled), the layout is said to be "set behind"; if the X is placed beyond the line, the layout is said to be "set ahead."

Laying out 16 in. on center

One of the first mistakes a newcomer to framing might make is to pull a tape measure from the end of the mud-

sill and mark at the highlighted 16-in. increments. Regardless of whether he sets the layout ahead or behind these marks, the first sheet of plywood then will have to be cut to break on the joists. But it's easy to set things up so that the first sheet of plywood falls right into place without being cut, thus saving time and material.

For a 96-in.-long sheet of plywood to break evenly in the center of a 1½-in.-thick joist, that joist must be laid out at 95¼ in., with the X set ahead. This layout places the center of the joist (which is ¾ in. in from the edge of 2x framing) at the 96-in. mark. To make the plywood break evenly on the joist, measure 15¼ in. from the corner and make your first mark (see the drawing on the facing page). Then pull the tape measure from the 15¼-in. mark and lay out the rest of the joists at the 16-in. increments, setting the Xs ahead. Whenever you're laying out on center (o.c.), you're shifting the layout over ¾ in. so that the centers (rather than the edges) of the 2x framing members are spaced on the specified module, which in this case is 16 in.

Laying Out Joists 16 in. On Center

When laying out on center (o.c.), shift the layout over ¾ in. so that the centers (rather than the edges) of 2x framing members fall on increments of 16. This can be done by either first measuring 15¼ in. to the first layout mark, and then measuring from that point in full 16-in. increments, or by measuring from the edge and subtracting ¾ in. from each full increment of 16.

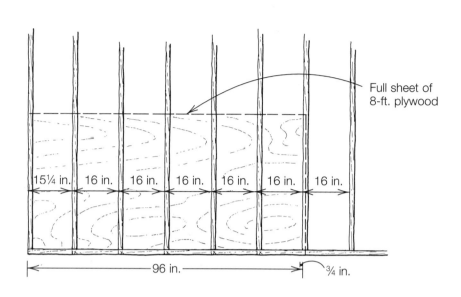

Full sheet of 8-ft. plywood

15¼ in. | 16 in. | 16 in. | 16 in. | 16 in. | 16 in. | 16 in.

96 in. ¾ in.

Leaving a path for the plumbing

It is certainly nice to be able to flop that first sheet of plywood into place without having to cut it. The layout that places the joists in the perfect position to receive the plywood, however, can also place a joist in the path of the toilet drain. This means that when the plumber arrives, the joist will have to be cut, and the frame will have to be modified to support it. In this case, it's much easier simply to cut the plywood instead. You can save a lot of time and maximize the structural integrity of the floor system if you think about the location of the toilets and tubs when you lay out floor joists (see the drawing on p. 96).

On a recent addition, I discovered that my normal layout procedure of starting at 15¼ in. placed a joist right in the path of both the toilet and the tub drains. To avoid this situation, I moved the starting point of my layout over 8 in. Although this meant that I'd have to cut the first sheet of plywood, both drains ended up close to the center of the bays between the joists. The key to this discovery? I looked at the plans. When the toilet and the tub are going to run parallel with the joists, you can scale the location of the drains and mark those locations right on the mudsill. (Use red keel—or lumber crayon—to make these marks stand out.) Then, as soon as you mark off the first joist at 15¼ in., pull the tape from that point and see immediately if the 16-in. increments land on top of the drains. If so, move the layout over as necessary.

When the plumbing fixture runs perpendicular to the floor joists, it helps to know exactly where the drain comes out of the fixture. For a standard toilet, allow 12 in. from the inside of the bathroom wall to the center of the drain. For a standard tub, allow 15 in. from the sidewall and 10 in. from the end wall. To lay out the position of these drains, don't forget to allow for the thickness of the framed walls.

Laying out stairwells

If a house has a basement, the first floor will probably incorporate a stairwell. Since requirements dealing with stairways have changed in recent years, make sure the width in the plans is in compliance with the local building code. In my area, basement stairs are typically 36 in.

Looking Out for the Plumber

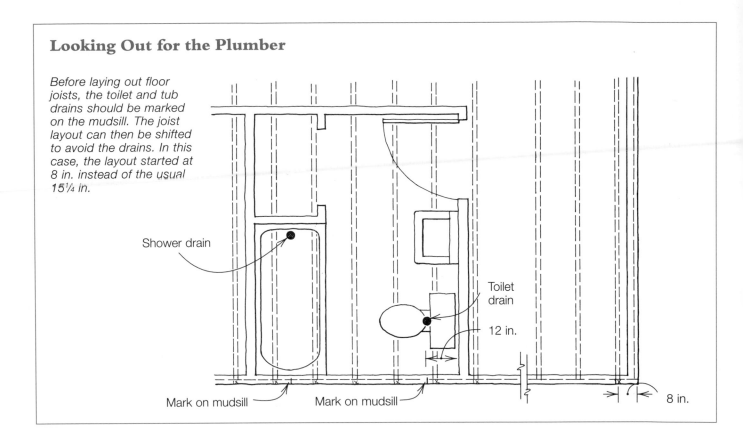

Before laying out floor joists, the toilet and tub drains should be marked on the mudsill. The joist layout can then be shifted to avoid the drains. In this case, the layout started at 8 in. instead of the usual 15¼ in.

Shower drain

Toilet drain

12 in.

Mark on mudsill

Mark on mudsill

8 in.

wide. In Chapter 7, I'll discuss how to calculate the length for a stairwell to provide the required headroom (usually 80 in.) above the stairs. Because the length needed varies according to the thickness of the floor system and the pitch of the stairs, it can be difficult at this early stage to determine how long to build the stairwell opening. When the stairs run parallel to the joists, that decision can be deferred until later, when the stairs are built (see the drawing on the facing page).

When the stairs run perpendicular to the joists, on the other hand, you must decide how long to make the opening during the framing stage. Since it's much easier to shorten the opening later than to make it longer, I always make the opening a bit longer than I estimate will be needed. For basement stairs that run perpendicular to the floor joists, I'm comfortable with a 128-in. opening, as shown in the drawing. This distance falls evenly between joists (128 ÷ 16 = 8), and after framing the opening, I run the plywood subfloor over it and leave it there until the stairs are built. This not only

makes it easier to adjust the length of the opening later but also eliminates a serious job-site hazard.

Straightening floor joists

If you install floor joists before the band joist, you'll notice that they are leaning every which way when they are all in place. This is because there's nothing to hold them vertically. To straighten these joists, I use a Speed Square and a tool called the Tweaker. This is a steel bar shaped a little like an "h" that fits over the edge of 2x lumber and can be used to leverage twisted lumber into line as you install the band joist.

At this point the locations of the joists are fixed, because they've been toenailed to the mudsill at the layout lines. As you nail through the band joist into the end of each floor joist, hook the Tweaker over the top of the joist and tilt the board until it's plumb (see the top right drawing on p. 98). To see when the joist is square to the mudsill, push your Speed Square into the intersection of the joist and mudsill. Two people working together—

Laying Out the Stairwell Opening

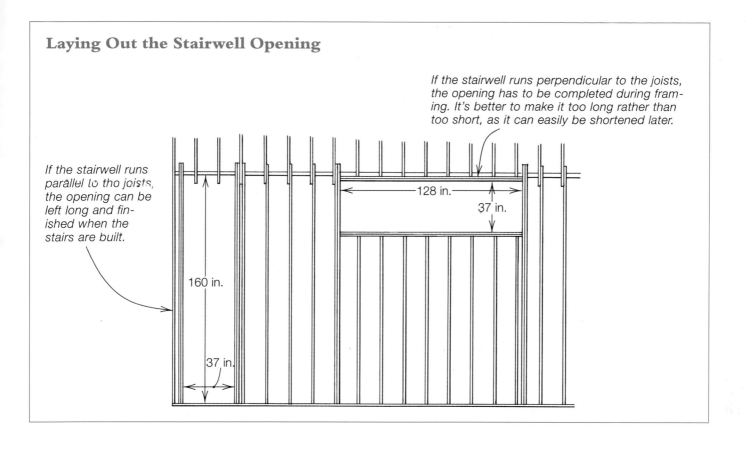

If the stairwell runs parallel to the joists, the opening can be left long and finished when the stairs are built.

If the stairwell runs perpendicular to the joists, the opening has to be completed during framing. It's better to make it too long rather than too short, as it can easily be shortened later.

128 in.

37 in.

160 in.

37 in.

one tweaking and squaring and the other nailing—seems to be the best way to handle this job.

If you install the band joist first, you should use the Speed Square to scribe plumb layout lines on the inside of the band joist. I've found that the Tweaker is also helpful here in levering the joists to the vertical lines. If you don't have a Tweaker, you can usually push and grunt the joists into place, and if you run into a particularly stubborn "leaner," you can use a bar clamp as a lever to straighten it out (see the bottom right drawing on p. 98).

In a floor system that is, say, 27 ft. wide, the band joist holds the ends of the floor joists plumb around the perimeter of the floor. In the center of the floor, where the joists overlap and are supported by a center beam or bearing wall, blocking is needed to stiffen and hold that end of each joist plumb. These spaces should be measured at the bottom of the joists, where they are nailed to the main beam or bearing wall. The tops of the joists will be leaning in all directions, and the purpose of the

blocks is to force them straight. I like to use a bar clamp to pull the joists snugly against the blocks as I nail them together (see the left drawing on p. 98).

There is one more element that is often used to help straighten joists: midspan bridging. When I first started doing carpentry work, bridging was considered an essential part of the floor structure that was needed to impart stiffness and to help straighten the floor. Numerous studies have shown, though, that the structural contribution of bridging is negligible. In my state, bridging is no longer required by code for floor systems built with joists smaller than 2x12s—which is to say, most floors.

Laying the plywood subfloor

The final step in building the floor is installing the plywood subfloor. While this is pretty straightforward, there are two things related to the layout worth mentioning. First, it is best to establish a baseline 48 in. from the edge with a chalkline so that you can follow it when installing the first course of plywood. Even if the outside edge of the frame looks quite straight, chances are it

Straightening Floor Joists

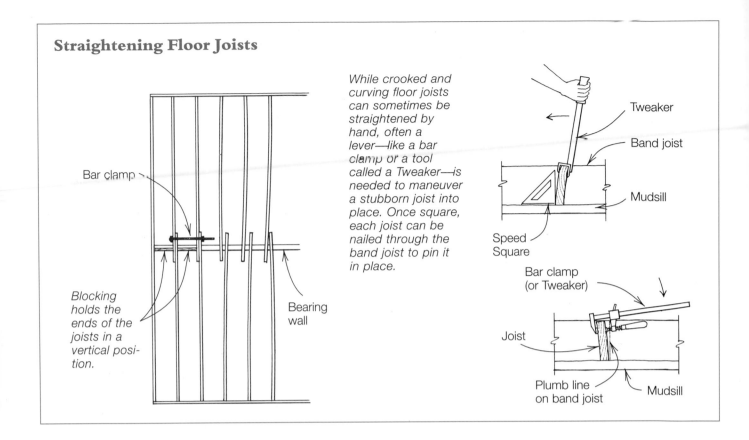

Bar clamp

Blocking holds the ends of the joists in a vertical position.

Bearing wall

While crooked and curving floor joists can sometimes be straightened by hand, often a lever—like a bar clamp or a tool called a Tweaker—is needed to maneuver a stubborn joist into place. Once square, each joist can be nailed through the band joist to pin it in place.

Tweaker

Band joist

Mudsill

Speed Square

Bar clamp (or Tweaker)

Joist

Plumb line on band joist

Mudsill

won't be as exact as a chalkline. The straighter you start out with plywood, a rigid and strictly dimensioned material, the faster and better it will go.

Second, don't count on the joists being straight, especially if you haven't used bridging. The plywood, in fact, should be used to straighten out the floor joists as you work. To do this, mark the joist layout (either 16-in. or 24-in. centers) right on the plywood and push or pull the joists to the marks as you nail off the plywood.

FRAMING WALLS AND CEILINGS

By the time you nail down the last sheet of plywood subfloor, any questions about plumb and square should be nailed down as well. This floor—upon which you will now build and erect the first-story walls—should be, for all practical purposes, a level and square platform. You should be able to lay out square rooms without having to pull diagonal measurements, and build level walls and level openings within those walls without using a level (see the drawings on the facing page). When you know the deck is level and square, you can simply trans-

fer those properties to the walls by measuring equal distances from the edge or top surface of the deck.

Laying out walls on the deck

After sweeping the sawdust off the newly framed and sheathed deck, you have what amounts to an enormous drawing board. All of the dimensions that are represented in scale on the plans can now be transferred full-size to the floor deck. Although it's not necessary, I like to lay out all of the walls right on the deck at this point. If I have a full crew, one person can help me with the layout while the others build corners, T-intersections, and headers (see the sidebar on p. 100). After measuring and marking all of the walls with a generously chalked line, preserve the layout lines by spraying them with a clear acrylic or other transparent coating.

First, lay out the exterior walls. Strike chalklines for these walls rather than use the edge of the floor system as a guide. This way, you avoid carrying over into the wall the imperfections built into the edge of the floor.

Framing from a Level and Square Deck

If the first-floor deck is properly framed, it will be level and square. This makes future framing tasks much easier, because level and square can be transferred by measuring equal distances.

Plan view

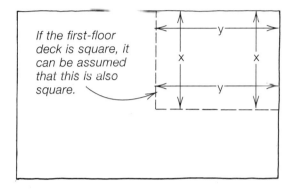

If the first-floor deck is square, it can be assumed that this is also square.

Elevation view

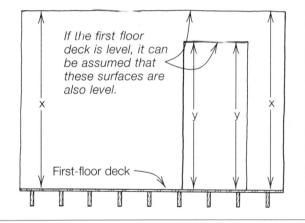

If the first-floor deck is level, it can be assumed that these surfaces are also level.

First-floor deck

In this case, measure in the thickness of the exterior wall at each corner of the floor and snap a chalkline from mark to mark. This width is generally 3½ in. or 5½ in., depending on whether the exterior walls are being built out of 2x4s or 2x6s, respectively. While laying out these exterior walls, take advantage of this one last chance to adjust the outside dimensions of the house, if necessary.

Measure the length, width, and diagonals after marking in the width of the floor plate, making any minor adjustments needed before snapping chalklines.

After snapping chalklines representing the exterior walls, lay out the interior walls, focusing on critical dimensions. If there's a bathroom, and one wall has to be exactly 60 in. long to accommodate a tub, for example, lay out that wall first. Experience has given me a working knowledge of details that aren't always specified in the plans but that can be important later on. One of these is the depth of closets. While inside dimensions aren't always provided and sometimes scale to 20 in. or so on the plans, I've learned that a full 24-in. depth (which will be reduced to 23 in. after the drywall is hung) is really needed if the client expects to hang a coat on a hanger. I try to point out items like this to the homeowner or architect when I first review the plans.

Sometimes the architect or designer makes mistakes or overlooks a detail. On more than one occasion, I've encountered drawings with hallways or landings that, when scaled, don't comply with the building code. When this is the case, the hallway or landing should be brought into compliance, even if an adjoining room loses an inch or so. Where the code and plans come into conflict, the code should always win. In fact, this principle is often stamped on each page of the plans, and it's the duty of the frame carpenters to be the last line of defense against noncompliance and the complications that come with it. Here, the frame carpenter can render a very valuable service by having a code book on hand and being alert to possible violations.

Drawing in window and door openings

Once the walls have been marked on the floor, begin to fill in the details. Start with the window and door openings. Here, concentrate on two things: getting the opening in the right place and of the right width.

To get the opening in the right place, don't just scale the drawing or follow the dimensions on the plans. It's also important to try to understand the intent of the designer and to anticipate trim and finishing details. If the designer obviously intended to place a window or door in the center of a wall, for example, place it there even if that location differs slightly from the numbers on the

Assembling the Components of a Wall

Corners (in plan)

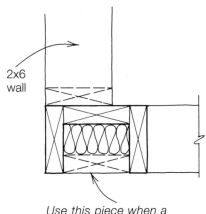

2x4 provides nailer here.

2x4 wall

To save wood, use scraps for the middle piece.

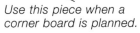

2x6 wall

Use this piece when a corner board is planned.

T-intersections (in plan)

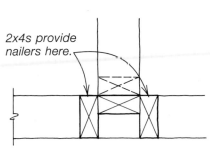

2x4s provide nailers here.

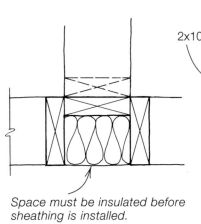

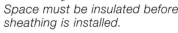

Space must be insulated before sheathing is installed.

Headers (in cross section)

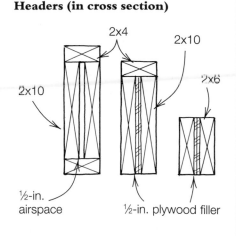

2x4

2x10

2x6

2x10

½-in. airspace

½-in. plywood filler

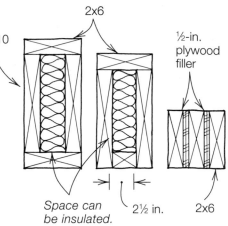

2x10

2x6

½-in. plywood filler

Space can be insulated.

2½ in.

2x6

The components that go into a wall can be assembled before it is framed or even laid out. Soon after you get the plans for a house or addition, count up the corners and T-intersections of the walls. These components are designed both to tie adjoining walls together and to provide a solid nailing surface for the finishing layers of the house, such as drywall, trim, and siding. Because they are usually identical in length and method of construction, they can all be built at the same time.

After you know how many corners and T-intersections will be needed, make up a list of headers. To determine the length of each header, refer to the door and window schedule on the plans. Add 3 in. to rough openings (R.O.s) smaller than 6 ft. (to allow for the width of a pair of supporting jack studs) and 6 in. to R.O.s wider than 6 ft. (to allow for a pair of doubled jack studs). Also, make note of the specific type of construction of each header.

I try to arrive on site with my list of necessary corners, T-intersections, and headers already prepared. This allows me to divide the crew and put everyone to work immediately. An experienced framing crew should look efficient and organized, and a job site should look like a small but productive factory. While everyone assembles the wall components, I can go ahead and lay out the walls.

plan. There are many decisions made along the way that can affect the dimensions, so rigid adherence to a number on the plans can be a mistake.

In my area, for instance, the wall behind a toilet now has to be 5½ in. thick to accommodate the pipe vent. This requirement is new and not reflected on many published plans. Making the wall thicker naturally affects the other dimensions of the plans and moves the center of the bathroom over an inch or so. In this case, then, it makes sense to move the window location slightly to center it in the room.

One of the things that isn't clearly specified in many plans but that can be important during the trim phase of the job is the distance between door openings and the inside corners of walls. Doors are often drawn so that they open along a wall. When these openings are framed, you must think ahead to when the door will be hung and the opening finished with trim. For a nice trim job, the opening should be far enough away from the corner of the room to allow for a full piece of casing (see the drawing below). For the 2¼-in.-wide casings that are often used, I make the opening 3 in. (the thick-

ness of two studs) away from the inside corner of the room. For wider custom casings, I allow the width of the casing plus ¾ in. While not as common a concern as with doors, the width of window casings sometimes needs to be considered during framing as well.

Getting the opening in the right place is only half the battle. The other half is laying out the opening to the correct width and height. At this point, concentrate on the width. For interior doors, allow for the actual size of the door specified plus 2 in. to allow room for the jambs and shims. If a 30 in. door is specified, in other words, lay out the opening to be 32 in. wide. Because exterior doors typically have thicker jambs, allow for the specified door width plus 2½ in. Window sizes and styles vary tremendously, so it's necessary to know the manufacturer-specified rough opening (R.O.) for each particular window. And as I mentioned in Chapter 1, I always use inches (rather than feet and inches) to lay out door and window openings. To avoid confusion, I cross out foot-and-inch designations on the window chart and on the plans and replace them with straight inches. I also use a ruler, which I find much easier to work with, rather than my tape measure.

Leave Room for the Door Casing

Doors that open along a wall should be framed so that a full piece of casing will fit when the door is trimmed out later. When a 2¼-in.-wide casing is planned, the R.O. should be built 3 in. from the wall. For larger, custom casings, ¾ in. should be added to the width of the casing to find the proper distance from corner to opening.

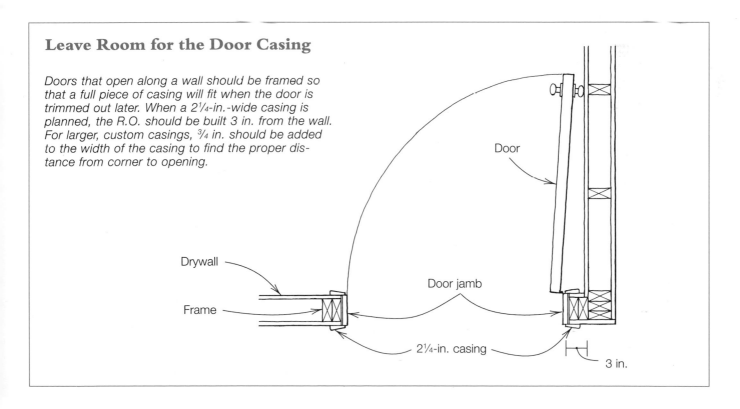

Because openings are often specified to be in the center of a given space, you'll need to have a routine for quickly and accurately finding centers. Here's a method I use that is fast and just about foolproof.

First, quickly measure the space. Don't be concerned about precision here; you just want to get within 1 in. or 2 in. of the total length. Let's say you need to find the center of a room that is exactly 171¹¹⁄₁₆ in. wide. Your quick-and-dirty measurement shows that it is a little over 170 in. wide, which you can easily divide by two to get 85. Then measure 85 in. from each side and mark. The center is midway between these marks, and you can usually just mark the center by eye. To check the accuracy of your eye, measure from each corner to the center mark and make sure both measurements are the same.

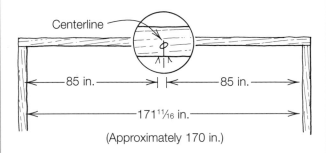

Centerline

85 in. — 85 in.

171¹¹⁄₁₆ in.

(Approximately 170 in.)

1. *Estimate or roughly measure the distance using a number that is easily divisible by 2 (170 in. in this example).*
2. *Measure half that distance (85 in. in this example) from each corner and mark.*
3. *The center of the room is midway between those marks.*

For example, let's say you need to lay out a 6-ft. 2¾-in. R.O. for a French door in the center of a dining-room wall. First convert the R.O. to 74¾ in., then mark the center of the wall (for a quick way to measure to the center of any space, see Tricks of the Trade at left). From this center point, measure out half of the R.O. (or 37⅜ in.) in both directions. To check your math, measure from mark to mark to verify that the two halves add up to the R.O. (74¾ in. in this case). Then, to clearly indicate the beginning and end of the R.O., draw a bracket, often with a brief note attached for later reference (see the drawing on the facing page). After you've laid out all of the walls and openings, make a final inspection of the layout, comparing the full-scale one you're standing on to the plans you're holding. When you're satisfied that everything is okay, spray a light coating of clear acrylic on the deck to preserve the layout. Now you're ready to lay out the wall plates.

Laying out wall plates

Begin this phase of the job by cutting and fitting the bottom plate of one of the long exterior walls. After you've cut the plate material and carefully placed it along the layout line at the edge of the floor, transfer the elements that you've already marked on the floor. These include wall corners, T-intersections, and door and window R.O.s.

There are different ways of assembling wall corners and T-intersections. The purpose of these components is twofold. First of all, they tie the intersecting walls together securely. Second, they provide a nailing surface at the inside corner of intersecting walls for drywall (on the interior of the house) and sheathing, siding, trim, or other treatments (on the exterior). The configuration I typically use is shown in the left drawing on p. 104.

Before laying out the components of door and window openings, let's review how they are framed. The design is basically post-and-beam construction, though the beam is typically called a header. The design of the header varies according to several factors, including the span, the load above it, concerns for energy conservation and the conservation of wood resources, the cus-

Laying Out a Centered Rough Opening

Rather than rely on plan measurements, the most accurate way to center a door or window in a wall is to find either the interior or exterior wall center (whichever is the more critical dimension) and lay out the R.O. from there.

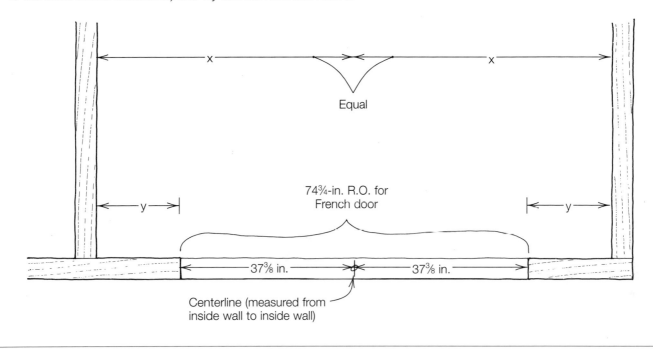

Equal

74¾-in. R.O. for
French door

37⅜ in.   37⅜ in.

Centerline (measured from
inside wall to inside wall)

toms of a given region, and the habits of individual carpenters. For our purposes here, you can use a header made with two 2x10s with either 2x4s or 2x6s laid flat and nailed to the top and bottom.

As the right drawing on p. 104 indicates, headers are always longer than the width of the opening because they have to rest on posts, called jack studs (also called trimmer studs). Typically, two supporting jack studs are required on both sides for headers over 6 ft. long, so a R.O. width of 74¾ in. requires a header length of 80¾ in. (74¾ in. plus the thickness of four 2x jack studs, or 6 in.). This post-and-beam assembly is always sandwiched between full-length studs, called king studs, which tie the header to the jack studs and build the whole assembly firmly into the wall.

After transferring the R.O. you've already laid out on the floor to the plate (in this case 74¾ in.), mark the positions of the jack and king studs with a rafter square. Though any square will do, it's better to use the rafter square because you can mark along both sides of the 1½-in. tongue of the square to represent each jack or king stud. When you're finished, the plate has four lines on each side of the R.O. To indicate the jack studs, print an O in the first two spaces; to indicate the full-length stud, mark an X.

You can lay out windows the same way you lay out doors. Of course, to complete the window, you would have to enclose the opening at the bottom only or, in some cases, at both the bottom and top. (I'll discuss techniques for laying out this part of the window opening in the section on building the walls.)

Studs and cripple studs in 2x4 walls are usually laid out on 16-in. centers; 2x6 walls are often laid out on 24-in. centers, both to save lumber and to allow for more insulation. Whether the increment is 16 in. o.c. or 24 in.

Marking Corners and T-Intersections on the Bottom Plate

After laying out the walls directly on the deck, 2x plates can be cut to length and the position of studs, corners, and T-intersections transferred directly from the floor to the plates.

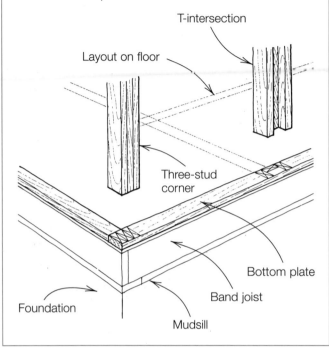

T-intersection

Layout on floor

Three-stud corner

Bottom plate

Band joist

Foundation

Mudsill

Framing a Wall Opening

Once the size and position of a door or window R.O. is known, the length of the header can be determined and the supporting jack and king studs can be laid out.

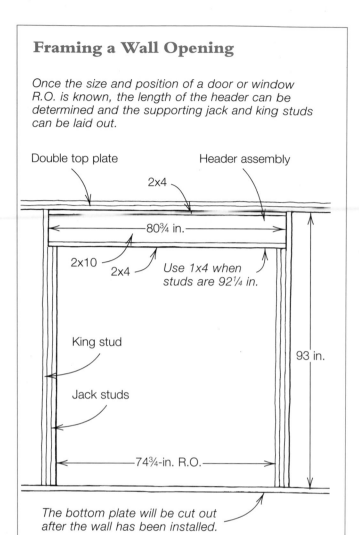

Double top plate

Header assembly

2x4

80¾ in.

2x10

2x4

Use 1x4 when studs are 92¼ in.

King stud

93 in.

Jack studs

74¾-in. R.O.

The bottom plate will be cut out after the wall has been installed.

o.c., the stud-placement pattern should be maintained from the beginning to end of each continuous wall section. On the exterior, this makes it easier to sheathe the walls without having to cut sheathing—which comes in 4-ft. or 8-ft. modules—to fit. Inside the house, this makes it easier to hang drywall and helps finish carpenters find studs to nail into.

For exterior walls laid out 16 in. o.c., start by measuring 15¼ in. in from the outside corner and mark, with the X set ahead (for more on laying out 16-in. centers, see p. 94). Then, from that mark, pull the tape measure and mark every 16 in., again setting the X ahead (see the drawing on the facing page). When this pattern enters a R.O., write C, for cripple, instead of X. If one exterior wall has already been built and set up, and you're laying out the adjoining exterior wall plate, hook the tape measure to the outside of the first wall and mark the 15¼-in. measurement from that source rather than from the end of the plate. This ensures that the center of the third stud will be 48 in. from the outside corner.

After laying everything out on the bottom plate, you're ready to lay out the top plate as well. Look for the straightest long 2x4 (or 2x6) material that you can find for both the bottom and top plates. The top plate is usually cut the same length as the bottom plate. On long walls, where the plate has to be spliced, offset the splices of the top plate from the splices of the bottom plate. While some carpenters like to make the splice over the

Laying Out Walls on 16-in. Centers

The layout for adjoining exterior walls should begin at the corner rather than at the end of the plate so that full sheets of sheathing will break in the center of a stud. Note that the corner construction of a 2x6 wall can't be a triple stud because it won't provide adequate thickness to serve as an interior corner nailer.

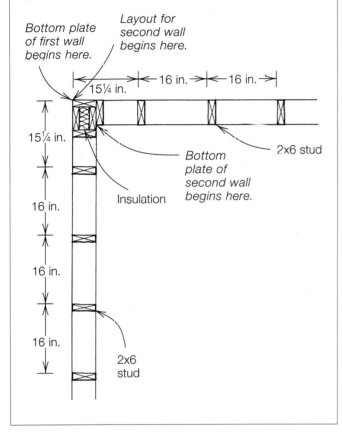

Bottom plate of first wall begins here.

Layout for second wall begins here.

15¼ in.

16 in.

16 in.

15¼ in.

16 in.

16 in.

16 in.

Insulation

Bottom plate of second wall begins here.

2x6 stud

2x6 stud

---

wall. To keep the plates from moving in relation to each other and to remove bows that might affect accuracy, clamp the plates together before transferring the layout. In addition to the layout lines, transfer the Xs and Os to indicate clearly on which side of the line to place the studs and jack studs when the wall is being nailed together. Because you usually don't have cripple studs at the top of the wall, you'll rarely transfer their layout to the top plate.

Building walls

As soon as the top plate has been laid out, separate the plates and place them just over 8 ft. apart, taking care to keep them in the same position relative to each other. Then place the studs, corners, T-intersections, jack studs, and headers in their appropriate positions as indicated by the layout on the plates.

Studs (as well as the corners and T-intersections that are made out of them) are often factory cut to length. The standard length of a precut stud in my area is 93 in. (in some areas, precut studs are 92¼ in.), which produces a 97½-in. wall once the bottom plate, studs, and double top plates have been assembled. Later, after drywall is added to the ceiling and floor covering to the floor deck, the net wall height ends up very close to 96 in. Other precut stud lengths are available for higher ceilings.

The height of door and window headers is a variable that needs to be determined before the walls are built (see the drawings on p. 107). A standard 6-ft. 8-in. interior door requires a header height of about 81½ in., while an exterior door needs a slightly larger header height of about 82¼ in. to allow for the height of the door sill. A very simple way to achieve the right height for doors is to make the headers out of 2x10s, with a 2x4 or 2x6 (depending on wall construction) nailed to the top and bottom of the header. This header assembly is nominally 12¼ in. high, and if placed below the double top plate, it will be about 80¾ in. up from the bottom plate (to achieve this figure, subtract 12¼ in. from 93 in.). Because of the variation in actual lumber dimensions, check the actual height of the header assembly before cutting the jack studs to length. Not infrequently, the header assembly totals 12½ in. or more. In areas where precut studs are 92¼ in., you'll need to substitute a 1x4 or 1x6 for the 2x at the top of the header.

middle of a stud, I prefer to make it in the middle of the space between the studs, where I can easily tie the two sections together with a 14-in. section of 2x blocking.

After you've either cut out or assembled a top plate to the same overall length as the bottom plate, place the plates side by side and transfer the entire layout from the bottom plate to the top plate with a square (see the drawing on p. 106). My tool of choice for this operation is the Speed Square. The original 7½-in. Speed Square spans across both plates when I'm building a 2x4 wall, while I'll use my Big 12 (which spans 12½ in.) for a 2x6

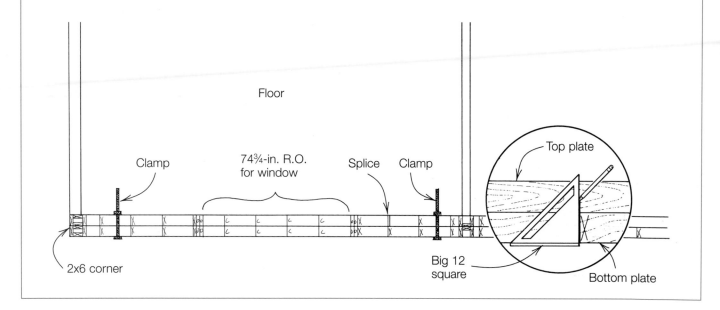

Laying Out the Top Plate on the Floor

A Speed Square makes a fast and accurate tool for transferring the bottom-plate layout to the top plate. Clamps help hold the plates in place and remove error-causing bows. Splices in long plates should be offset as shown, either in the center of a stud or in the center of a stud bay, where 2x blocking can tie it together.

Floor

Clamp

74¾-in. R.O.
for window

Splice   Clamp

Top plate

2x6 corner

Big 12
square

Bottom plate

Adding 1½ in. for the thickness of the bottom plate leaves the top of the rough opening 82¼ in. off the plywood subfloor. When the floor covering is installed, this height is reduced to about 81½ in., which is just about perfect for a standard 6-ft. 8-in. (80-in.) door. When using this system for standard exterior doors that have sills, leave one of the 2x4s off the header because the R.O. needs to be slightly taller. The jack studs for exterior door openings, then, should be 82¼ in. long.

This system is simple, but it's also overbuilt. You can save wood on narrow openings by using smaller-dimensioned headers and filling the space with short cripple studs. Using cripple studs requires more labor, though. In either case, jack-stud lengths of 80¾ in. for interior doors and 82¾ in. for exterior doors yield acceptable R.O. heights.

Windows often have the same header heights (and therefore jack-stud lengths) as doors. Here, I'll use this height to explain how I lay out and build window open-

ings (note that actual window heights can vary far more frequently than door heights). And since you build window openings as you build the wall, let's pause and look at how the wall goes together.

After you've marked off both plates and distributed the studs, jack studs, corners, T-intersections, and headers to their respective places, begin nailing the walls together (I build one wall at a time on the deck and then raise it into place). Hold each piece to its layout line on the top plate and nail through it into the end of the stud, corner, or other vertical component. At openings, begin by installing the king studs, then nail the header into position through the sides of the studs and the top of the top plate. After the header is in position, wedge the jack studs into place under it, nailing straight into the stud and at an angle into the header.

Previously, when you laid out the plates, you laid out just the widths for windows. After assembling the rest of the wall, then, window openings look the same as

Framing Door Openings

Standard-size interior doors

A 6-ft. 8-in. interior door requires a R.O. height of about 82¼ in. to leave room for the jamb and the height of the finish floor. The R.O. is achieved with 80¾-in.-long jack studs. Headers can be either a 2x10 assembly with 2xs on top and bottom or a 2x6 header with cripple studs. The R.O. width is 32 in.

Standard-size exterior door

A 6-ft. 8-in. exterior door requires more clearance than interior doors to allow for a threshold. Making the header smaller and cutting the jack studs 82¼ in. long will allow for a 83¾-in. R.O. height. The R.O. width is 38½ in.

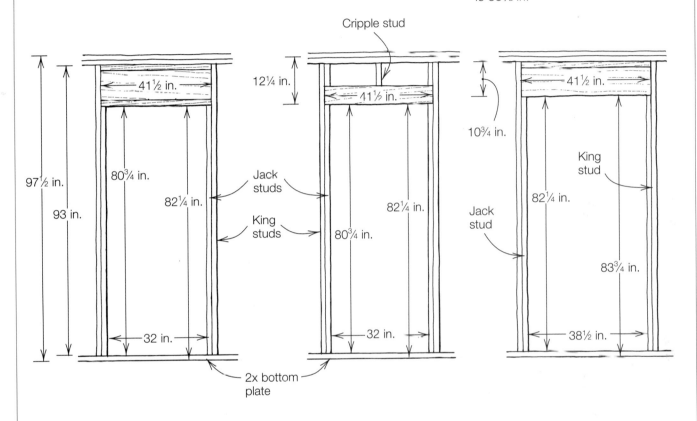

Headers in cross section

Use a 1x4 at the top if 92¼-in. studs are used.

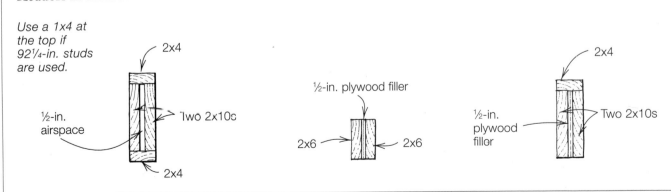

door openings. To finish the window openings, you have to lay out and build the bottom. First, determine the window's R.O. length and measure this distance down from the underside of the header. Then measure down from this mark another 1½ in. and 3 in. (which represent the double 2x horizontal rough windowsill) and scribe lines across the width of the jack stud with a combination square set to just under 3½ in. If the cripple studs haven't already been laid out on the bottom plate, hook your tape measure to a stud laid out in the 16-in.-o.c. pattern and continue the layout through the window area. After scribing square lines with the combination square and marking Cs (for cripple studs) on the appropriate side of the line, cut the windowsills and transfer the layout on the plate to one of the sills.

Next, set the sills aside and measure the length needed for the cripple studs, which is the distance from the top of the bottom plate to the lowest line for the sills (the line that is 3 in. below the R.O. mark). Cut the cripple studs to length and install them by first nailing through the bottom plate into the end of each stud. Then nail the rough windowsill with the layout on it onto the cripple studs, pushing or pulling the cripple studs as necessary to get them into the right position. The final step is to nail the second sill on top of the first (see the drawing at right). The second sill provides better nailing for window trim later on.

Prepping walls for sheathing and raising

After the frame of the wall has been nailed together, it has to be straightened, squared, sheathed, raised, and straightened again. Begin by dragging, pushing, tapping, and levering the wall precisely into position along the layout line. Once the wall has been positioned, nail through the bottom plate and into the floor deck every 5 ft. or so to pin it in place. Try to get the nails to exit the plate as closely as possible to the corner along the layout line so that they will allow the plate to rotate as the wall is tilted up (see the drawing on the facing page).

Once the bottom plate is anchored to the layout line, square it up by measuring the diagonals of the assembly. If one diagonal is longer than the other, the top corner of the long measurement should be knocked over with a sledgehammer until the diagonals are equal. I like to take the guesswork out of this process by actual-

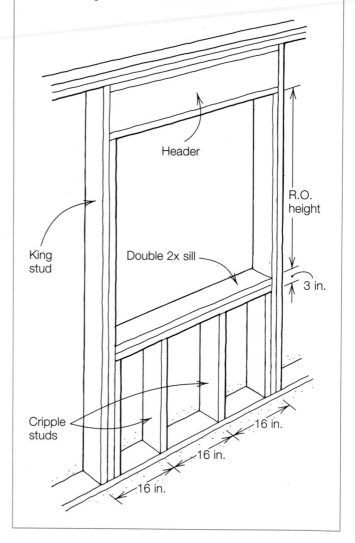

Framing a Window Opening

A window is framed like a door, except that rough sills and cripple studs are needed to complete the R.O. Cripple studs are laid out on the same centers as the rest of the wall, and the double sill provides better nailing for future window trim.

Header

R.O. height

King stud

Double 2x sill

3 in.

Cripple studs

16 in.

16 in.

16 in.

ly measuring the height and length of the wall and calculating the diagonal. Here is another instance when having a tape measure laid out in a decimalized foot comes in handy. It's not too difficult to convert the height of a 97½-in. wall to 8.125 ft., but it's easier to measure it directly. If the wall you're building here were 48 ft. long and 8.125 ft. high, the hypotenuse (or diagonal) would be 48.683 ft. long. Once the diagonals are equal, the wall can be held square with a temporary brace until it's been sheathed.

Sheathing usually serves a serves a structural function because it braces the wall and prevents it from racking. This means you should follow the recommended nailing schedule, even if it seems excessive. In my part of the country, the schedule calls for fasteners every 6 in. along the edges and 12 in. in the field for ½-in. CDX plywood or oriented-strand board (OSB). When I install sheathing, I usually let it run right over any openings and cut them out later with a router.

Although not required by code, I run plywood horizontally and, by extending it below the wall plate, use it to anchor the wall tenaciously to the floor structure. To do this with an 11½-in.-thick floor system, measure 36½ in. up from the bottom of the wall on each end, strike a chalkline and run the first course of plywood to that line. Because plywood or OSB sheathing is 48 in. wide, this leaves 11½ in. hanging over the bottom. It's a good idea to lay out stud centers on the sheathing before installing it, which makes it easier to straighten curved studs as well as to find them when nailing the sheathing. After enough sheathing has been run to hold the wall rigid, you can remove the temporary brace.

Raising walls

Because the wall is nailed to the floor along the layout line, it should rotate into place as it's being lifted. Walls don't always do what they're supposed to do, however, and small alignment adjustments are often necessary after the wall is upright. You can make these adjustments with a sledgehammer, and after the wall is positioned correctly on the layout line, have one of your crew members nail the plate securely to the deck, making an effort to nail into solid framing rather than just subfloor. Use temporary 2x braces to hold the wall safely in an upright position until it can be plumbed and straightened (see the top drawing on p. 111).

The usual procedure for getting the wall plumb and straight along the top plate is to plumb and carefully brace each end, then stretch a stringline from end to end to plumb up the rest of the wall. First nail 2x4 blocks to the inside edge of the top plate and pull a stringline from block to block along the length of the wall. You can then use a third 2x4 scrap as a gauge as you carefully pull the top of the wall into position. Starting at one end and working down the length of the wall, hold the 2x4 scrap against the inside of the top plate just below the stringline (see the bottom drawing on p. 111). At the same time, push or pull the wall until the edge of the block is even with the stringline. As you

Nailing the Bottom Plate to the Deck

Nailing the bottom plate to the deck along the layout line keeps it in the proper position during wall assembly yet allows the plate to safely and accurately swing into place as the wall is raised. As the wall rotates into the upright position, the nails pinning it to the layout line bend.

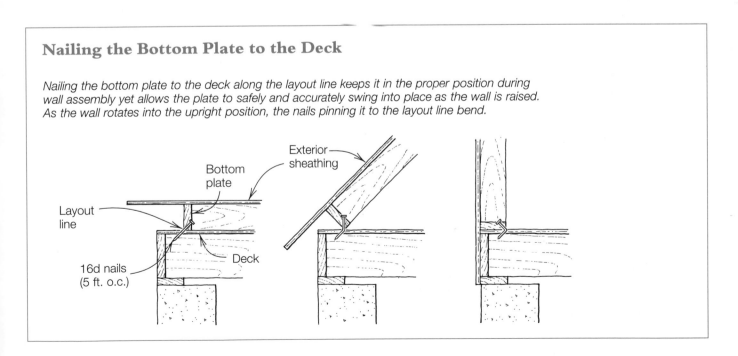

struggle to hold the wall in place, have a helper install a 2x4 brace running diagonally from just below the top of the wall to a block nailed to the deck. Typically, a brace is installed every 8 ft. or so.

Each wall built this way depends on three logical assumptions. First, if the floor is level and all of the studs are cut the same length, the top of the wall will be level. Second, if the floor is level and the wall is built square, the two edges of the wall will be plumb. And third, if each corner of the wall is braced plumb and the rest of the wall is set to a stringline stretched corner to corner, the wall will be plumb throughout its length.

The rest of the walls are built using the same layout techniques and depend on the same basic assumptions as those I've just discussed. The interior walls are attached to the exterior walls in two ways. The first is by nailing through the adjoining stud of the interior wall into the T-intersection of the exterior wall. The second is by overlapping the second top plate over the exterior wall and nailing down into the first top plate. Traditionally, these two methods have been used together to secure interior partitions to exterior walls. In recent years, however, the uppermost top plate has sometimes been eliminated (to save lumber) and this, in turn, obviates the use of interlocking top plates. The only other difference between interior walls and exterior walls is that interior walls are almost always left unsheathed.

Framing ceilings

The ceiling frame is usually made up of one of the following three systems: ceiling joists built in conjunction with a raftered roof; the underside of floor joists with living space above; or the bottom chord of roof trusses. All three of these systems accommodate the 4-ft. module drywall and plywood are manufactured in. Ceiling and floor joists are usually laid out in 16-in. increments and roof trusses in 24-in. increments. Where heavy snow loads are encountered, an extra truss per 8 ft. is often specified, which divides the layout into 19.2-in. increments. This accounts for the markings that you'll often find every 19¾₆ in. or so on many tape measures.

The main layout challenge for ceilings is to make sure there is a nailer (for the ceiling drywall) at every point where a wall intersects the ceiling. When a wall runs perpendicular to the ceiling frame, the drywall on the ceiling can be fastened every 16 in. or 24 in. along the wall-ceiling intersection. Here, the only place a nailer might have to be added is at the end of a wall that terminates somewhere in the middle of the ceiling span.

When a wall runs parallel to the ceiling structure, on the other hand, additional framing at the ceiling level is almost always required. One solution is to cap the wall with a board wider than the wall. The part that projects over the edge of the wall serves as a nailer for the ceiling drywall. The main shortcoming of this method is that the top of the wall is not secured to the ceiling frame. In some circumstances, it is better to install a series of 2x4 blocks laid out 16 in. o.c. across the ceiling joists in the bay above the interior wall. The top plate of the wall can then be nailed to the blocks, which are installed flush with the bottom of the ceiling frame.

Another important consideration when laying out the structure that forms the ceiling is plumbing vent pipes. Whether laying out second-story floor joists, roof trusses, or ceiling joists in conjunction with rafters, you need to keep a pathway clear for these pipes. Sometimes it's necessary to shift the layout over a few inches to accommodate them.

THINKING AHEAD DURING FRAMING

One of the most important skills of the frame carpenter is forethought—the ability to anticipate the requirements of subsequent stages of the job. You not only have to be mindful of later carpentry tasks, but you also must concern yourself with the needs of the mechanical trades, masons, drywall hangers, and others. Here are some of the most important things you should keep in mind as you lay out and build walls.

Provide nailers

Newcomers to carpentry are often surprised at the amount of wood that goes into a framed wall. That's because they're only thinking in terms of structural load. A lot of the wood that goes into a closet, for example, is placed there solely to accept the screws and nails of drywall hangers and finish carpenters. Besides being structurally adequate, then, one of the main concerns during wall framing should be to provide solid nailing surfaces at every corner and T-intersection.

Plumbing and Straightening a Wall

After plumbing and bracing both ends of the wall temporarily, an offset stringline is stretched from end to end. The top plate is then pushed or pulled into position along the stringline and held in place with intermediate braces nailed every 8 ft. or so.

Bracing a wall

Nail 2x4 braces to the deck every 8 ft. or so to hold the wall plumb and straight.

Sheathed wall

2x4 braces

Blocking (nailed to deck)

Rooms laid out on deck

Testing for plumb

Once the corners of the wall are plumb, nail 2x4 blocks to the ends. Stretch a stringline from one end to the other and use a gauge block to make sure that the wall is plumb and straight.

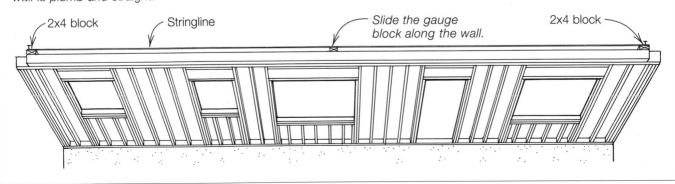

2x4 block

Stringline

Slide the gauge block along the wall.

2x4 block

Providing Nailers

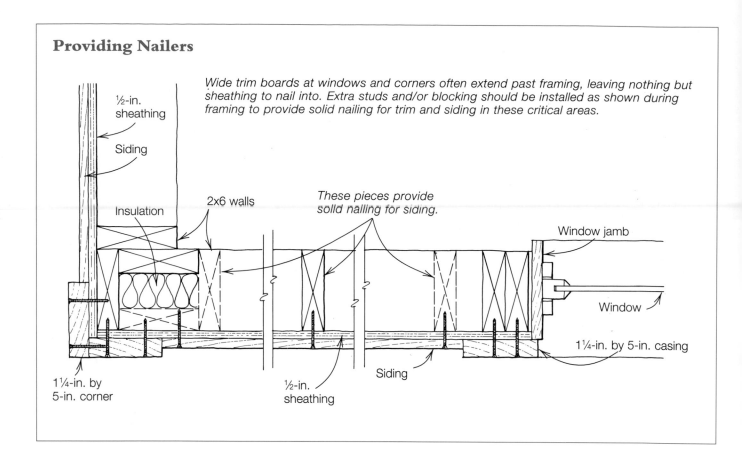

Wide trim boards at windows and corners often extend past framing, leaving nothing but sheathing to nail into. Extra studs and/or blocking should be installed as shown during framing to provide solid nailing for trim and siding in these critical areas.

½-in. sheathing

Siding

Insulation

2x6 walls

These pieces provide solid nailing for siding.

Window jamb

Window

1¼-in. by 5-in. casing

1¼-in. by 5-in. corner

½-in. sheathing

Siding

One of the most common framing mistakes is failing to provide nailers for the ends of siding. Often, corner boards and window casings extend past the solid nailing surfaces provided by conventional framing, leaving nothing but sheathing to nail into. And since some sheathings provide a very poor nailing surface, the ends of the siding are basically held in place by wishful thinking. To avoid problems like this, check the various trim details during the framing stage and install extra studs and blocking as necessary (see the drawing above).

Leave room for the plumber

A 2x4 wall behind a toilet can present significant problems later on. The plumber has to install a 3-in. vent pipe in the wall, which means he has to put a 3-in. hole in the top and bottom of 3½-in.-wide plates. This does not leave much wood in the plate to hold it together and can cause a number of headaches, including a wobbly wall, a bulge in the finished wall (caused by the pipe), and screws finding and penetrating the vent pipe.

In my area, code now requires a 2x6 wall behind toilets to provide for the 3-in. vent pipe that must be run through it—an excellent idea, even where not required by code.

Another area of concern is the valve wall at the end of the tub. To make it easier for the plumber to install the valve, diverter, and showerhead, measure 15 in. in from the sidewall and mark. This represents the centerline of the tub, the area that should be left clear. Now measure 7¼ in. to one side of the centerline, mark, and set the X ahead (see the left drawing on the facing page). You can then lay out the rest of the wall on 16-in. centers from this point. Another way to help out both the plumber and the electrician is to nail the second top plate into the first only above the studs. This keeps nails out of the path of their drill bits.

Laying Out the Valve Wall of a Tub

Centering a stud bay around the center of the tub will leave plenty of room for the plumber to install the valve and showerhead. Start the layout to either side and 7¼ in. away from the tub's centerline.

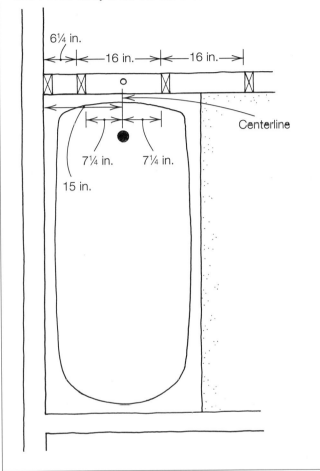

6¼ in.

16 in.

16 in.

Centerline

7¼ in.

7¼ in.

15 in.

Framing around a Chimney

Because masons work most efficiently with even brickwork, the size of the chimney and required clearances should be determined before any openings are framed. In this chimney, none of the bricks that enclose the 13-in. by 13-in. flue need to be cut.

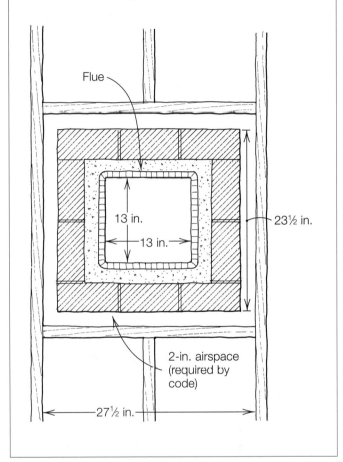

Flue

13 in.

13 in.

23½ in.

2-in. airspace (required by code)

27½ in.

Keep framing away from the chimney

In a wood-framed house, fire is and always has been a tremendous hazard. The first building codes in this country were focused almost entirely on this hazard, and the first building inspector in most communities was the fire chief. Because the threat of fire remains a primary concern, framers should stay clear of the chimney. Framing materials should never be built hard against a chimney. While the required clearance varies, it is usually between 1 in. and 2 in. and is strictly enforced (see the right drawing above).

In new construction, the frame carpenter usually precedes the chimney mason, and it is his responsibility to build openings through floors, ceilings, and roofs with the proper clearance. To lay out the openings, first find the chimney dimensions, being sure to add the code-required clearances. If there is also a fireplace, you'll need to frame an opening in the wall. Because the height and width of these openings varies according to the size and style of the fireplace, it is imperative to find out what the mason intends to build and what the code requires for clearances before framing the opening.

Chapter 6

LAYING OUT BASIC ROOFS

Perhaps no measuring and marking task in all of carpentry has been the subject of more bloated and misleading claims than the layout of roof rafters. Contrary to what certain tool manufacturers, the publishers of rafter tables, and the makers of construction calculators would have you believe, there is no gadget, table, or formula that can lay out the frame of a roof for you. Instead, these tools simply give you the hypotenuse of a right triangle after you have provided specific information about the length of the base of the triangle and the pitch or angle of the hypotenuse in relation to that base. In other words, these tools give you stored geometry and trigonometry.

While these are powerful tools, the information that comes from them is only as good as the dimensions fed into them. Furthermore, after the calculations have been completed, they still have to be applied correctly to the timber you are working with. You must know precisely where to begin and end your measurements and how to superimpose your geometry, which is as flat as this page, on your wood, which is 1½ in. thick.

Roof layout begins with careful measurement and the ability to visualize and marshal several details at once. And as you'll see in this chapter, it's possible to lay out even complex roofs without using any of the special tools so highly touted by manufacturers and publishers. It is very difficult to lay out a roof frame, however, without being able to see clearly how the components fit together and are joined to the building.

As is often the case in construction layout, there are many ways to approach the task of laying out a roof. The system I'll present in this chapter is not the only way, but it is an efficient and easily understood method of approaching a complex task. It works well for laying out gable roofs and hip roofs (both regular and irregular), as well as for laying out valleys. What I like most about this system is that it provides an overview of the mechanics of the process. Knowing *why* this method works, I've found, makes it easy to remember and simple to use.

LAYING OUT SIMPLE GABLE ROOFS

In this section, I'll discuss how to lay out the rafters and ridge of a roof with an 8-in-12 pitch on a building 27 ft. 1 in. wide (27 ft. from plate to plate, plus ½-in. sheathing on both sides). The walls on this hypothetical house are made out of 2x6s and sheathed with ½-in. plywood, so they are 6 in. thick.

The layout of a rafter for any roof consists of three parts: first, laying out the top—or plumb—cut, where the rafter meets the ridge beam; second, laying out the bottom—or seat—cut; and third, measuring the rafter's length. In addition, the tail of the rafter is often fully or partially shaped to conform to the design of the eaves at the same time that the seat cut is laid out and cut. Once the rafters have been laid out, you can select and prepare the ridge beam and begin laying out the rafter locations on it.

Laying out the plumb and seat cuts of the rafter

While there are several easy ways to lay out the plumb cut at the top of a common rafter and the seat cut at the bottom, the first way I learned to do this was with a rafter square (see the left drawing on p. 116). If the plan calls for an 8-in-12 roof pitch, simply hold the square so that the 8-in. and 12-in. marks are lined up with the edge of the rafter. To get the plumb cut, scribe along the side where the 8-in. mark engages the edge of the board; scribe along the other side, where the 12-in. mark engages the edge of the board, to find the seat cut (which is also called the level cut).

In addition to the traditional rafter square, there are also several other squares available designed primarily for laying out the angled cuts on rafters. Inspired by the Swanson Speed Square, these squares employ the "one-number" method. Instead of lining up two numbers, as is required by the rafter square, you can rotate the Speed Square on its pivot point until the desired pitch number is aligned with the edge of the rafter (see the right drawing on p. 116). For an 8-in-12 pitch, align the mark at the number 8 along the common-rafter scale to get the plumb cut for an 8-in-12 rafter cut. To lay out the seat cut at the bottom of the rafter, start with the plumb-cut layout, then scribe another line perpendicular to the plumb line. Since using the Speed Square is awkward for this, I generally use a rafter square to make this second, seat-cut line.

For laying out several identical plumb and seat cuts, there are a number of squares that have an adjustable arm that can be locked into position at the desired pitch angle. One of these is the Stanley Quick Square, and like the Speed Square, it uses the one-number method (see the left drawing on p. 117). To set this square for an 8-in-12 roof pitch, rotate the arm until it lines up with the mark at 8 in the common-rafter scale and lock it in place. Once the square has been set up, use the arm as a fence. To lay out the plumb cut, just push the fence against the edge of the rafter stock and scribe along the edge of the square. By flipping the square over, you can make seat cuts. One of the best features of the Quick Square is the ease with which you can convert pitch to degrees and vice versa. If you set the arm for an 8-in-12 pitch, for example, you can glance down the arm and see that the pitch is just shy of 34°.

Over the years, I've accumulated all of these squares, but my tool of choice for laying out rafter cuts is a site-built rafter jig. You can make this type of jig in 10 minutes or so out of three scraps of wood. For an 8-in-12 roof, start with a scrap of plywood about 18 in. to 20 in. wide. Because you need a square corner, look for a scrap cut off the end of a sheet of plywood and double-check it for square with your rafter square. To make an 8-in-12 rafter jig, measure 8 in. up and 12 in. across from the 90° factory corner. Connect those marks with a pencil and a straightedge, make a second, parallel line about 2 in. above the first, then cut out the triangular-shaped piece along this second line. To finish the jig, attach a 1x2 fence on both sides of the plywood along the first line you scribed. To use the jig, hold the fence against the edge of the board and scribe along the vertical side for

Four Methods of Laying Out Plumb and Seat Cuts

Using a rafter square

A rafter square can be used to mark the plumb and seat cuts for any given pitch (8-in-12 in this example).

To lay out the plumb cut, scribe a line where the 8-in. mark engages the edge of the rafter.

Using a Speed Square

For an 8-in-12 pitch, align the mark at 8 along the common-rafter scale to find the plumb cut.

To lay out the seat cut, scribe where the 12-in. mark engages the edge of the rafter.

8 in.

12 in.

Plumb cut

Pivot point

8 in.

Plumb cut

8 in.

Plumb cut

8 in.

12 in.

12 in.

Seat cut

Seat cut

After making the plumb-cut line with the Speed Square, use a rafter square to mark the seat cut.

the plumb cut or the horizontal side for the seat cut (see the right drawing on the facing page). Then mark the pitch on the jig and save it for future projects.

If wide stock is going to be used for the rafters, the jig can be enlarged without changing the pitch simply by multiplying the rise and run figures by the same dimension. For example, to bridge the width of 2x10 rafters, it's convenient to build a slightly larger jig. Multiplying both 8 and 12 by 1.5 enlarges the jig to a more manageable triangle with a rise of 12 and a run of 18.

There are at least four reasons why I go through the trouble of making this jig. First of all, I find it easier to visualize the cuts with the jig than with any manufactured tool. Second, identical layouts for both the top and bottom cuts can be made in rapid succession. Third, I use the plumb edge as a cutting guide for my circular

saw. And finally, I return to the rafter jig again and again later on, while I'm framing the gable, finishing the eaves and rake, installing siding on the gable, or marking any material that follows the pitch of the roof (see the bottom drawing on the facing page). I've never invested time in making a rafter jig that wasn't returned several-fold by the end of the job.

Before moving on to the next section, I should mention one other way to "lay out" the plumb cut. Instead of using a pencil and a straightedge to lay out the angle on the rafter, you can simply use the scale on any of the several sliding compound-miter saws that are now available. Of course, to do this you'll first have to convert pitch to degrees, either by using one of the specialty squares described previously or by consulting a conversion table (see Appendix C on p. 211). Then you simply set the saw to the proper angle.

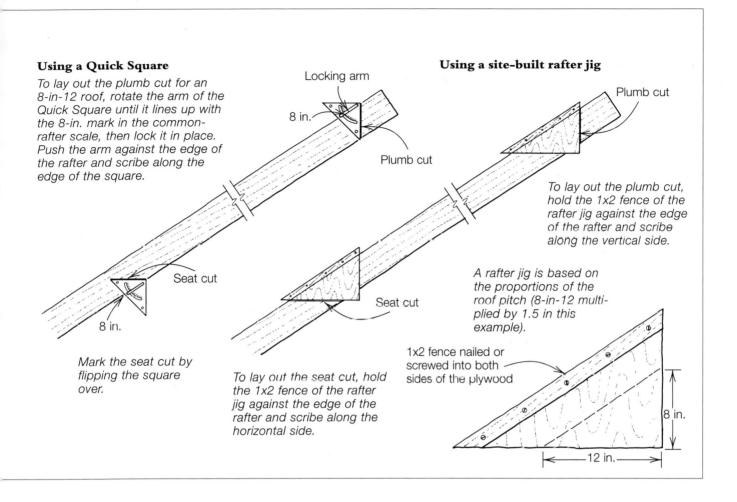

Using a Quick Square

To lay out the plumb cut for an 8-in-12 roof, rotate the arm of the Quick Square until it lines up with the 8-in. mark in the common-rafter scale, then lock it in place. Push the arm against the edge of the rafter and scribe along the edge of the square.

Locking arm

8 in.

Plumb cut

Seat cut

8 in.

Mark the seat cut by flipping the square over.

Using a site-built rafter jig

Plumb cut

Seat cut

To lay out the seat cut, hold the 1x2 fence of the rafter jig against the edge of the rafter and scribe along the horizontal side.

To lay out the plumb cut, hold the 1x2 fence of the rafter jig against the edge of the rafter and scribe along the vertical side.

A rafter jig is based on the proportions of the roof pitch (8-in-12 multiplied by 1.5 in this example).

1x2 fence nailed or screwed into both sides of the plywood

8 in.

12 in.

Other Uses for a Rafter Jig

Besides being useful for laying out rafters, a rafter jig can be used as shown for other framing and trimming tasks that rely on the roof pitch.

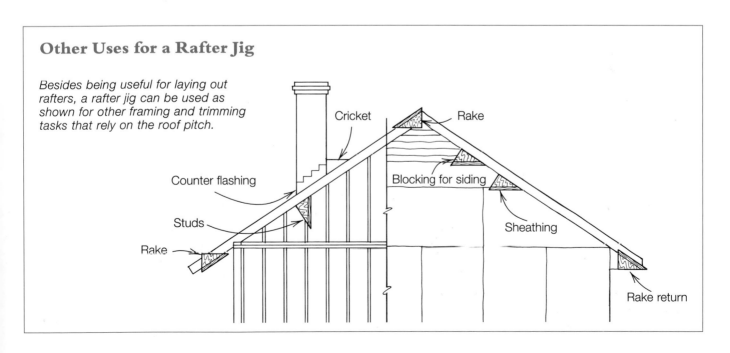

Cricket

Rake

Counter flashing

Blocking for siding

Studs

Sheathing

Rake

Rake return

Laying out the bird's mouth and rafter tail

So far, I've limited the discussion of the bottom cut of the rafter to a straight seat cut. In most cases, though, the bottom cut is an elaboration of the seat cut, called a bird's mouth. The rafter tail is often shaped at this time as well in anticipation of the framing of the eaves.

To make a bird's mouth in a 2x10 rafter that rests on a 2x6 wall, for example, begin by drawing a level seat-cut line using the rafter jig (see the drawings at right). Then measure along that line from the edge of the underside of the rafter a distance equal to the thickness of the wall (or 6 in., in this example). From that point, scribe a plumb line down to the edge of the rafter using the jig. The resulting triangular-shaped cut enables the rafter to sit securely on the plate while extending out over it to provide framing for building the eaves.

To lay out the rafter tail for the same 2x10 rafter, hold the jig at the plumb line of the bird's mouth (see the drawings on the facing page). Measure out the width of the eaves (16 in. in this example) and mark along the bottom (seat-cut) edge of the jig, then transfer that mark to the rafter. Scribe a plumb line at the mark. When the plumb cut has to be made near the end of the rafter, you can set the jig against the bottom edge to mark the line.

Measuring the rafter length

Before going any further, I want to state emphatically that for any rafter measurements that we produce here to have meaning, there must be a clear understanding of the beginning and ending points of that measurement. Rafters vary in design and don't have natural beginning and ending points, so the process of assigning a "length" to a rafter is arbitrary. You have to decide where to measure from and where to measure to, in other words. While rafter manuals, the tables on rafter squares, and calculators excel at providing rafter lengths, they often do a poor job of explaining where these measurements begin and end relative to the plumb and seat cuts. My goal in this section, then, is to identify the rafter's measuring line, to establish the exact points along that line where rafter measurements begin and end, and to demonstrate how plumb and seat cuts should be laid out from those points.

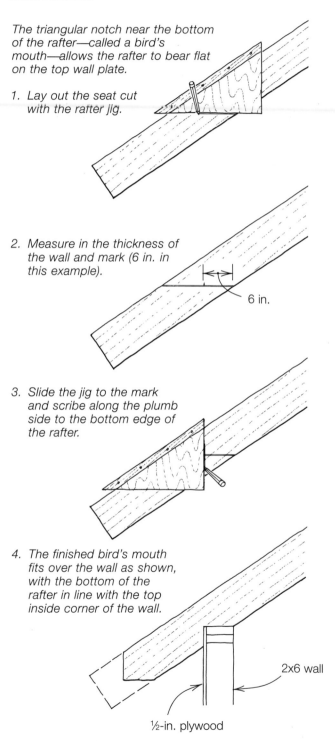

Using a Rafter Jig to Lay Out the Bird's Mouth and Rafter Tail

Bird's mouth

The triangular notch near the bottom of the rafter—called a bird's mouth—allows the rafter to bear flat on the top wall plate.

1. Lay out the seat cut with the rafter jig.

2. Measure in the thickness of the wall and mark (6 in. in this example).

6 in.

3. Slide the jig to the mark and scribe along the plumb side to the bottom edge of the rafter.

4. The finished bird's mouth fits over the wall as shown, with the bottom of the rafter in line with the top inside corner of the wall.

2x6 wall

½-in. plywood

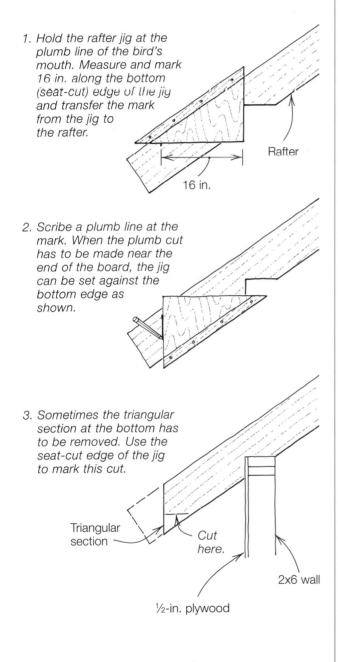

Rafter tail

Oftentimes the rafter tail is laid out and cut right after the bird's mouth, before the rafter is installed.

1. *Hold the rafter jig at the plumb line of the bird's mouth. Measure and mark 16 in. along the bottom (seat-cut) edge of the jig and transfer the mark from the jig to the rafter.*

Rafter

16 in.

2. *Scribe a plumb line at the mark. When the plumb cut has to be made near the end of the board, the jig can be set against the bottom edge as shown.*

3. *Sometimes the triangular section at the bottom has to be removed. Use the seat-cut edge of the jig to mark this cut.*

Triangular section

Cut here.

2x6 wall

½-in. plywood

Many rafter manuals place the measuring line somewhere near the middle of the board, rather than at the top or bottom edge of the rafter. However, the exact location of this measuring line on the rafter varies because it begins at the point where the rafter intersects the outside edge of the wall, which changes from job to job. Although the location along the depth of the rafter varies, the line always runs parallel to the top and bottom edges. While the beginning point of the measuring line is where the rafter intersects with the outside edge of the building, the ending point actually lies beyond the end of the rafter, in the center of the ridge beam. So when rafter manuals provide the length of a rafter, they mean the distance between these measuring points (see the top drawing on p. 120).

This can be confusing. To begin with, the rafter length provided by manuals is simply not really the length of the rafter, at least according to conventional English usage. Second, this measuring line makes it difficult to visualize how the cuts should be made in relation to the marks. Carpenters are used to measuring and marking along the edge of a board, and they usually begin the layout of their cuts at the marks they've made along that edge. When they use the measuring line offered by rafter manuals, however, they have to start the layout of angled cuts uphill from the mark so they can catch it along the measuring line. Finally, there is the "ridge reduction" ritual. Many carpenters wonder, with good reason, why they should make careful measurements and calculations, then, at the last minute, subtract "half the thickness of the ridge." Why not just begin the whole process where the rafter actually meets the ridge? I've never found a good reason not to do so.

In the bottom drawings on p. 120, there are three different measuring lines used to lay out the same 8-in-12 pitch rafter for a 27-ft.-wide building. Along each of those measuring lines, the measurement of length has different beginning and ending points. There are two things worth noting here. The first is that the final layout of all three rafters is identical. It doesn't matter which measuring line and which reference points along that line are used, as long as there is a clear picture of how the line should fit into the final layout. The second thing to note is that each example employs an imaginary right triangle to lay out the rafter. Being able to see these measuring triangles can be very helpful when you

Defining the Length of a Rafter

According to standard English, the length of this rafter is 213⅝ in., while rafter manuals insist on calling its length 195¼ in. Referring to the 195¼-in. dimension as the measuring length (the distance from the center of the ridge beam to the outside of the wall) is more accurate and less confusing.

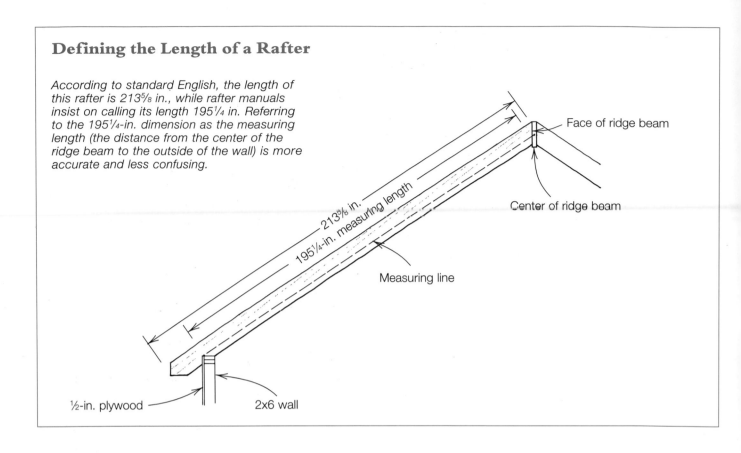

Face of ridge beam

Center of ridge beam

213⅝ in.

195¼-in. measuring length

Measuring line

½-in. plywood

2x6 wall

Deciding on the Measuring Line

While the measuring lines (and the lengths along them) of the rafters in the three examples below are different, their finished rafters are identical. (Walls are 2x6 with ½-in. sheathing.)

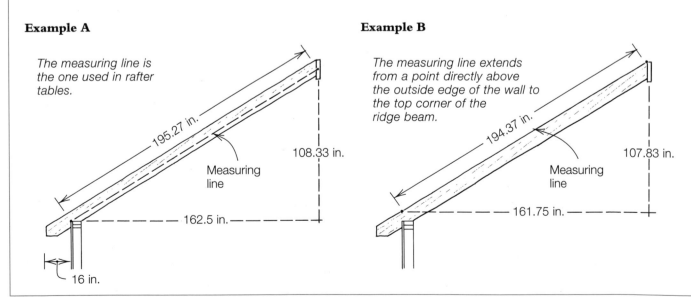

Example A

The measuring line is the one used in rafter tables.

195.27 in.

Measuring line

108.33 in.

162.5 in.

16 in.

Example B

The measuring line extends from a point directly above the outside edge of the wall to the top corner of the ridge beam.

194.37 in.

Measuring line

107.83 in.

161.75 in.

are trying to visualize where to begin and end your layout. This is especially true when you're confronted with a roof that is not covered by the rafter manuals and the tables on the rafter square.

For measuring common rafters, my own preference is to use the method shown in example C. Here, the measuring line is along the bottom of the rafter, and the beginning and ending points are at the inside edge of the wall (the heel of the seat cut) and the bottom corner of the ridge beam (the heel of the plumb cut), respectively. As you'll see, this method not only simplifies rafter layout, but it also makes it easy to set the ridge beam at the correct height. As the drawing indicates, the same measurement and the same measuring triangle can be used along the top edge of the rafter.

Laying out a common rafter

While it shouldn't be difficult to lay out an actual rafter for a 27-ft.-wide building with an 8-in-12 pitch roof, often there is confusion about where the measuring triangle actually is relative to the ridge beam and wall plates. I use the following steps to quickly and accurately find the measuring length of rafters and to lay out their plumb and seat cuts.

1. Establish the run of the rafter The term "run" can be very confusing, especially when used in connection with roof framing (see the sidebar on p. 122). But it can also be very useful if it is well defined. When carpenters speak of the run of a rafter or the run of a staircase, they simply mean the horizontal distance that an inclined piece of wood spans. In this chapter, when I refer to the run of a rafter, I'll always be referring to the base of the measuring triangle as defined in the drawing on p. 123.

On many jobs, this length can be found simply by measuring along the top plate of the end wall after laying out the position (in plan view) of the ridge beam. When the end wall hasn't been built, I measure the distance between the sidewalls (313 in. in this example), subtract the width of the ridge beam (1½ in.), and divide the remainder (311.5 in.) in half to get the run of the rafter. In this example, then, the run of the rafter (and therefore the base of the measuring triangle) is 155.75 in.

2. Determine the measuring length of the rafter After establishing the run, or base of the measuring triangle, you can quickly find the altitude and the hypotenuse of the triangle and then lay out the plumb and seat cuts. Because the roof pitch is 8-in-12, you know that the rafter should rise 8 in. for every 12 in. of run. The total rise (or the altitude of the measuring triangle) can thus be obtained by dividing the run by 12 (155.75 ÷ 12 = 12.979) and then multiplying the result by 8 (12.979 × 8 = 103.83), or 103.83 in. You can also determine the fourth proportional (as described in on p. 46) to find the altitude, as follows:

$$\frac{8}{12} = \frac{x}{155.75}, \text{ where } x = 103.83.$$

The measuring length of the rafter (from the heel of the plumb cut to the heel of the seat cut) is actually the hypotenuse of the measuring triangle. To find the hypotenuse, you can use the geometry on the rafter tables of the rafter square. Under the number 8, the "length common rafters per foot run" is given as 14.42 in. To use this table, all you have to do is find out how many feet are in the run, then multiply the result by 14.42. In this case the run is 155.75 in. Here's the math:

Example C

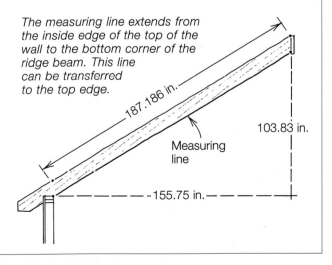

The measuring line extends from the inside edge of the top of the wall to the bottom corner of the ridge beam. This line can be transferred to the top edge.

187.186 in.

103.83 in.

Measuring line

- 155.75 in. -

Just What is the Run of a Rafter, Anyway?

The language of roof framing is filled with vague, archaic and confusing words, one of which is "run." Somehow, the term "total run" has come to mean half the width of the building (this is like saying a "total half-dozen"). From this run, the roof builder then calculates the "theoretical" or "mathematical length" of the rafter, from which he deducts half the thickness of the ridge beam to arrive at the "actual length" (which is actually not the length of the rafter at all if it runs past the wall and helps form the eaves).

Things get even more confusing when the ridge of the building is not in the center of the house or if the roof has two pitches on each side (as would be the case if the house has a gambrel roof). In these circumstances, the idea of the total run being half the width of the house has to be abandoned and substituted with a temporary expedient, such as "total run of each section."

Because rafter squares let you use the run of the common rafters to compute the length of hip and valley rafters, furthermore, the terms "apparent run" (the total run of the common rafter) and "actual run" (the total run of the hip) have entered the vocabulary. Either of these can be used to compute the theoretical or mathematical length of the hip, which does not become the actual length of the hip until you deduct half the thickness of the ridge beam (which is actually more than half the thickness of the ridge because the hip intersects it at an angle). Of course, the actual length of the hip is not the real length of the hip, unless you pretend that the part that extends beyond the wall doesn't exist. Sort of confusing, isn't it?

It's not too difficult to see how we ended up with this tortured use of the term run. Somehow, a system evolved that was supposed to make things easy for the simple but earnest carpenter: Find the pitch of the roof, measure the width of the house, look up half that number in a table, and get the length of the rafter. Thus, a carpenter could make perfect rafters without really understanding what he did. Problem is, this effort to simplify actually makes roof framing more complicated; the more effort spent trying to make this system work, the more confusing the process and the accompanying language has become.

On many roofs—shed roofs, mansard roofs, gambrel roofs, roofs that have an off-center ridge, and roofs where the ceiling joists cantilever over the sidewalls—the run, as half the width of the building, is a useless concept, and the fiction has to be abandoned temporarily. I propose that we abandon the fiction altogether, and along with it terms like "mathematical, theoretical, and actual length," "apparent and actual run," and "ridge reduction." Instead, the run should reflect the actual length of the base of the measuring triangle that is used to compute the rise and measuring length of the rafter.

155.75 ÷ 12 = 12.979 ft.

12.979 × 14.42 = 187.157 in. (or 187³⁄₁₆ in.).

(For more on converting sixteenths to decimals, see Tricks of the Trade on p. 127.)

When I first learned this technique, I was disturbed by the fact that I was multiplying something by feet (in this case 12.979 ft.) and ending up with inches. This mystery worried my feeble mind until I finally figured out that I was working out a simple proportion with the help of the table. From the information on the rafter square, you know that a right triangle with a base of 12 in. and an altitude of 8 in. has a hypotenuse of 14.42 in. If you expand the same triangle until it has a base of 155.75 in., you'll end up with a hypotenuse of 187.57. This problem can be written as follows:

$$\frac{14.42}{12} = \frac{x}{155.75}, \text{ where } x = 187.159.$$

When you use the table on the rafter square, you multiply the number of feet, not the length in feet, by the length—14.42 in.—in the table. In this case, the table tells you, in imperfect English, that for every 12 in. of run, there are 14.42 in. of rafter length (see the drawing below).

There are two other approaches to finding the measuring length. One way is to install the ridge beam after calculating the total rise. In this example, the bottom of the ridge beam should be installed 103.83 in. above the top plate of the wall. After the ridge beam has been installed and accurately centered between the plates, you can find the distance from the bottom of the beam to the inside edge of the wall with a tape measure. This method requires a little climbing but no geometry (for other non-mathematical approaches to roof framing, see the sidebar on p. 124).

A third approach is to use the geometry stored in rafter-length tables or in construction calculators. Both of these devices work the same way: You supply the pitch and the run, and they supply the hypotenuse of the tri-angle. If you have a rafter-length table, for example, all you have to do is look up the "total run" of 155¾ in. under the 8-in-12 pitch to find the hypotenuse of the triangle—in this case 187³⁄₁₆ in. The same information punched into a construction calculator will yield the same result.

There is no one correct way to calculate the measuring length of a rafter. Instead, there are several correct ways. Many excellent carpenters swear by rafter-length tables or construction calculators. I prefer to calculate the rise, then solve for the measuring length using the Pythagorean theorem. Then, to double-check my work, I use the table on my rafter square. This process is just about fool proof and takes less than five minutes.

3. Measure and mark the rafter You now have all of the essential ingredients for laying out this rafter: a well-understood measuring line (the bottom of the rafter); the exact measuring length (187³⁄₁₆ in.); and a clear understanding of how the plumb and seat cuts should be made in relation to the beginning and ending points of the measuring length (from the heel of the plumb cut at one point and the heel of the seat cut at the other). Now you can go ahead and lay out and cut this rafter (see the drawing on p. 126).

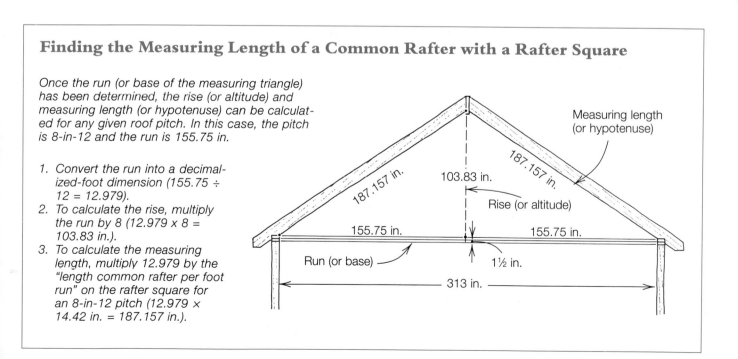

Finding the Measuring Length of a Common Rafter with a Rafter Square

Once the run (or base of the measuring triangle) has been determined, the rise (or altitude) and measuring length (or hypotenuse) can be calculated for any given roof pitch. In this case, the pitch is 8-in-12 and the run is 155.75 in.

1. *Convert the run into a decimalized-foot dimension (155.75 ÷ 12 = 12.979).*
2. *To calculate the rise, multiply the run by 8 (12.979 x 8 = 103.83 in.).*
3. *To calculate the measuring length, multiply 12.979 by the "length common rafter per foot run" on the rafter square for an 8-in-12 pitch (12.979 × 14.42 in. = 187.157 in.).*

187.157 in.

Measuring length (or hypotenuse)

103.83 in.

187.157 in.

Rise (or altitude)

155.75 in.

155.75 in.

Run (or base)

1½ in.

313 in.

Selecting and preparing the ridge beam

Most building codes require that rafters bear for the full length of the plumb cut against the ridge beam. To comply with this requirement, you must use wider lumber for the ridge beam than you use for the rafters. If you want to make the ridge beam the same width as the plumb cut, all you have to do is draw the plumb cut on a piece of the rafter material and then measure that line. The plumb cut for an 8-in-12 roof drawn on a 2x10 is about 11¹⁄₁₆ in. long. To make the ridge beam flush with the rafters, then, you need to use a 2x12, ripped to 11¹⁄₁₆ in. With a crew of three or more, it's possible to set the ridge beam to the proper height without making any measurements. While two people hold each end of

---

Non-Mathematical Approaches to Roof Framing

Most of the carpenters I know are not well versed in the geometry of roof framing. The fact is, they don't have to be to earn a living as carpenters. For one thing, most roofs today are built with trusses. For another, it's possible to get by on a stick-built roof with a few simple tools and a lot of common sense.

The first carpentry crew I worked with couldn't find the hypotenuse of a right triangle and didn't know how to use the tables on their rafter squares, yet they routinely put together perfectly sound stick-built roofs. Here's how they did it. From the drawing, they scaled the height of the ridge beam and installed it. Then they held the rafter stock in place, letting it run past the ridge beam on the top and the wall plate on the bottom, and scribed both the plumb cut and the bird's mouth (see the drawing at right). After cutting this rafter, they used it as a pattern for the rest of them. This technique wasn't elegant, but it worked, and over the years, many solid roofs have been laid out the same way. And I've found that many of these are either slightly less or slightly more than the intended pitch, presumably because the carpenters didn't get the ridge beam at the correct height.

Another non-mathematical way to figure out the length of a common rafter is to lay it out full-size on the floor deck. To draw a 6-in-12 pitch, for example, snap a chalkline and mark a 12-ft. length of it. Next, draw a perpendicular line at one of the marks, using a sheet of plywood as a square or one of the entries on the brace table on your rafter square (for more on the brace table, see Chapter 3). Then measure and mark 6 ft. up the perpendicular line and snap a chalkline from the first mark along the baseline through the 6-ft. mark. This gives you a full-scale picture of a 6-in-12 roof pitch. You can now measure and mark the run of the rafter along the baseline, draw another perpendicular line at that point, and then get the measuring length of the rafter right off the layout.

Laying out a common rafter without geometry

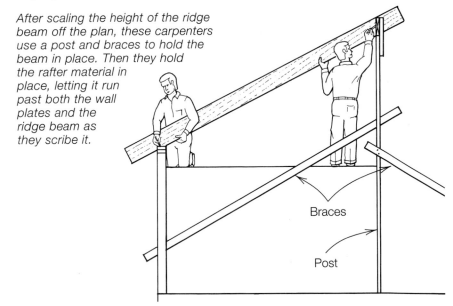

After scaling the height of the ridge beam off the plan, these carpenters use a post and braces to hold the beam in place. Then they hold the rafter material in place, letting it run past both the wall plates and the ridge beam as they scribe it.

Braces

Post

the ridge beam, plus the top end of a rafter, a third person can quickly toenail the bottom of the rafters into the top plate. After affixing a pair of opposing rafters to the top plate in this manner, you can set the ridge beam to the right height by holding it even with the plumb cuts of the opposing rafters. Here you get an assist from gravity, which pulls the rafters down and against the

ridge beam. As soon as the ridge beam is in the proper position, you can nail the rafters to it.

While this technique is simple enough, it requires at least three people, and when the ridge beam is a substantial timber (as it is in the example here), it also requires a lot of physical exertion. To save my back, I pre-

---

The measuring length of a valley or hip rafter can also be determined without using geometry, because it can be measured in place right on the roof. Although it's not essential, it simplifies matters if you know the pitch of the hip or valley rafters. On a regular hip or valley, all you have to do is take the pitch of the common rafters and substitute 16.97 for 12. Where the common rafters have a pitch of 6-in-12, in other words, the hip or valley will have

a pitch of 6-in-16.97 (usually rounded to 6-in-17).

Another way to determine the pitch of a hip or valley rafter is to set up a stringline from the ridge beam to the plate. At the plate, you must devise some means of holding the stringline at the same "height above the plate" as are the top edges of the common rafters. With a bevel square, you can then take the angle of the plumb cut at the ridge beam, transfer this

measurement to a board, and measure the angle with a Speed Square. This gives you the correct angle in degrees as well as in roof pitch.

After you know the pitch of the hip or valley, you can lay out and cut short test pieces for both the bottom and top. As soon as you're satisfied with the fit of these test pieces, you can establish one measuring point at the top (on the king common rafter) and another on the bottom on the test piece. Now, instead of calculating the measuring distance, you can physically measure the distance between these two points and transfer that measurement to the hip or valley stock (see the drawing at left).

The empirical method—using stringline, a tape measure, scraps of wood, a bevel square, and a straightedge—often takes more time and physical exertion than using geometry and trigonometry. Still, it gets the job done. And on complex and irregular roofs, and where buildings are out of square, the empirical method can be the most effective one.

Measuring the hip rafter in place

On irregular roofs and out-of-square buildings, sometimes an empirical measurement is faster and more accurate than geometry for finding the length of a hip rafter. A stringline is pulled from the ridge and held at the proper height at the plate by a test scrap of rafter stock.

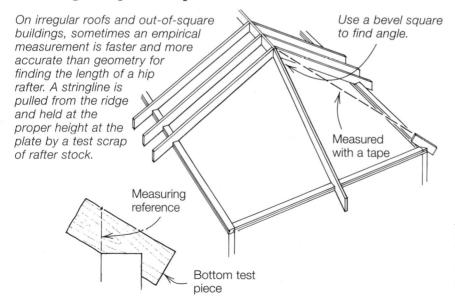

Use a bevel square to find angle.

Measured with a tape

Measuring reference

Bottom test piece

Measuring and Marking a Common Rafter

Once you have a well-understood measuring line, the exact measuring length, and a clear understanding of how the plumb and seat cuts should be made in relation to the beginning and ending points of the measuring length, you can lay out and cut the rafter.

1. Mark the measuring length.

Crown

187³⁄₁₆ in.

2. Mark the plumb and seat cuts.

Seat cut

187³⁄₁₆ in.

Plumb cut

3. Lay out the bird's mouth and shape the rafter tail.

Seat-cut line

6 in.

9¼ in.

11¹¹⁄₁₆ in.

Plumb cut

187³⁄₁₆ in.

Rafter tail shaped in accordance with eave design

Bird's mouth

Rip the ridge beam to 11¹¹⁄₁₆ in.

fer to cut a post to the correct height and let it carry the weight of the ridge beam. Here is where using the measuring triangle (as seen in the drawing on p. 123) really pays off. As the drawing shows, the bottom of the ridge beam must be the same height above the top plate (103¹³⁄₁₆ in.) as the altitude of the measuring triangle. If the end wall is in place, all you have to do is cut a post 103¹³⁄₁₆ in. long, center it on the wall, nail it at the bottom, and brace it plumb. The ridge beam can then be set on top of the post. To hold it safely there, nail a scrap of 2x4 to the post that runs several inches past the top of the ridge beam that is nailed or clamped to it. If the end wall isn't in place, the support post should be 103¹³⁄₁₆ in. long plus the height of the walls (typically 97 in. in my area).

Laying out rafter locations on the ridge beam

After the ridge beam has been set, the location of the outside edge of the house must be transferred up from either the floor system or the end wall (if it is already in place and has been carefully straightened and braced). This mark then serves as a starting point for the rafter layout, which has to be marked in an identical pattern on the wall plates beginning at the outside of the same end wall. To plumb up from the outside edge of the floor system or the end wall, you can plumb and brace the permanent post that supports the ridge beam. If a temporary support post has been set up inside the house, you can use a straightedge and a level.

When the ridge beam is quite a distance above the top plate and the end wall hasn't been built, I like to use a plumb bob to transfer the position of the outside edge of the floor to the beam. To do this, drive a nail at an angle into the side of the ridge beam a few inches in from where you estimate the outside edge of the house is located. Lower the bob from this nail and mark where it engages the floor, then measure from that point to the outside of the floor system. Then measure the same distance out from the nail you've used to hold the bob and mark. You can then commence your rafter-position layout from that reference point.

LAYING OUT REGULAR HIP ROOFS

On a hip roof, the roof slants down at the end of the building instead of terminating at the gable. At the intersection of the main roof and this end roof, the carpenter installs a hip rafter. On a regular hip roof, the hip rafter is set at a 45° angle, in plan view, from the common rafters in the main roof. On an irregular hip roof, the hip rafter is set at an angle other than 45°. The rafters that run from the top of the wall to the hip rafter are called hip jack rafters. In this section I'll discuss the layout of a regular hip roof. Next, I'll examine the layout of an irregular hip roof.

A hip roof starts out by looking like a typical gable roof. The center section of the roof is formed by common rafters exactly like those I just discussed. As the ridge beam approaches the end of the house, however, it surrenders to an end king common rafter, which dives

down to the top plate of the end wall. This end king common rafter may have a regal name, but it is exactly like all of the other common rafters in the roof (see the drawing on p. 128).

To lay out the end king common rafter, first find the center of the end wall and mark ¾ in. to each side. Next, holding the end king common rafter in place along the outside of one of the layout lines on the wall plate and overlapping the ridge beam, which has been left long, scribe along the plumb cut of the king common. Cut the ridge beam in place and install the end king common rafter in line with the ridge beam.

The next step is to lay out and install the two side king common rafters. To do this, first measure the distance from the corner of the house to the edge of the end king common rafter, then transfer this measurement, with the layout set ahead, to each sidewall. The top layout is at the end of the ridge beam, with the thickness of the rafter set in.

Determining the pitch of hip rafters

From a plan view, the end of the house is now divided into two equal squares by the three king common rafters. The next task is to divide each square diagonally with a hip rafter. If you look at the plan view shown in the drawing on p. 129, you can see that the run of the hip rafter is quite a bit longer than the run of the com-

King Common Rafters of a Hip Roof

King common rafters are identical to common rafters. Side king common rafters define the boundary of the common rafters of the main roof, while end king common rafters are centered on either end wall and butt into the ridge beam.

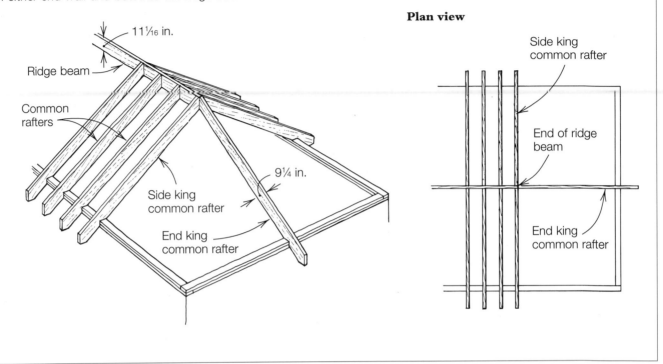

Plan view

11⁷⁄₁₆ in.

Ridge beam

Common rafters

9¼ in.

Side king common rafter

End king common rafter

Side king common rafter

End of ridge beam

End king common rafter

mon rafters. It is, in fact, 1.414 times longer. As I explained in Chapter 3, the formula for finding the diagonal of a square is 1.414 ($\sqrt{2}$) times the length of one of the sides. For example, a square that is 12 in. wide has a diagonal of 16.968 (12 × 1.414 = 16.968). Rounding off this number to 16.97 gives you the same number that is listed for a 12-in-12 roof on the "length common rafter per foot run" scale of a rafter square.

This is very useful information for two reasons. First, you can now calculate the run of the hip rafter by multiplying the run of the common rafter by 1.414. Once you have the length of the run of the hip rafter, you can then compute the measuring length of the hip rafter. But before going any further with this process, let's look at the second reason the above information is useful.

On a hip roof, the rise is fixed by the height of the ridge beam. When you install a hip rafter, however, the run

changes. The run of the hip rafter, as you've just seen, is 1.414 times longer than the run of the common rafter. This means that the pitch of the hip rafter is more gradual than the pitch of the common rafters. Fortunately, because of the above information, you know exactly what that pitch is. Instead of rising 8 in. for every 12 in. of run, the hip does not rise 8 in. until it has traversed 16.97 in. of run. The pitch of the hip on an 8-in-12 roof, then, is 8-in-16.97. On a regular hip roof, where the hip is set at a 45° angle to the common rafters, this rule holds true no matter what pitch is used. On a 4-in-12 roof, for example, the pitch of the hip rafter will be 4-in-16.97; on a 7-in-12 roof, it will be 7-in-16.97.

Laying out a hip rafter

Let's return now to the 27-ft.-wide house used as an example earlier, again using 2x10 rafters and 2x6 stud walls. Assuming that the common rafters and end and

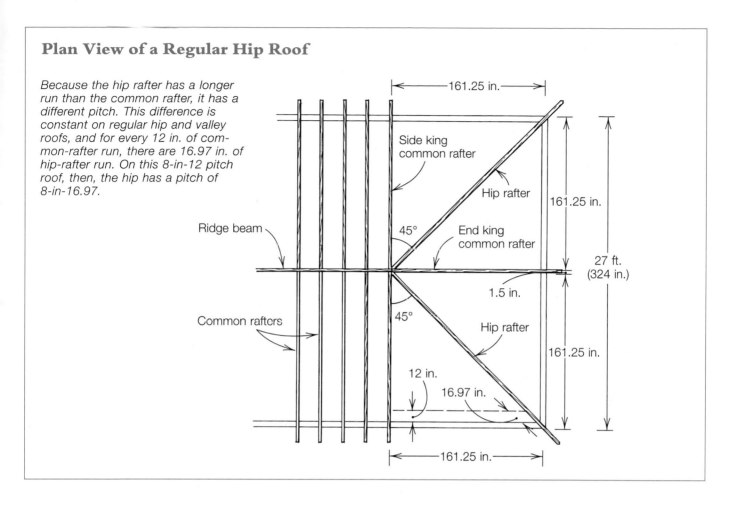

Plan View of a Regular Hip Roof

Because the hip rafter has a longer run than the common rafter, it has a different pitch. This difference is constant on regular hip and valley roofs, and for every 12 in. of common-rafter run, there are 16.97 in. of hip-rafter run. On this 8-in-12 pitch roof, then, the hip has a pitch of 8-in-16.97.

Ridge beam

Common rafters

Side king common rafter

Hip rafter

End king common rafter

Hip rafter

45°

45°

161.25 in.

161.25 in.

161.25 in.

161.25 in.

161.25 in.

27 ft. (324 in.)

1.5 in.

12 in.

16.97 in.

side king common rafters are already in place, here are the steps I follow to lay out and install the hip rafters.

1. Make a hip-rafter jig On a rectangular building, only four hip rafters are required. Because they are the most difficult rafters to visualize and lay out on the entire roof, it's worthwhile to spend a few moments to make a jig. This jig is identical to the one on p. 117, except that the pitch is now 8-in-16.97. As before, you can enlarge these numbers by multiplying everything by 1.5 so that the jig size is more useful. In this case, the jig ends up with a rise of 12 (8 × 1.5) and a run of 25.455 (16.97 × 1.5).

2. Lay out the position of the hip rafter at the ridge beam and at the wall plate The hip rafter runs from the juncture of the king common rafters at the ridge beam to the intersection of the side and end wall at the plate. To lay out these points, you need to mark ¾ in.

out from a line that connects both of these points. It's really not necessary to mark the layout at the ridge beam because when the hip is properly cut, it will jam tightly into the intersection of the king common rafters.

You need to know exactly where the top edge of the hip will engage the top edge of the king common rafters, however, because this will be the top point of your measuring line. And you need to know exactly how far away from the ridge beam, in plan view, this point is. On a regular hip, this is easy to determine: it is always 1¹⁄₁₆ in. As the drawing on p. 130 indicates, this distance can be derived by drawing a double 45° bevel on the top of a 2x scrap and then measuring the length of the bevel. Here, that isn't necessary, because you know that this dimension is always 1¹⁄₁₆ in. when there is a 45° bevel. On an irregular hip roof, as you will see, you will indeed draw out the bevel and measure its length. But, of course, in those cases it's never a 45° bevel.

Laying Out the Position of a Hip Rafter

While the layout of a regular hip rafter at the plate and ridge beam is straightforward, it's important to locate and mark the 1¹⁄₁₆-in. offset at the junctions of both the plates and the king common rafters as shown. These mark the beginning and ending points of the measuring line of the hip rafter.

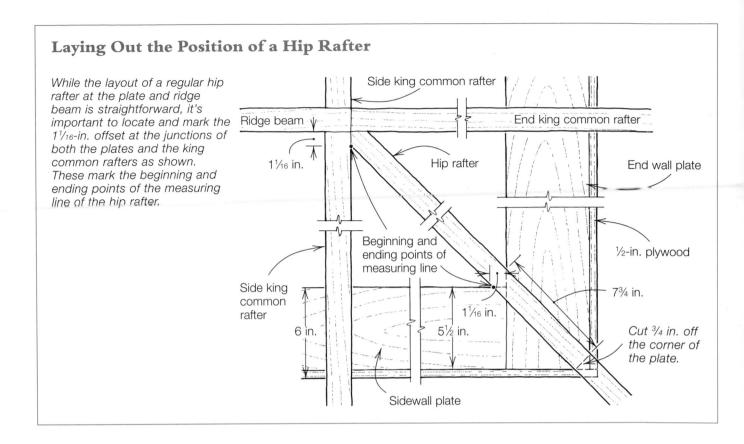

Side king common rafter

Ridge beam

End king common rafter

1¹⁄₁₆ in.

Hip rafter

End wall plate

Beginning and ending points of measuring line

½-in. plywood

Side king common rafter

7¾ in.

6 in.

1¹⁄₁₆ in.

5½ in.

Cut ¾ in. off the corner of the plate.

Sidewall plate

At the top plate of the walls, the layout of the hip is straightforward. Just scribe a 45° line from the inner corner to the outer corner of the plate, then measure out ¾ in. from that line on both sides and draw two more lines. After the hip location has been marked, I like to clip ¾ in. off the outside corner of the wall with my circular saw. This way, the bird's mouth of the rafter can be smaller and will not have to contend with the sharp corner of the plate.

3. Select and prepare hip-rafter material Hip rafters need to be as wide as the plumb cut of the jack rafters that will bear against it. Because the plumb cut of the jack rafters will be greater than the width of a 2x10, however, in this instance you'll have to use 2x12s for the hip rafters. The hip rafters should fit evenly with the jack rafters, however. To find out exactly how wide to make the hip rafters, first take a scrap of 2x10 and make a sample cut at the same compound miter/bevel angle that you'll be using later when you fit the jack rafters against the hip rafter (see the drawing on the facing page). You can lay out the miter using the plumb side of

the 8-in-12 rafter jig. The bevel is simply 45° and can be laid out by setting the table of your circular saw to 45°. A sliding compound-miter saw, of course, would be ideal for this cut. Simply set the miter to 34° (the equivalent of an 8-in-12 pitch) and the bevel to 45°.

After making this cut, draw a layout line on the 2x12 to represent the juncture of the jack and hip rafters. To make this line, which must be like a plumb line on the hip rafter after it's installed, use an 8-in-16.97 rafter jig. Now hold the scrap with the test cut of the jack rafter up to the line to find just how wide to rip the hip (about 10⅛ in. in this case).

4. Decide on the measuring line Most rafter tables position the measuring line of a hip rafter in the center of its top edge. This line extends from a point directly above the outside corner of the wall to the center of the ridge beam so that, eventually, the thickness of the ridge beam has to be deducted. This task is complicated by the fact that the hip rafter intersects the ridge beam at a

Preparing Hip-Rafter Material

Because the full width of jack rafters should bear against the hip rafters, they must be made of wider stock. To determine the proper width for a hip rafter, first make a test cut of a 2x10 scrap (as shown), then place the scrap to a layout line on 2x12 hip stock and mark the width (10⅛ in. in this example).

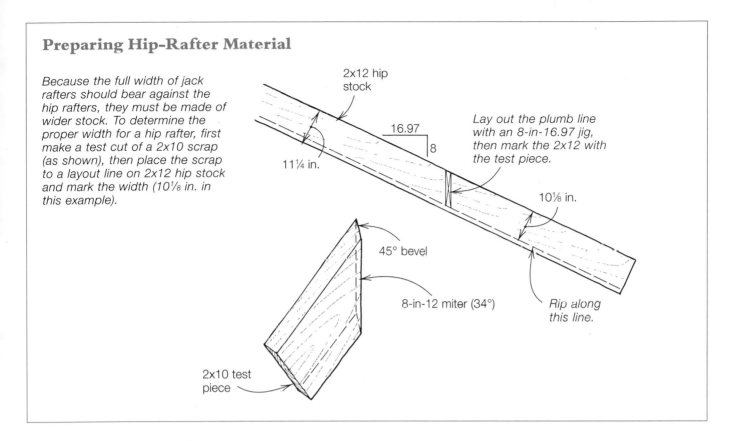

2x12 hip stock

16.97

8

Lay out the plumb line with an 8-in.-16.97 jig, then mark the 2x12 with the test piece.

11¼ in.

10⅛ in.

45° bevel

8-in.-12 miter (34°)

Rip along this line.

2x10 test piece

45° angle; as a result, the reduction has to be 1 1/16 in. rather than ¾ in.

In addition to this, the hip rafter has to be dropped slightly by deepening the seat cut, because if the center of the hip rafter is left in the same plane as the rest of the roof, the edges of the hip will poke about 5/16 in. above the roof plane. In fact, I find the process of using the center of the hip rafter as a measuring line to be so cluttered and confusing that I don't even use it. By establishing a measuring line along the top outside *edge* of the rafter—instead of the center—you can unload the unnecessary cargo of ridge reduction and hip dropping now, at the beginning of the layout (see the left drawing on p. 132).

5. Determine the "adjusted run" Previously, I mentioned that determining the length of the base of the measuring triangle was the key to laying out rafters. This is true for all rafters, including hip rafters. And as I mentioned in my discussion of the use (or perhaps I should say misuse) of the word run, rafter squares have a table that lets you use the run of the common rafter to com-

pute the "length" of the hip rafter. This is a marvelous shortcut that I will discuss later. First, though, I want to go through the process "longhand" because I think it's important to see the mechanics of the entire process and because it will be necessary to use this longer process when we get into irregular hip roofs.

To compute the length of a hip rafter the long way, I use two measuring triangles. The first one lies horizontally and employs the run of the common rafters to determine a hypotenuse that, in turn, represents the run of the hip rafter. The second measuring triangle stands vertically, with the run of the hip rafter as a base and the rise, determined by the rise of the common rafters, as the altitude. The trick here, as always, is to form a clear picture of the beginning and ending points of the run.

Because the beginning and ending points are on the edge (and not the center) of the hip rafter, the base of the first measuring triangle is 1 1/16 in. shorter than the base of the measuring triangle used on the common rafters. A simple way to get this dimension is to measure from the edge of one of the king common rafters to the

Establishing the Measuring Line of a Hip Rafter

Locate the measuring line on the top outside edge of a hip rafter rather than along the centerline. This eliminates the need to deduct the thickness of the ridge beam and deepen the seat cut later on to drop the edge of the hip rafter into the same plane as the rest of the roof.

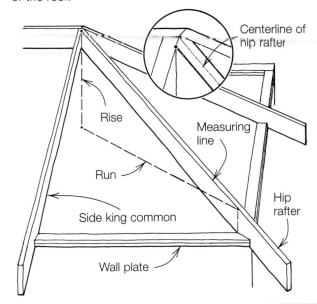

Centerline of hip rafter

Rise

Measuring line

Run

Hip rafter

Side king common

Wall plate

Determining the Adjusted Run of a Hip Rafter

Before the actual run of the hip rafter can be determined, you need to calculate the "adjusted run." Because the measuring line is on the top edge of the hip rafter (rather than the center), the run is shortened by 1¹⁄₁₆ in. Here the adjusted run is the same dimension (154.69 in.) as the measurement between the layouts for the king common and hip rafters.

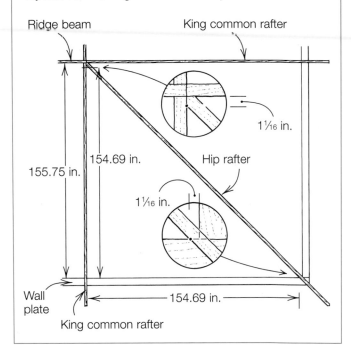

Ridge beam

King common rafter

1¹⁄₁₆ in.

154.69 in.

Hip rafter

155.75 in.

1¹⁄₁₆ in.

Wall plate

King common rafter

154.69 in.

hip layout line on the wall plate. In this example, the dimension is 154.69 in. (155.75 – 1.06). Once you have this length, things fall right into place. I call this distance the "adjusted run" (see the right drawing above).

6. Calculate the measuring length of the hip rafter
Once you have the length of the adjusted run, you can calculate the length of the run of the hip rafter by multiplying the adjusted run by 1.414. In this case, the run of the hip rafter is 218.73 in. (154.69 × 1.414 = 218.73). Now you have the base of the second, vertical measuring triangle, and you can determine the length of the hypotenuse, and thus the measuring length of the hip rafter, by using the Pythagorean theorem.

But hold your calculators: There's been a slight modification of the rise. The rise used when you calculated the common rafters was 103.83 in., but you moved the top point of that rise down slightly when you took

1¹⁄₁₆ (or 1.06) in. off the run. The required adjustment can be determined by scribing an 8-in-12 pitch on a board (you can use the seat cut on your 8-in-12 jig for this), measuring 1¹⁄₁₆ in. along the base and measuring the altitude (see the drawings on the facing page). It comes to about ¾ in. The "adjusted rise" then, is 103.08 in. (103.83 – 0.75 = 103.08).

Another way to figure the adjusted rise is to calculate it. By taking the length of the adjusted run, 218.73 in., and the pitch, 8-in-16.97, it's possible to ascertain the rise by solving for the fourth proportional. Here's how:

$$\frac{8}{16.97} = \frac{x}{218.73}, \text{ where } x = 103.11.$$

Determining the Adjusted Rise of a Hip Rafter

The edge of the hip rafter engages the king common rafter 1¹⁄₁₆ in. (1.06 in.) away from the ridge beam, so the rise must also be adjusted. To find the amount to adjust the rise, follow these steps.

1. On a scrap of 2x4, draw an 8-in-12 pitch with the seat-cut edge of the rafter jig.
2. Measure and mark 1¹⁄₁₆ in. (1.06 in.) along the edge.
3. Square down from that mark.
4. Measure the altitude (³⁄₄ in.).

8-in-12 pitch

2x4 scrap

1¹⁄₁₆ in.

³⁄₄ in.

The measuring line has been transferred to the top of the rafter.

1¹⁄₁₆ in.

³⁄₄ in.

Ridge beam

King common rafter

103.08-in. adjusted rise

Heel of the bevel on the hip rafter engages the side king common rafter here.

103.83-in. rise

154.69-in. adjusted run

Now you have the base (218.73 in.) and the altitude (103.11 in.) of the measuring triangle for the length of the hip rafter. Using the Pythagorean theorem, you can now compute the hypotenuse, which is the measuring length of the hip rafter. This comes to 241.81, or 241¹³⁄₁₆ in.

For a regular hip, like the one here, the second table—called the "length hip or valley rafter per foot run" table—on the rafter square provides a nice little shortcut to the hip-rafter length you've just solved for. "Foot run" here refers to the run of the common rafters. Thus, you can jump right from the adjusted run of the common rafter to the measuring length of the hip rafter without stopping to figure out the run of the hip rafter. The entry in this table for an 8-in-12 roof is 18.76 (18.76

is the hypotenuse of a right triangle with sides of 8 and 16.97). To get the length of the hip rafter in this example, you simply convert the adjusted run of the common rafter (154.69 in.) into 12-in. increments and multiply that result by 18.76 (see the drawing on p. 134).

7. Measure and mark the hip rafter With the measuring length in hand, you can now lay out and cut the hip rafter. Begin by laying out the plumb cut with the 8-in-16.97 rafter jig. The cut must be a double bevel, with both bevels at 45°, so that the hip fits snugly into the intersection of the king common rafters. If you're using a circular saw, mark the miter with the jig and "lay out" the bevel by setting the saw to a 45° bevel. If you have a sliding compound-miter saw, set the miter to 25° and the bevel to 45°. (You can make the conversion

Calculating the Measuring Length of a Hip Rafter with a Rafter Square

Under the entry that describes the pitch of the common rafters (8-in-12), the "length hip or valley rafter per foot run" table allows you to use the adjusted run of the king common rafter to find the measuring length of the hip rafter.

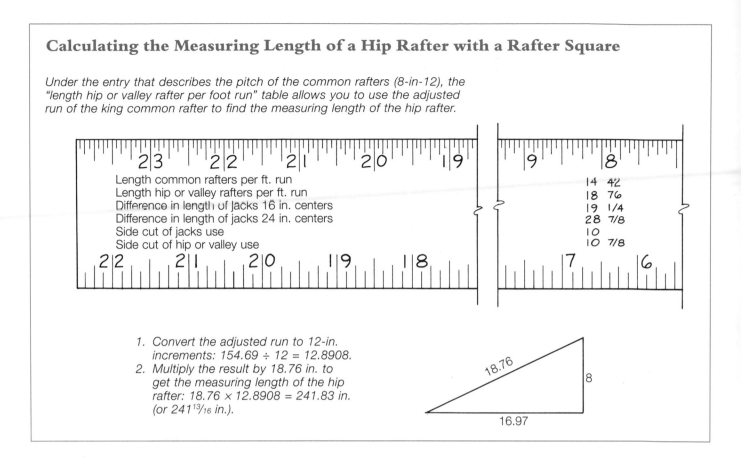

Length common rafters per ft. run — 14 42
Length hip or valley rafters per ft. run — 18 76
Difference in length of jacks 16 in. centers — 19 1/4
Difference in length of jacks 24 in. centers — 28 7/8
Side cut of jacks use — 10
Side cut of hip or valley use — 10 7/8

1. Convert the adjusted run to 12-in. increments: 154.69 ÷ 12 = 12.8908.
2. Multiply the result by 18.76 in. to get the measuring length of the hip rafter: 18.76 × 12.8908 = 241.83 in. (or 241¹³⁄₁₆ in.).

from an 8-in-16.97 pitch to 25° with the use of a Stanley Quick Square. Simply set the arm to 8 on the hip-valley scale and read the corresponding degrees.) Both sides of the plumb cut must be laid out and cut, of course, since the hip rafter is beveled on both sides.

After making the plumb cut, measure 241¹³⁄₁₆ in. down the top edge of the rafter, starting at the top outside edge of the bevel cut, and mark. Using the 8-in-16.97 jig, draw a second plumb line at the mark. Since the hip rafter crosses the top plate at a 45° angle (see the drawing on p. 130), the bird's mouth must be cut about 1.414 times deeper than the bird's mouth of the common rafters. To make sure the top edge of the hip rafter is the same height above the plate (HAP) as the common rafters, measure that distance at the bird's mouth on one of the common rafters that you've previously installed. This measurement should be the same as the HAP on the hip rafter. With the jig, scribe the horizontal seat cut through the intersection of the plumb line and the bottom edge of the rafter. Finish the bird's

mouth by measuring in the thickness of the wall (about 8½ in.) and scribing a plumb line down from that point (see the top drawing on the facing page).

Laying out the hip-rafter tail

At this time, it's often convenient to shape fully or partially the rafter tail according to the design of the eaves. As you've seen, the overhang (measured horizontally) for the hip rafters has to be 1.414 times longer than the overhang of the common rafters. You can draw the whole business out, in plan view, on a sheet of plywood in a couple of minutes. Then, while you're laying out the bird's mouth, simply square over the correct amount from the plumb line that represents the outside of the house (see the bottom drawing on the facing page).

Alternatively, you can use a mathematical approach in which you divide the run of the eaves (the desired width) into 12-in. increments and multiply that number by the numbers found in the rafter tables (in this case, 14.42 for the common rafters and 18.76 for the hip rafters).

Laying Out a Hip Rafter

After marking the measuring length along the top edge of the hip rafter, use the 8-in-16.97 jig to lay out the plumb and seat cuts. Because the hip rafter crosses the top plate of the wall at a 45° angle, the seat cut must be about 1.414 times deeper than the seat cut of the common rafters (1.414 × 5.5 = 7.77). You can take this measurement directly from the layout on the plate. If the hip rafter is ripped to the correct width, the height above the plate (HAP) should be the same as the HAP of the common rafters.

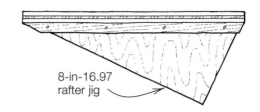

8-in-16.97
rafter jig

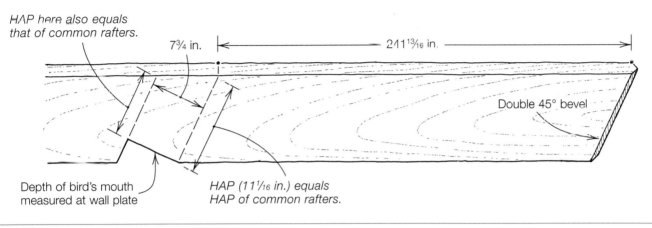

HAP here also equals
that of common rafters.

7¾ in.

241¹³⁄₁₆ in.

Double 45° bevel

Depth of bird's mouth
measured at wall plate

HAP (11¹⁄₁₆ in.) equals
HAP of common rafters.

Graphic Approach to Laying Out a Hip-Rafter Tail

1. Draw a plan view of the overhang full size and measure the amount needed for the hip overhang.
2. Square over that amount from the plumb cut of the bird's mouth to mark the hip rafter.

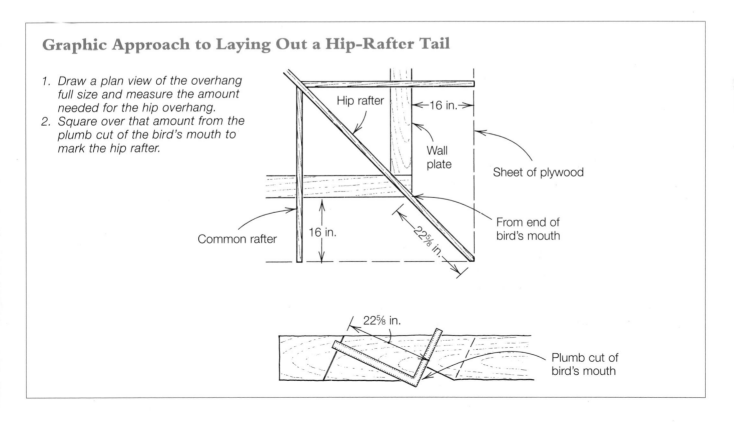

Hip rafter

16 in.

Wall
plate

Sheet of plywood

Common rafter

16 in.

22⅝ in.

From end of
bird's mouth

22⅝ in.

Plumb cut of
bird's mouth

Let's say that on this roof, you wanted a 16-in. overhang. To get the correct distance running down the top edge of the rafters, first divide 16 by 12 to find the number of 12-in. increments. Then multiply the result—1.333—by 14.42 to get the distance running down the common rafter and by 18.76 to get the distance running down the hip rafter (25 in.).

Laying out and installing hip jack rafters

For plywood sheathing to continue to break evenly on the middle of rafters even after it passes over the king common rafter and into the triangle below the hip rafter, the jack rafters have to continue the layout pattern established by the common rafters. Laying out the plate is easy, of course, since the centers are consistent along the length of the wall. The top layout is more difficult, though, because it is made on the hip rafter, which both runs at a 45° angle to the common rafters and is sloped, in this case at an 8-in-16.97 pitch. The simplest way to lay out the position of the top of a jack rafter is to pull a tape measure from one of the common rafters on the other side of the king rafter, mark the hip rafter at one of the 16-in. centers, and set the X ahead. This method can be inexact, however, both because the common rafter you're pulling from will probably not be perfectly straight and because it is not likely that you'll pull your measurement at a 90° angle to the rafter.

It's more accurate to calculate the length of the first jack rafter. Begin this process by measuring from the layout of the hip rafter to the layout of the first (longest) jack rafter along the plate. In the drawings on the facing page, the jack-rafter layout on the plate is 139⁷⁄₁₆ in. (with the X set back) from the hip-rafter layout. This length is also the run of the jack rafter. Once again, knowing the exact run is the key to all further calculations, and the length of the jack rafter can now be determined using either the first table on the rafter square or the Pythagorean theorem (after calculating the rise).

I prefer using the rafter square table. Begin by changing 139⁷⁄₁₆ into 139.44 and divide it by 12 to find the number of 12-in. increments (or 11.62). Next, look under the number 8 in the common-rafter table and multiply the entry—14.42—times 11.62 to get the length of the first jack rafter (or 167.56 in.).

At this point, it's possible to calculate the layout along the hip rafter by figuring for the hypotenuse of a right triangle with sides of 139.44 in. and 167.56 in. This calculation really isn't necessary, however. If the jack rafter is the correct length, it should stay on the layout when it's installed, provided the hip rafter is kept arrow straight. To straighten the hip rafter and keep it that way, use a stringline as a guide and temporary braces to hold it in place.

The next hip jack rafter is located 123.44 in. from the corner. You can figure the length of this rafter using the same technique I just described. Divide 123.44 by 12 and then multiply the result by 14.42 to get 148.33 in. The difference in length between the first jack rafter and the second is 19.23 in. (167.56 – 148.33 = 19.23). This difference will be constant through the whole set of jack rafters; the next one, in other words, will be 129.1 in. long (148.33 – 19.23 = 129.1). Incidentally, this handy tidbit of information is stored in the third table, "difference in length of jacks 16 in. centers" on the rafter square. (The 0.02 difference between the dimension on the rafter square, 19¼, and the dimension I just used is the result of rounding numbers and is inconsequential for frame carpentry.)

Plumb- and seat-cut layout of hip jack rafters is the same as for common rafters, with one notable exception. Unlike a common rafter, which butts squarely into the ridge beam, the jack rafter joins to the hip rafter at a 45° angle. In addition to being cut at an angle that reflects the pitch, the jack rafter has to be beveled at a 45° angle to conform to the angle (in plan view) of the hip. So while the seat cut of a jack rafter is identical to the seat cut of a common rafter, the plumb cut is a compound miter/bevel cut. The miter reflects the pitch and can be laid out with the 8-in-12 rafter jig or by setting a sliding compound-miter saw to 34°. The bevel reflects the orientation, in plan view, of the hip, which for regular hips is always 45°. I normally organize my layout so that the measuring line is at the sharp point (rather than at the heel) of the bevel, but it can be placed on either side of the jack.

Laying Out Hip Jack Rafters

Measuring length of hip jack rafters

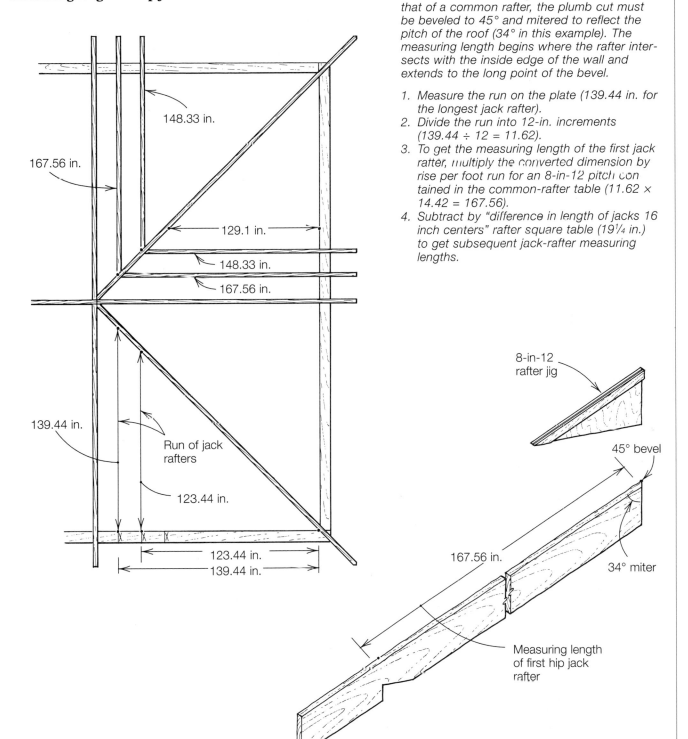

148.33 in.

167.56 in.

129.1 in.

148.33 in.

167.56 in.

139.44 in.

Run of jack rafters

123.44 in.

123.44 in.

139.44 in.

8-in-12 rafter jig

45° bevel

167.56 in.

34° miter

Measuring length of first hip jack rafter

While the seat cut of a jack rafter is identical to that of a common rafter, the plumb cut must be beveled to 45° and mitered to reflect the pitch of the roof (34° in this example). The measuring length begins where the rafter intersects with the inside edge of the wall and extends to the long point of the bevel.

1. *Measure the run on the plate (139.44 in. for the longest jack rafter).*
2. *Divide the run into 12-in. increments (139.44 ÷ 12 = 11.62).*
3. *To get the measuring length of the first jack rafter, multiply the converted dimension by rise per foot run for an 8-in-12 pitch contained in the common-rafter table (11.62 × 14.42 = 167.56).*
4. *Subtract by "difference in length of jacks 16 inch centers" rafter square table (19¼ in.) to get subsequent jack-rafter measuring lengths.*

LAYING OUT IRREGULAR HIP ROOFS

The information regarding hip and valley roofs that is etched on a rafter square applies only to regular hips and valleys. This is also true for the information printed in rafter manuals. So, what do you do when you have to build a hip roof that runs at an angle other than 45°, in plan view, from the common rafters? One way to tackle this job is to break the problem down into two or more measuring triangles, a process I touched on previously. To see how this works, let's frame the 12-in-12 pitch roof of a 12-ft.-wide octagonal building (see the drawings at right). The walls of this building are 3½ in. thick (2x4 construction) with 2x10s for the rafters.

Laying out the common rafters

My strategy for framing an octagonal roof is to have all of the common rafters bear against an octagonal ridge piece set in the center of the roof. After the common rafters have been installed squarely against the ridge piece, you can then fit eight hip rafters in the 45° intersection formed by the common rafters.

To determine the overall width of this ridge piece, whereby each side of it is exactly 1½ in. wide (to accommodate the width of each 2x rafter), it's best to make a full-scale drawing on a board with your Speed Square. From the drawing, you can determine that the overall width should be 3⅝ in. Since making each side exactly 1½ in. wide will simplify the top cuts for both the common and the hip rafters of this roof, it's important to make this ridge piece up with care (see the right drawings on the facing page).

After this eight-sided ridge has been fabricated, it has to be installed in the center of the building, in plan view, and positioned so that the flat sides are parallel to the flat sides of the building. To lay out the location of the common rafters on the plates, determine the center of each wall and mark ¾ in. to each side. There's no need to lay out the top locations of the common rafters, since each common rafter meets at the flats on the ridge piece. To lay out the bottom positions of the eight hip rafters, scribe a 22.5° angle at each corner and mark a parallel line ¾ in. to each side. The top of the hip rafters don't need to be laid out either: They fall at the intersection of the common rafters.

Laying Out an Octagonal Roof

Basic building dimensions

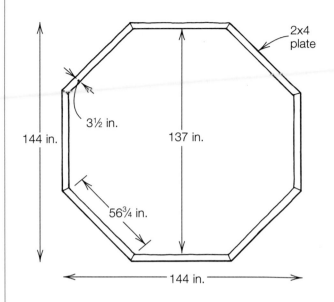

Plan view of common rafters

The eight common rafters are installed against the flats of the ridge piece.

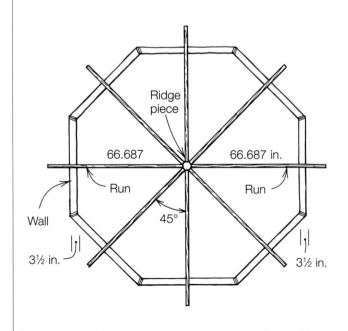

Rafter layout

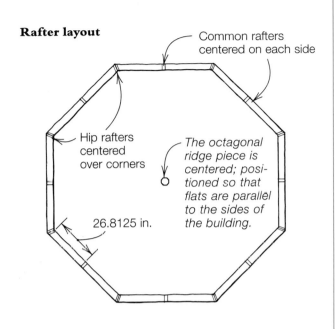

Common rafters centered on each side

Hip rafters centered over corners

The octagonal ridge piece is centered; positioned so that flats are parallel to the sides of the building.

26.8125 in.

Plan view of hip rafters

The eight hip rafters are installed in the 45° space between the common rafters (shaded). To bisect this angle, each side of the hip rafters must be beveled at 67.5° (the complement to a 22.5° angle).

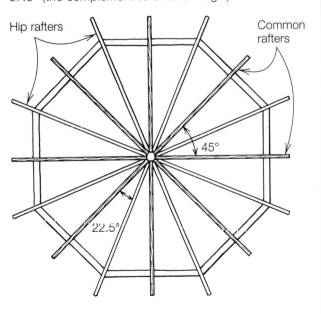

Hip rafters

Common rafters

45°

22.5°

Getting the Ridge Right in an Octagonal Roof

Installing 16 evenly spaced rafters in a radial pattern is difficult enough without having to make extra cuts at the ends of the rafters. To avoid complicated cuts, each flat side on the ridge piece should be 1½ in. wide (or the thickness of the rafter stock being used).

Ridge piece correct size

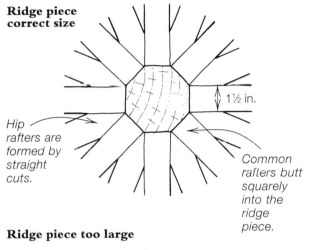

Hip rafters are formed by straight cuts.

1½ in.

Common rafters butt squarely into the ridge piece.

Ridge piece too large

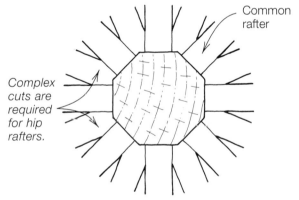

Common rafter

Complex cuts are required for hip rafters.

Ridge piece too small

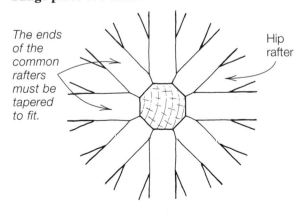

The ends of the common rafters must be tapered to fit.

Hip rafter

Common-rafter lengths are determined just like the common rafters of a gable roof, a process that was discussed at length in the first part of this chapter. In a nutshell, determine the run, divide it into 12-in. increments, and multiply that dimension by the listing in the common-rafter table for a 12-in-12 pitch roof. As the drawing below shows, the run of a common rafter is 66.687 in. Divide that number by 12, which equals 5.55725. Multiply that number by 16.97 (the listing in the common-rafter table) and you get 94.3072 (or 94⁵⁄₁₆). Therefore, the measuring length of a common rafter for this building is 94⁵⁄₁₆ in.

Laying out an irregular hip rafter

After installing the eight common rafters, you need to lay out the hip rafters. Here are the six steps I follow:

1. Determine the adjusted run The first task is to find the adjusted run of the common rafter. As I noted in the last section, the adjusted run begins at the inside edge of the plate and ends at the point, in plan view, where the side of the hip rafter engages the king common

rafter. As the drawing on the facing page indicates, the adjusted run is 64.812 in.

This figure is a little tricky to get. Here's how to do it. First, draw a double 67.5° degree bevel on a scrap of 2x lumber. How did I arrive at this angle for the bevel? After the eight common rafters have been installed radially around the ridge piece, there are eight 45° spaces left between them. For the hip rafters to bisect these spaces, each side must be cut at a 22.5° angle as measured from the face of the board. When carpenters cut a bevel, however, the angle is customarily measured from an imaginary line that runs perpendicular to the face of the board. Set your saw to 0° and you get a cut that is 90° to the face of the board; set your saw to 10° and your cut is 80° from the face of the board. Notice that all these angles—called complementary angles—always add up to 90°. The angled cut required for this hip rafter is 22.5° from the face of the board, but in the standard parlance of carpenters, it is called a 67.5° bevel. The two angles—22.5° and 67.5°—add up to 90° and thus are complementary.

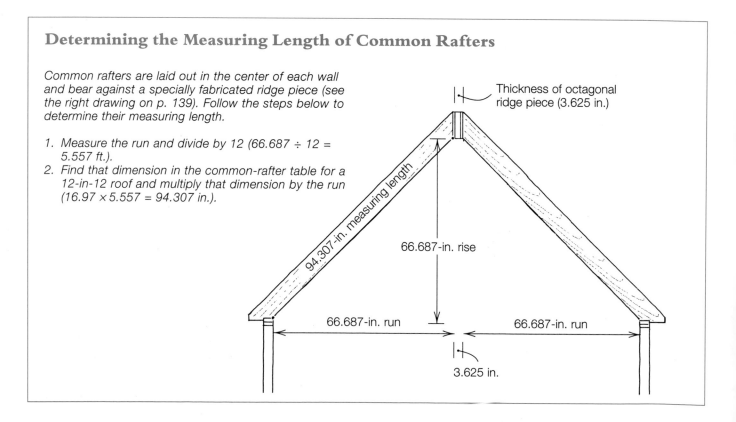

Determining the Measuring Length of Common Rafters

Common rafters are laid out in the center of each wall and bear against a specially fabricated ridge piece (see the right drawing on p. 139). Follow the steps below to determine their measuring length.

1. *Measure the run and divide by 12 (66.687 ÷ 12 = 5.557 ft.).*
2. *Find that dimension in the common-rafter table for a 12-in-12 roof and multiply that dimension by the run (16.97 × 5.557 = 94.307 in.).*

Thickness of octagonal ridge piece (3.625 in.)

94.307-in. measuring length

66.687-in. rise

66.687-in. run

66.687-in. run

3.625 in.

Finding the Adjusted Run of a Common Rafter

The measuring length of a hip rafter can't be determined without knowing the adjusted run of a common rafter. Follow the steps below to find the adjusted run.

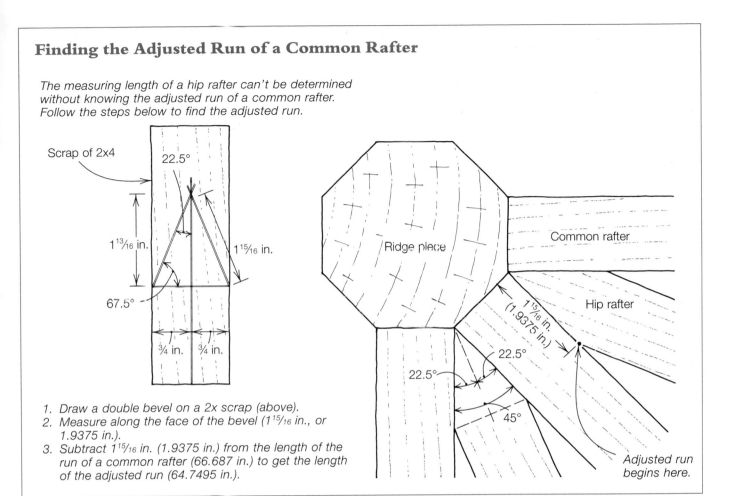

Scrap of 2x4

22.5°

1 13/16 in.

1 15/16 in.

67.5°

3/4 in. 3/4 in.

Ridge piece

Common rafter

Hip rafter

1 15/16 in. (1.9375 in.)

22.5°

22.5°

45°

Adjusted run begins here.

1. Draw a double bevel on a 2x scrap (above).
2. Measure along the face of the bevel (1 15/16 in., or 1.9375 in.).
3. Subtract 1 15/16 in. (1.9375 in.) from the length of the run of a common rafter (66.687 in.) to get the length of the adjusted run (64.7495 in.).

Next, measure the length of the bevel—1 15/16 in., or 1.9375 in.—which is the amount that you have to deduct from the run of the common rafter to get the adjusted run. The adjusted run here is 66.687 − 1.9375 = 64.7495 in. Once again, this dimension is the key to all further calculations.

2. Determine the run The neat shortcut you employed in the last section, where you jumped directly from the adjusted run of the common rafter to the measuring length of the hip rafter, can't be used here. Because this is an irregular hip roof, the calculation has to be done in two steps. First, calculate the length of the run of the hip rafter by using a horizontal measuring triangle. The adjusted common-rafter run that you just calculated, 64.7495 in., is the base of the horizontal measuring triangle, while the distance between the

common-rafter layout and the hip-rafter layout along the inside of the wall, 26.8125 in. (or 26 13/16 in.), is its altitude. The easiest way to get the altitude is simply to measure it at the top of the wall.

With the base and altitude in hand, you can then calculate the hypotenuse of this measuring triangle using the Pythagorean theorem:

$$64.7495^2 + 26.8125^2 = 4911.4078.$$

Find the square root of 4911.4078 to get the hypotenuse. The run of the hip rafter, then, is 70.081 in. (see the drawing on p. 142).

3. Determine the adjusted rise As you saw in step 1, the adjusted run ended up 1 15/16 in. (or 1.9375 in.) shorter than the common-rafter run. This shortened run

Finding the Run of a Hip Rafter

A horizontal measuring triangle (shaded area) can be used to determine the run of a hip rafter. The altitude is the measured distance on the plate between the layout for the common rafter and the hip rafter, while the base is the adjusted run. Use the Pythagorean theorem to calculate the hypotenuse.

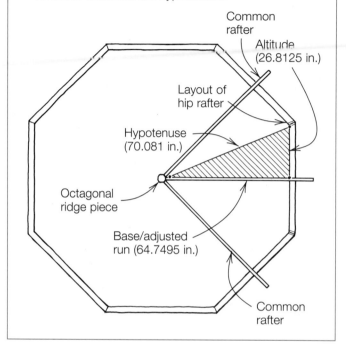

Common rafter

Altitude (26.8125 in.)

Layout of hip rafter

Hypotenuse (70.081 in.)

Octagonal ridge piece

Base/adjusted run (64.7495 in.)

Common rafter

makes the rise slightly less, so now you also need to determine the adjusted rise.

To calculate the adjusted rise, all you have to do is draw the pitch of the common rafter (12-in-12), measure and mark 1.9375 in. along the base where the pitch line starts, square up from that point, and measure the length of the altitude of this small triangle. Because this is a 12-in-12 pitch, the altitude will be the same as the base, or 1.9375 in. By deducting this amount from the common-rafter rise, you'll find the adjusted rise: 64.7495 in. In this case, the adjusted rise is the same as the adjusted run. But things aren't always so easy. If you were working with any other pitch, the adjusted rise and adjusted run would be different.

4. Determine the measuring length and pitch You now have the run of the hip (70.081 in.) and the rise of the hip (64.7495 in.). With these two dimensions, you can find both the measuring length and the pitch of the hip rafter. To find the length, use the Pythagorean theorem to calculate the hypotenuse of the right triangle with a base of 70.081 in. and an altitude of 64.7495 in.:

$$64.7495^2 + 70.081^2 = 9103.9055.$$

Find the square root of 9103.9055 to get 95.414 in. (or 95$\frac{7}{16}$ in.), the hypotenuse.

To find the pitch, write the problem in the form of a proportion:

$$\frac{64.7495}{70.081} = \frac{x}{12}, \text{ where } x = 11.1.$$

The pitch of the hip, then, is 11.1-in-12, or 11$\frac{1}{8}$-in-12, and the measuring length is 95$\frac{7}{16}$ in. (see the top drawing on the facing page).

5. Select and prepare hip material A 2x10 is usually 9$\frac{1}{4}$ in. wide. When you draw the plumb cut for a 12-in-12 pitch on a 2x10, the layout line measures 13$\frac{1}{16}$ in. To get the same length in a plumb cut that is laid out using an 11$\frac{1}{8}$-in-12 pitch, the board would have to be 9$\frac{9}{16}$ in. wide. Therefore, you have to use 2x12s ripped to 9$\frac{9}{16}$ in. for the hip rafters.

6. Lay out and cut the hip rafter The easiest way to lay out the hip rafter is to make an 11$\frac{1}{8}$-in-12 pitch jig (for more on making a rafter jig, see p. 117). After making the jig, begin the layout process by marking two plumb-cut lines 95$\frac{7}{16}$ in. apart on the hip material (see the bottom drawing on the facing page); this is the measuring length of the hip rafter. The layout at the bottom of this irregular hip rafter is like the layout of a regular hip rafter. Make sure the HAP is the same as it is for the common rafters, which is 13$\frac{1}{16}$ in. above the bottom point along the measuring line (see the top drawing on the facing page). To check this, measure the length of the plumb line, then scribe the seat cut with the 11$\frac{1}{8}$-in-12 jig. At the same time, mark the depth of the bird's mouth. You can get the depth by measuring along the layout at the top plate; it should be about 5 in.

Determining the Measuring Length of a Hip Rafter

Once the rise and run have been calculated, use the Pythagorean theorem ($64.7495^2 + 70.081^2 = 9103.9055$) to determine the measuring length of the hip rafter ($\sqrt{9103.9055}$, or 95.414).

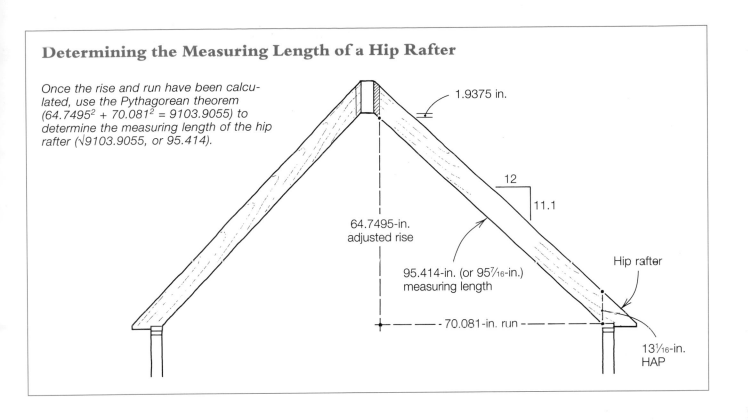

1.9375 in.

12

11.1

64.7495-in. adjusted rise

95.414-in. (or 95⁷⁄₁₆-in.) measuring length

Hip rafter

— 70.081-in. run —

13¹⁄₁₆-in. HAP

Measuring and Marking the Hip Rafter

1. *Mark two plumb-cut lines 95⁷⁄₁₆ in. (the measuring length) apart on the hip material. At the bottom of this irregular hip rafter, make the HAP the same as for the common rafters (13¹⁄₁₆ in.).*
2. *Measure down 13¹⁄₁₆ in. along the plumb line, mark, then scribe the seat cut with an 11⅛-in-12 rafter jig. At the same time, mark the depth of the bird's mouth (about 5 in.).*

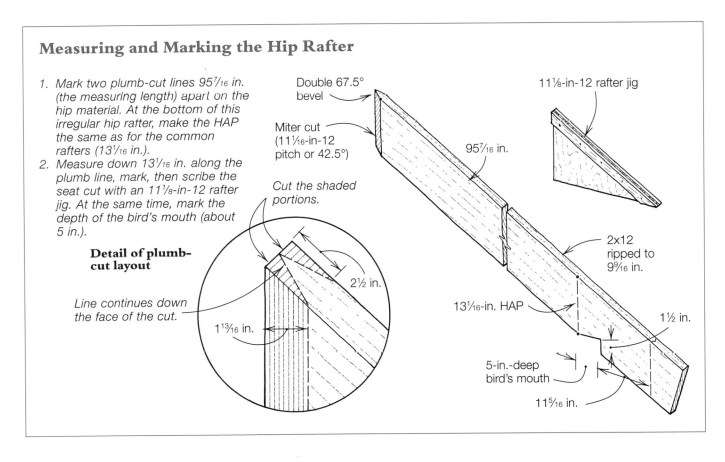

Double 67.5° bevel

11⅛-in-12 rafter jig

Miter cut (11¹⁄₁₆-in-12 pitch or 42.5°)

95⁷⁄₁₆ in.

Detail of plumb-cut layout

Cut the shaded portions.

Line continues down the face of the cut.

2½ in.

1¹³⁄₁₆ in.

2x12 ripped to 9⁹⁄₁₆ in.

13¹⁄₁₆-in. HAP

1½ in.

5-in.-deep bird's mouth

11⁵⁄₁₆ in.

Another consideration when laying out and cutting the hip rafter would be to make the height *below* the plate the same on all of the rafter tails. In the drawing on p. 140, the tail of the common rafter is cut level at a point 1½ in. below the plate; this serves as the framing for the underside of the eaves. Laying this level line out on the hip rafter tail is easy. However, laying out and cutting the plumb cut at the very end of the rafter tail is a little trickier, because the overhang of the hip rafter must be longer than the overhang of the common rafters. In this case, the overhang of the common rafters is 8 in. To determine the short overhang of this hip, the easiest course is simply to draw out full-scale both overhangs in plan view (see the bottom drawing on p. 135) and get the dimensions right off the drawing (it comes to 11⁵⁄₁₆ in. from the outside wall).

At the top of the rafter, the layout begins at the plumb line you made earlier (at the end of the 95⁷⁄₁₆-in. measuring length). From this line, you have to lay out a double 67.5° bevel to follow the plumb cut of the 11⅛-in-12 pitch. In the last section on laying out regular hips, you were able to lay out the bevel simply by setting your saw to 45°. Here, the bevel is too sharp to use that technique (I don't own a power saw that can be set to that acute an angle). So, you have to lay out the compound miter/bevel cut with a pencil and cut it the old-fashioned way—with a handsaw.

Begin the layout of this cut by looking at the plan view of the double-bevel layout. Earlier, you measured the length of the bevel (which was 1.9375 in.); here you want to measure the depth of the bevel. As the bottom drawing on p. 141 shows, it is 1.8125 in. (or 1¹³⁄₁₆ in.) deep (the length of the centerline). Using the rafter jig, draw a second plumb line parallel to and exactly 1¹³⁄₁₆ in. beyond the first. Now, make a standard, square cut along this second plumb line with a circular saw. When you're finished with this cut, draw two "side-cut" lines. On the top of the rafter, these lines angle from the first plumb-cut line to the center of the board at the cut. After the two lines converge, a single line continues down the center of the face of the cut. With a sharp handsaw followed by a sharp plane or a belt sander, you can remove the wedge-shaped pieces in five minutes or so to complete the hip rafter.

LAYING OUT TRADITIONAL VALLEYS

If you look at a rafter square, you'll see that the tables for hips and valleys have been combined. This is because the lengths and cuts are virtually identical, the main difference being the way in which they are oriented toward each other. To a certain degree, the valley of a roof is like a hip turned inside out. To see how this works, let's return to our 27-ft.-wide building, strip off the hip, and have the building turn at a right angle so that there are two intersecting roofs (see the drawings on the facing page).

Preparing the valley stock

After running the common rafters of the two intersecting roofs, it's necessary to fit a valley rafter on each side from the intersection of the ridge beams to the corner of the top plate. While a valley rafter is very similar to a regular hip rafter, there are a few differences between the two. For one thing, the valley rafter needs to be prepared to receive sheathing on the top edge and, in some cases, drywall along the bottom edge. And like a regular hip rafter, the valley rafter must come from stock that is wider than the common-rafter stock. For example, if the common rafters are made out of 2x10 stock, then the valley rafter should be made out of 2x12 stock.

In addition to making a valley rafter the right width so that valley jack rafters bear against it correctly, it's necessary to make a V-notch in the top edge of the valley rafter so that it stays in plane with the common rafters. The sides of the notch are angled at the same pitch as the valley rafter, which, in this case, is 8-in-16.97. You can use either a Speed Square or a Stanley Quick Square to convert this pitch to 25° by simply setting the square to the number 8 in the hip/valley scale and by reading the corresponding degrees. Then set your saw to 25° and cut the V-notch in the top of the valley rafter (see the bottom drawing on the facing page).

Next, you have to determine how wide to rip the valley rafter. Start by making a trial valley jack cut in scrap 2x10 stock (see p. 131). Like the hip jack rafter, this cut is a compound miter/bevel cut consisting of an 8-in-12 (or 34°) miter and a 45° bevel. After making this cut, draw a plumb (8-in-16.97) layout line on the notched 2x12 valley stock and test-fit the scrap piece. This experiment reveals that you need about 10⅛ in. of board

Components of a Traditional Valley

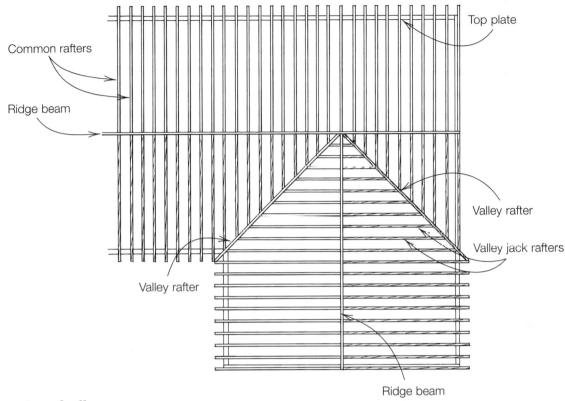

Common rafters

Ridge beam

Top plate

Valley rafter

Valley jack rafters

Valley rafter

Ridge beam

Cross section of valley

If interior and exterior finish materials are to sit correctly, a valley rafter must be notched and beveled before installation. The top V-notch and bottom bevel angle both equal the slope of the valley, while the width is determined by the width of the cut valley jack rafter.

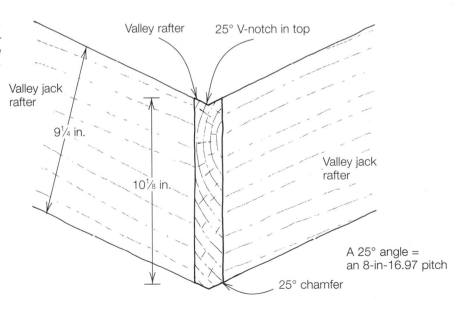

Valley rafter

25° V-notch in top

Valley jack rafter

9¼ in.

10⅛ in.

Valley jack rafter

A 25° angle = an 8-in-16.97 pitch

25° chamfer

width (the same amount required for the hip rafter). If the underside of the roof structure is going to be finished with a ceiling applied directly to the rafters, however, it's necessary to bring the bottom edge of the valley in line with the bottom edge of the rafters. To do this, use a circular saw to chamfer the bottom at the same angle, 25°, that you notched the top. In its final form, the valley rafter has the heel of the chamfer 10⅛ in. down from the top edge of the valley.

Determining the measuring length of the valley rafter

Another difference between hip and valley rafters is the way the measuring length is determined. If you look at the bottom drawing on the facing page, you can see that the plumb cut does not shorten the run as it did when you installed hip rafters. As a result, there is no need to calculate an adjusted run. While the bevel cut at the top of the hip rafter moves the edge of the hip rafter downhill and thus shortens the measuring length of it, the bevel on the top of the valley rafter runs along the ridge beam and doesn't shorten the measuring length.

To determine the measuring length of the valley rafter in this example, divide the run of the common rafter (155.75 in.) by 12 and multiply the result by the entry in the hip/valley rafter table (18.76). Here's the math:

$$155.75 \div 12 = 12.979,$$

$$12.979 \times 18.76 = 243.49.$$

After calculating this dimension, lay out the plumb and seat cuts using the 8-in-16.97 jig (which presumably you've saved from the 8-in-12 hip roof you did earlier). Aside from the measuring length, which is about 1⅝ in. longer here, the layout of the valley rafter is exactly the same as the layout of the hip rafter.

Laying out valley jack rafters

In the section on regular hip roofs, I discussed how to maintain the 16-in. on center (o.c.) layout pattern of the common rafters in the triangular section below the hip rafter. There, it was necessary to carry the layout pattern through on the wall plate, then calculate the proper length of the hip jack rafters. Here, the triangular sec-

tion is above the valley rafter, and you need to maintain the layout pattern at the ridge beam. Then you can calculate the length of the valley jack rafters that extend from the ridge beam down to the valley rafter.

To calculate the length of the first jack rafter above the valley rafter, use the measurement from the edge of the jack-rafter layout to the edge of the valley rafter where it intersects the ridge beam. This is equal to the jack-rafter run. As always, knowing the run is the key to the rest of the calculations. In the top drawing on the facing page, the measurement is 141.375 in. By dividing this dimension into 12-in. increments, then multiplying the result by 14.42 (the "length common rafter per foot run" entry for an 8-in-12 pitch roof on the rafter square), you can determine the length. The math looks like this:

$$141.375 \div 12 = 11.781,$$

$$11.781 \times 14.42 = 169.88 \text{ in.}$$

To get the lengths of the rest of the valley jack rafters, all you have to do is subtract 19.25, the entry under an 8-in-12 pitch roof for the "difference in length of jacks, 16 in. centers" on the rafter square. The cut at the top is a standard plumb cut, laid out with the plumb edge of the 8-in-12 rafter jig. The seat cut is also laid out with the plumb edge of the jig, but it needs to be cut with the circular saw set to a 45° bevel.

LAYING OUT BLIND VALLEYS

When the area directly under the roof deck is not going to be seen or used, a traditional valley is often unnecessary. Builders can save time and money by building one gable roof through and then grafting a second, intersecting gable roof onto the roof deck of the first. This simplified valley is called a blind valley, perhaps because it can't be seen from underneath. Because a blind valley is particularly convenient for remodeling projects, such as a doghouse dormer (see the sidebar on p. 148), where a new roof structure has to be built onto an existing roof, I'll use the roof of an addition as an example in this section. In this case, the addition is 14 ft. 1 in. wide with 4-in.-thick walls (2x4 studs and ½-in. sheathing).

Determining the Measuring Length of a Valley Rafter

While a valley rafter shares the same length table on a rafter square as a hip rafter, its measuring length is determined slightly differently. Here are the steps I follow.

1. *Divide the run of the common rafter by 12 (155.75 ÷ 12 = 12.979).*
2. *Multiply the result by the entry in "length hip or valley per foot run" table on the rafter square (18.76) under the appropriate roof pitch, 8-in-12, in this case (12.979 × 18.76 = 243.49).*

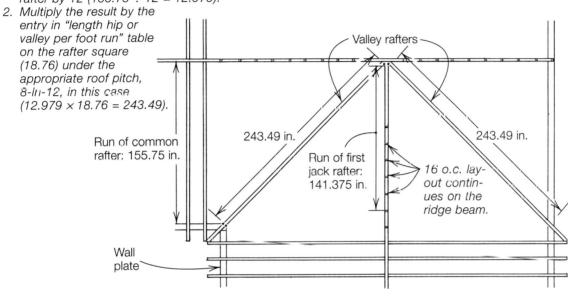

Valley rafters

243.49 in.   243.49 in.

Run of common rafter: 155.75 in.

Run of first jack rafter: 141.375 in.

16 o.c. layout continues on the ridge beam.

Wall plate

No adjustments needed

The run of the common rafter doesn't need to be adjusted to calculate the measuring length of the valley rafter. The run of the common rafter and run of the valley rafter both start at the edge of the ridge beam.

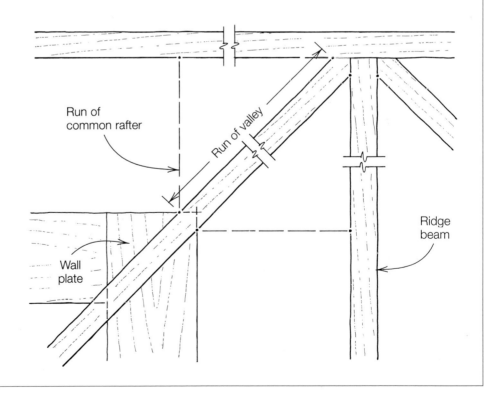

Run of common rafter

Run of valley

Wall plate

Ridge beam

Laying Out a Doghouse Dormer

The easiest way to build the roof of a doghouse dormer is to lay out a blind valley where the dormer roof intersects the main roof of the house and have a flat ceiling inside the dormer. But sometimes a cathedral ceiling is desired inside the dormer. In this case a blind valley is as useless as a coon dog on a quail hunt. Here, the dormer needs a traditional valley with the bottom edge of the valley in plane with the inside ceilings. To show you how to do this, I'll discuss how to build a roof on a 4-ft.-wide dormer setting on a 10-in-12 roof. The sides and the bottom of the opening and the front and sidewalls of the dormer have already been built, and it's at this point that the roof of the dormer has to be framed into the main roof.

The first difficulty is to get the header at the top of the opening at the correct height. The object is to place the ridge beam of the dormer where it will intersect smoothly with both the top and the underside of the rafters on the main roof. To simplify the layout, use plywood templates to hold the ridge beam temporarily at the correct height for locating the header. The templates make it easier to build a smooth transition from the room ceiling to the ceiling of the dormer.

Draw the layout of the dormer rafters and ridge beam on the template, then cut a slot for the ridge beam. You can now set a temporary ridge beam in the slot and slide it right through the opening in the main roof. Using a straightedge and a pencil, find and mark the header location across the opening in the main roof (see the drawing below). Install the header, remove the templates, and save them for the next dormer down the line.

Once the header is in place, install the permanent ridge beam and the common rafters, then locate the point on the double trimmer of the main roof opening where the plane of the dormer roof intersects with the plane of the main roof. To do this, hold a straightedge across the top surface of the common rafters (on the dormer) and mark where it engages the edge of the trimmer. The length of the valley can now be measured from this point to the intersection of the ridge beam and the plane of the main roof. Techniques for preparing the valley material are discussed later. Briefly, however, the V-notch on the top edge and the chamfer on the bottom edge of the valley rafter would be 30.5° (10-in-16.97 pitch); the plumb cut would have a 10-in-16.97 miter and a double 45° bevel; the seat cut would have a 10-in-16.97 miter and a 45° bevel.

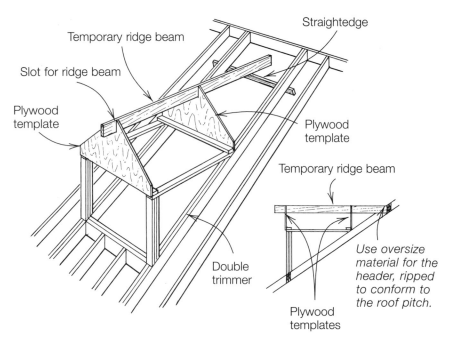

Save the templates and reuse them on the next dormer.

Straightedge

Temporary ridge beam

Slot for ridge beam

Plywood template

Plywood template

Double trimmer

Temporary ridge beam

Plywood templates

Use oversize material for the header, ripped to conform to the roof pitch.

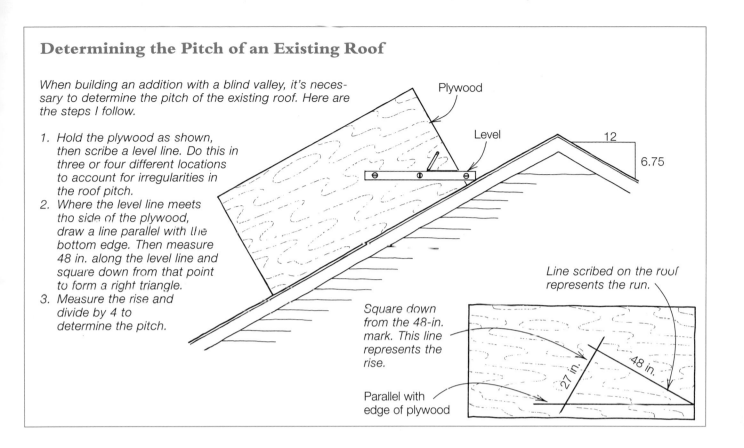

Determining the Pitch of an Existing Roof

When building an addition with a blind valley, it's necessary to determine the pitch of the existing roof. Here are the steps I follow.

1. *Hold the plywood as shown, then scribe a level line. Do this in three or four different locations to account for irregularities in the roof pitch.*
2. *Where the level line meets the side of the plywood, draw a line parallel with the bottom edge. Then measure 48 in. along the level line and square down from that point to form a right triangle.*
3. *Measure the rise and divide by 4 to determine the pitch.*

Plywood

Level

12

6.75

Line scribed on the roof represents the run.

Square down from the 48-in. mark. This line represents the rise.

Parallel with edge of plywood

27 in.

48 in.

Measuring the pitch of an existing roof

Before you can build the blind valley, you need to know the pitch of the existing roof. In this example, the existing building has a roof that can be walked on with some difficulty. It appears to have a pitch between 5-in-12 and 7-in-12, but the exact pitch is anybody's guess. The first order of business, then, is to measure the pitch of the existing roof. For this, you'll need to bring a sheet of plywood, a pencil, and a 4-ft. level up to the roof.

Hold the plywood on its edge and running vertically down the roof, then scribe a level line on it. Because of the irregularities found on most roofs, it's a good idea to do this three more times: once on the other side of the sheet, and twice more after flipping the sheet end-for-end. With these four lines, you can accurately determine the existing roof pitch (see the drawing above).

First, measure the distance along the side of the plywood from the bottom edge to the point where the level line starts. Then make a line at this height that runs parallel to the bottom to represent the surface of the roof. Next, carefully measure and mark 48 in. along the level line you had drawn while up on the roof to represent a run of 4 ft. Using a rafter square, square down from the level line at the mark; this line represents the rise. Now measure the distance along this vertical line from the level line to the roofline. Let's say that, in the four pitch readings you've taken, the average rise is 27 in. This total, divided by 4, reveals that the existing roof has a pitch of 6.75-in-12, which is an odd pitch.

Working with an odd pitch

In my experience, such odd pitches are fairly common. Carpenters frequently use non-mathematical techniques to lay out roof structures and this results in roofs that are close to —but not exactly—the desired pitch (see the sidebar on p. 124). In this circumstance, I wouldn't hesitate to build the roof of the addition at the same 6.75-in-12 pitch. Over the straight area, before the valley, I could even use trusses because my supplier can order them to the ¼ in. per foot of pitch.

But let's say that, to prevent delays, you've decided to build the roof of this addition out of 2x6 rafters. The layout of the common rafters is straightforward, even though you can't use the tables on a rafter square. The first step, as always, is to determine the run. If the measurement from inside wall to inside wall is 161 in., all you have to do is subtract 1½ in. for the 2x ridge beam, then divide the remainder in half to get a common-rafter run of 79.75 in. (or 6.646 ft.).

With this dimension, you can determine the rise by multiplying the number of feet—6.646—by the rise per foot—6.75 in.—to get 44.859 in. The measuring length of the rafter (the hypotenuse of a right triangle with a base of 79.75 and an altitude of 44.859) is 91.5 in. Now you can lay out the rafters with the 6.75-in-12 rafter jig, a process I described earlier.

Laying out the ridge beam and valley rafters

After installing the common rafters, strip the shingles off the existing roof in the addition area and extend the addition ridge beam to the deck of the main roof. First, make the angled cut on the ridge-beam extension where it will engage the existing roof deck, laying out the cut with the level or seat-cut edge of the rafter jig. After making this cut, clamp a level on the top of the ridge-beam extension and, keeping it even with the section of the ridge beam you've already installed, slide it up the roof until it's level. Then mark where it overlaps the other section of ridge beam and cut this final section to length. You can then install it in line with the rest of the ridge beam, using a stringline stretched the length of the ridge beam as a guide.

To lay out the blind valley, make a strongback out of two straight 2x4s nailed together in a cross-sectional L. The strongback serves as a long straightedge, and you can use it to extend the plane of the addition's common rafters over to the deck of the existing roof. To keep the strongback perpendicular to the common rafters, measure an equal amount up from the end of the rafters in two places and nail a block of wood at each mark (see the top drawing on the facing page). Then slide the strongback laterally toward the existing roof, resting it on the blocks, and mark where the corner of the strongback touches the deck. After doing this on both sides, strike chalklines on the existing roof deck from the marks to the edge of the ridge beam.

You're not finished laying out the valley, though. The jack rafters of the new roof need to bear on a plate. Usually I make this plate out of 2x material. To get the top edge of the plate in the same plane as the common rafters, set the strongback in place again and slide a length of 2x blocking under it, keeping it parallel (by eye) with the chalkline. When the block touches the strongback, mark the deck along its edge. This is the distance inside the initial chalkline that you need to install the plates, so measure the same distance at the top (near the ridge beam) and snap a second chalkline.

Laying out jack rafters

While the plumb cut of jack rafters is identical to the plumb cut of common rafters and laid out the same way, the seat cut on the jack rafters is a compound miter/bevel cut (see the bottom drawing on the facing page). The miter can be laid out with the seat cut of the rafter jig. The bevel, which needs to conform to the 6.75-in-12 pitch of the existing roof, must be "laid out" by setting the table of your saw to the proper angle. According to the Stanley Quick Square, a 6.75-in-12 pitch equals 29°, so set your saw to that angle before making the seat cut.

To lay out the positions of the jack rafters, continue the 16-in. o.c. pattern along the ridge beam and square down from the ridge beam to lay out the plate. In this situation, a sheet of plywood aligned with the ridge beam works well as a giant square. Align the top corner of the plywood with a layout mark, then simply measure from the plate to the ridge beam along the vertical edge of the plywood. After you've installed two or three of the shorter jack rafters in this fashion, you can measure the difference in length of these installed jacks and continue the pattern without having to square down.

Laying Out a Blind Valley

A strongback can be used as shown to find the position of a blind valley where an addition's roof intersects with an existing roof deck. A 2x block placed underneath the strongback will indicate the actual position of the 2x plate that extends from the ridge beam along the valley and on which the jack rafters will bear.

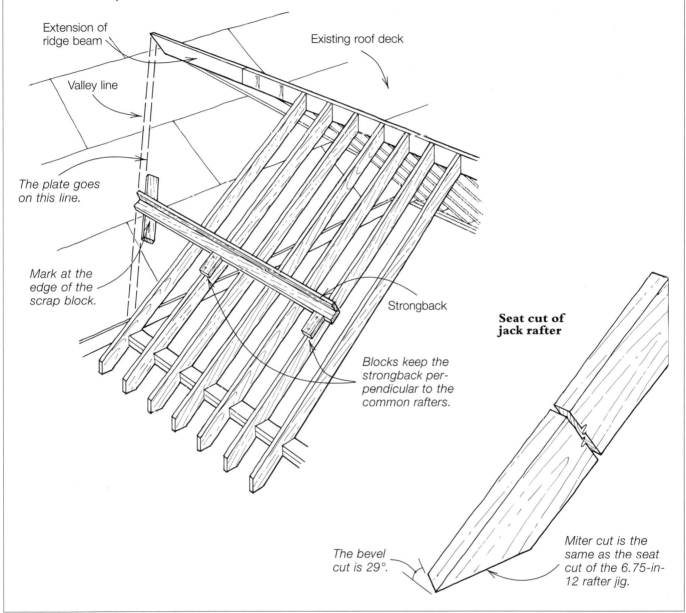

Extension of ridge beam

Existing roof deck

Valley line

The plate goes on this line.

Mark at the edge of the scrap block.

Strongback

Blocks keep the strongback perpendicular to the common rafters.

Seat cut of jack rafter

The bevel cut is 29°.

Miter cut is the same as the seat cut of the 6.75-in-12 rafter jig.

Chapter 7
BASIC STAIR LAYOUT

There is a logic and order in stairbuilding that I find very appealing, and the basic theory underlying it is easy enough to grasp. But it doesn't take long to figure out that building stairways requires attention to an array of details, each of which has a particular place and function. Some of these details are nettlesome and confusing, while others are simple enough to deal with but easy to overlook. Like a jigsaw puzzle, all of these details have an impact on each other, and all need to be resolved during the design and construction of stairs.

The stairbuilder's job is to arrange the many and varied details of a stairway into a harmonious and unified whole. This isn't just an aesthetic exercise, either. Because stairs are inherently dangerous, they need to be made as predictable underfoot as possible so that all of the risers are the same height and so that all of the treads are the same depth. Like the stairbuilding process, stairways need to be consistent, orderly, and precise.

DESIGNING STAIRS

While there are a number of different types of interior and exterior stairways, the two most common interior stairways (and the two that will be discussed in this chapter) are open stringer (see the top drawing on the facing page) and closed stringer (see the bottom drawing on the facing page). The basic dimensions—the depth of the stair tread, the height of the riser, the total width of the staircase—of any type of stairway usually present different (and sometimes conflicting) goals to the people designing, building, and using them.

Open-Stringer Stairway

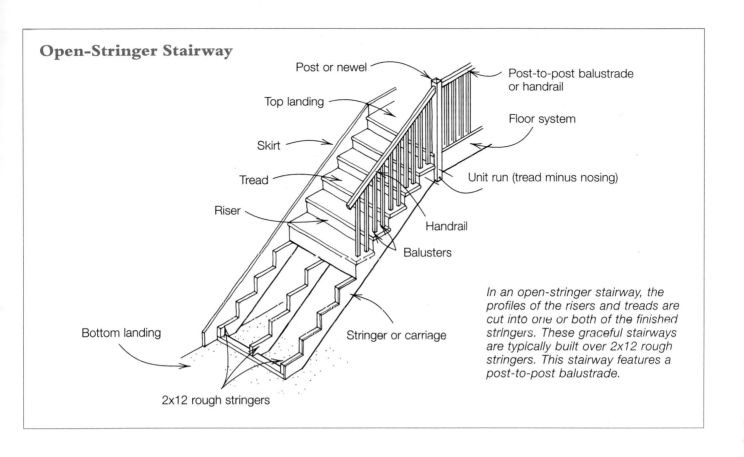

Post or newel

Top landing

Skirt

Tread

Riser

Bottom landing

Post-to-post balustrade
or handrail

Floor system

Unit run (tread minus nosing)

Handrail

Balusters

Stringer or carriage

2x12 rough stringers

In an open-stringer stairway, the profiles of the risers and treads are cut into one or both of the finished stringers. These graceful stairways are typically built over 2x12 rough stringers. This stairway features a post-to-post balustrade.

Closed-Stringer Stairway

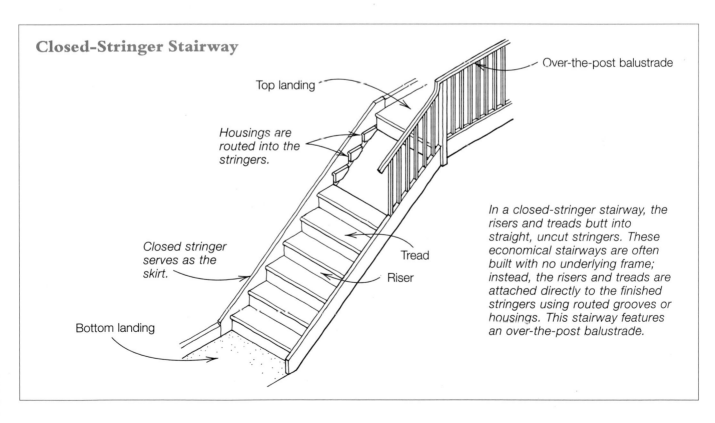

Top landing

Housings are routed into the stringers.

Closed stringer serves as the skirt.

Bottom landing

Over-the-post balustrade

Tread

Riser

In a closed-stringer stairway, the risers and treads butt into straight, uncut stringers. These economical stairways are often built with no underlying frame; instead, the risers and treads are attached directly to the finished stringers using routed grooves or housings. This stairway features an over-the-post balustrade.

On the one hand, contractors and homeowners are often driven both to use as little space as possible and to keep costs down. Safety engineers, on the other hand, would like to stretch stairs out in a kinder, gentler pitch that they insist would save lives. Architects and stairbuilders are sometimes at odds with both of these groups over aesthetic concerns. So before construction on any type of stairs can begin, the stairbuilder, homeowner, general contractor, and the architect must decide how to balance the issues of safety, aesthetics, budget, and space.

Building to code

The choices are not unlimited. Most building codes have sections covering stairs, handrails, and balustrades that impose sensible restrictions on designers and builders. These minimum safety and design standards help ensure that safe and functional stairways are built, but they still leave plenty of room both for creativity and frugality. Unfortunately, the national model codes don't always agree entirely on basic stairway dimensions. While sorting through the differences here would be a tedious and highly forgettable exercise, there is enough agreement that it's possible to compile a general picture of acceptable standards (see the drawing below). At the same time, I would urge anyone planning a stairway to check their local building code for specific requirements, which vary from region to region (and sometimes from year to year).

It's important to keep in mind that there is no law against exceeding the minimum standards set forth in

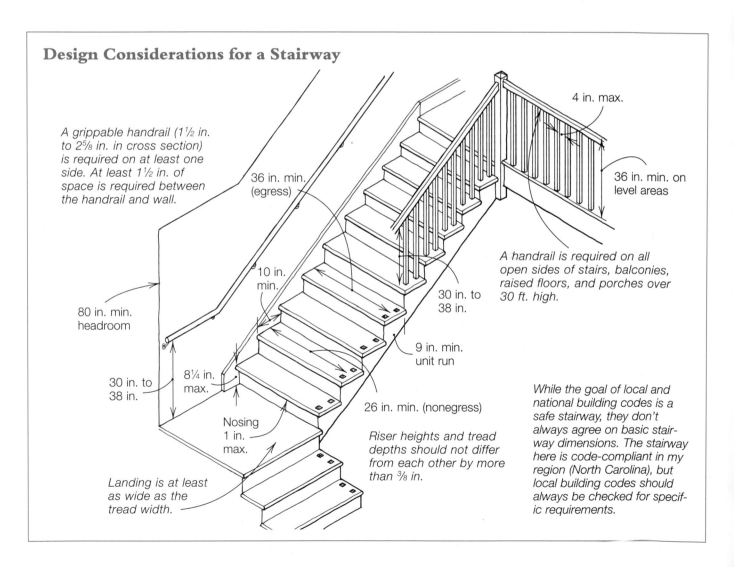

Design Considerations for a Stairway

A grippable handrail (1½ in. to 2⅝ in. in cross section) is required on at least one side. At least 1½ in. of space is required between the handrail and wall.

36 in. min. (egress)

4 in. max.

36 in. min. on level areas

10 in. min.

80 in. min. headroom

A handrail is required on all open sides of stairs, balconies, raised floors, and porches over 30 ft. high.

30 in. to 38 in.

9 in. min. unit run

30 in. to 38 in.

8¼ in. max.

Nosing 1 in. max.

26 in. min. (nonegress)

Riser heights and tread depths should not differ from each other by more than ⅜ in.

Landing is at least as wide as the tread width.

While the goal of local and national building codes is a safe stairway, they don't always agree on basic stairway dimensions. The stairway here is code-compliant in my region (North Carolina), but local building codes should always be checked for specific requirements.

the building codes. If money and floor space weren't factors, however, the ideal stairway would not be too far removed from the minimum that the code permits. A single inch per riser and tread separates a basic stairway from a luxurious one: A no-nonsense, utility stairway is made up of stairs about 8 in. high and 10 in. deep, while a sumptuous stairway is composed of stairs about 7 in. high and 11 in. deep. This "7-11" stairway produces a very comfortable slope and is strongly recommended by safety engineers. Unfortunately, a 7-11 stairway requires close to 3 ft. more in overall length than an 8-10 stairway to rise one story. This floor-space requirement makes a 7-11 stairway unfeasible or impractical in many houses. As might be expected, most stairways are laid out in the range between the basic 8-10 stairway and the space-devouring 7-11 stairway (see the drawings below).

Avoiding common stairway flaws

To a large extent, building a fine stairway is an exercise in avoiding mistakes, since a stairway doesn't easily forgive blunders and oversights. When errors occur, they're hard to hide and almost impossible to fix. What makes matters worse is that those mistakes usually don't show up until late in the game, when starting over would be expensive and painful. Usually, mistakes made during stairway construction become stairway flaws: annoying, unsightly, and permanent. But these flaws contain valuable lessons, and it's worthwhile to examine them carefully and, more importantly, to identify what caused them so that they can be avoided in the future. It might sound strange, but to be successful, a stairbuilder must be constantly aware of what can go wrong.

Tread and Riser Dimensions Determine Stairway Length

While differences in tread and riser heights may seem minimal, their effect on the total length of a stairway can be significant. Here, a stairway with 10-in.-wide, 8-in.-high treads is almost almost 3 ft. shorter than a stairway with more comfortable 11-in.-wide, 7-in.-high treads.

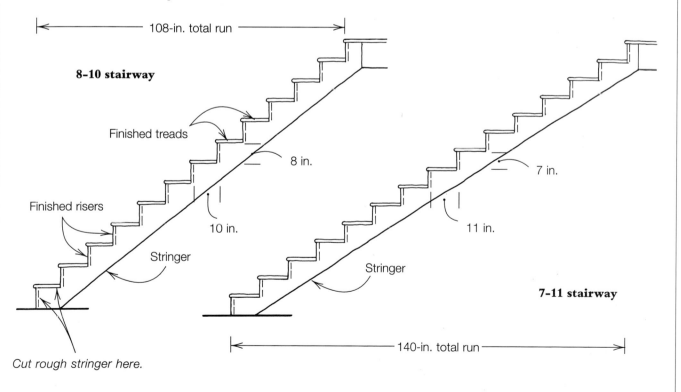

108-in. total run

8-10 stairway

Finished treads

8 in.

Finished risers

10 in.

Stringer

Cut rough stringer here.

7 in.

11 in.

Stringer

7-11 stairway

140-in. total run

Most stairway flaws show up in the top or bottom step of each run of stairs or are related to incorrectly built landings or stairwells. The reason for this is not too difficult to discern. More often than not, the carpenter's attention is focused almost entirely on the heart of the job: laying out and cutting the stringers. Unfortunately, stringers that are cut or mortised into perfectly uniform risers and treads don't guarantee a perfect stairway.

To get a stairway right, carpenters need to think about the big picture and how all of the details fit into it (see the drawings below and on the facing page). For example, how will the stairs be attached at the bottom and top? What is the finished floor on the landing and first and second floors, and how much thickness will it add to the subfloor? What is the thickness of the materials used for risers and treads? If there are any landings, pre-

Common Stairway Flaws

Weak stringer attachment

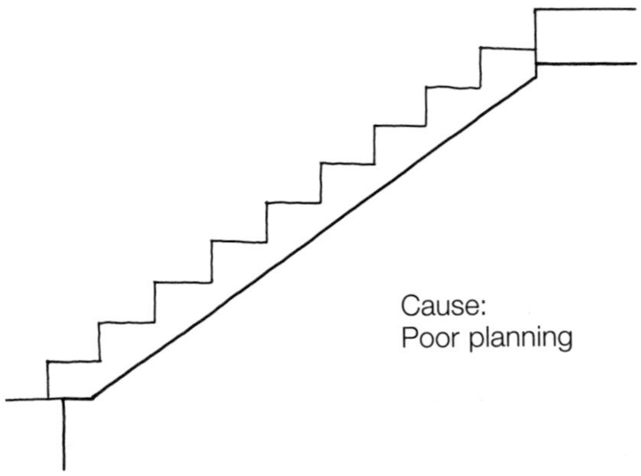

Cause:
Poor planning

Inconsistent riser sizes (usually top or bottom step)

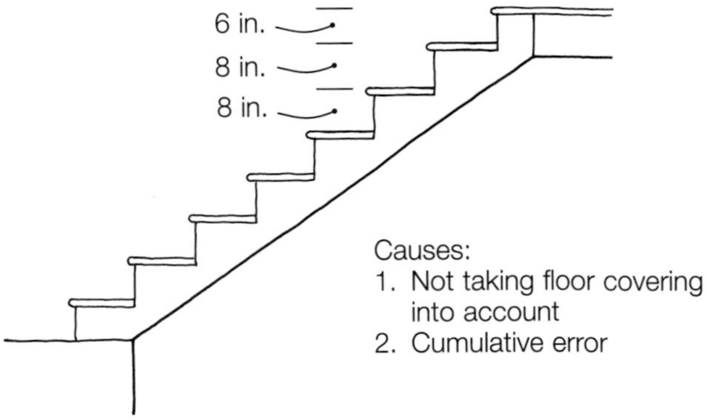

6 in.
8 in.
8 in.

Causes:
1. Not taking floor covering into account
2. Cumulative error

Inconsistent riser height from one run in split flight to the next

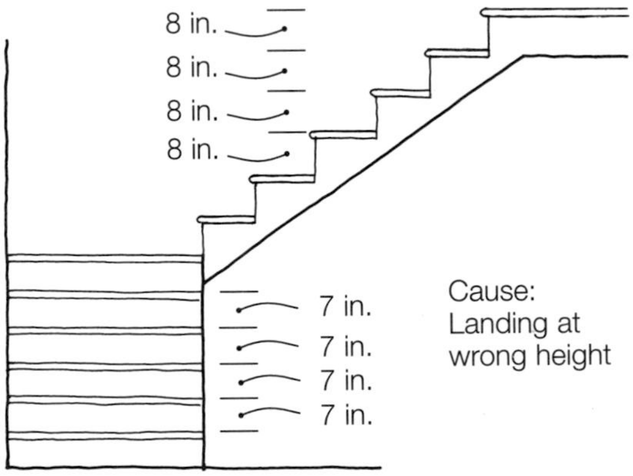

8 in.
8 in.
8 in.
8 in.

7 in.
7 in.
7 in.
7 in.

Cause:
Landing at wrong height

Inadequate headroom

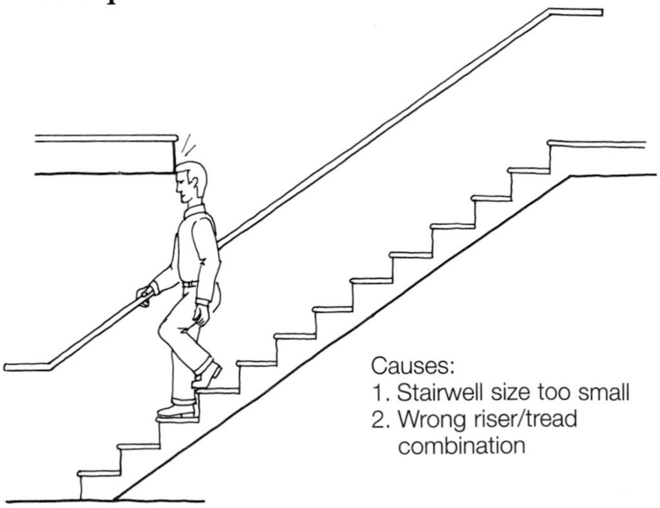

Causes:
1. Stairwell size too small
2. Wrong riser/tread combination

cisely how big will they be and how high off the finished floor? How much space is available for the length of the stairway? How much room will be needed for sufficient clearance above the stairway? Where will the newels for a balustrade be installed, and how will they be attached? These are all questions that need answering during the design stage.

LAYING OUT STAIRS

Like other complex jobs, stair layout can be divided into several steps. Breaking the job down into manageable parts helps the stairbuilder spot problems before committing saw to wood. Before discussing these steps, however, I want to emphasize an important feature of this process. The neatly divided steps presented here are actually quite interrelated. A change in one step often cre-

Inconsistent tread size (usually top tread on deck or porch)

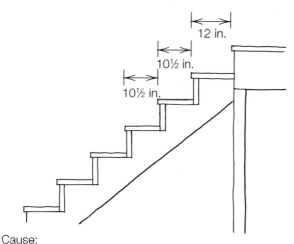

12 in.

10½ in.

10½ in.

Cause:
Not taking thickness of riser into account

Stairway too long (intrudes into doorway)

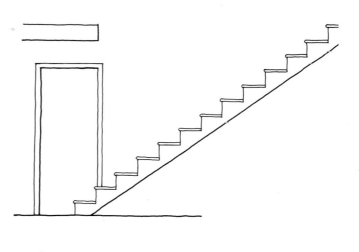

Causes:
1. Incorrect riser/tread combination
2. Single run of stairs not feasible in that space

Stairway too long (approach too small)

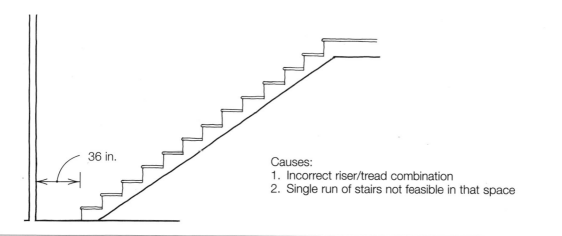

36 in.

Causes:
1. Incorrect riser/tread combination
2. Single run of stairs not feasible in that space

ates a chain reaction that forces changes in other steps. This phenomenon, of course, is not unique to stair layout, but the degree to which the various parts of this job are interconnected is very high.

1. Determine the total rise

The total rise in a set of stairs is the distance from the top of one finished floor to the top of the next finished floor. In the case of outdoor structures, the rise is the distance from ground level to the top of the finished deck, porch, or stoop (see the drawings below). When this measurement isn't taken correctly, an odd-size riser at the top or bottom of the stairs is the result. Missing this measurement is a common mistake in stairbuilding because the carpenter often has to measure something that is not yet in place. Typically, stairs are built when the house or addition is still in the framing stage and

long before the finished floors have been installed. But to measure the rise accurately, it's vital to confirm the type and thickness of the finished-floor material. Because the possible combination of flooring materials can vary quite a bit, any assumptions on the part of the stairbuilder about the actual floor configuration can be disastrous (see the top drawing on the facing page).

After confirming the type and thickness of the finished floor, make up a set of "floor-thickness" blocks. These blocks are about 16 in. long and are equal in thickness to each finished floor that will have an impact on the proposed stairway. Mark these blocks clearly, because you'll refer back to them several times in the course of building a flight of stairs. Not infrequently, my floor-thickness blocks are ready-made: An anticipated ¾-in.-thick floor covering, for example, could easily be repre-

Measuring the Total Rise

The total rise is the distance between finished floors. Floors shouldn't be assumed to be level; instead, level over from the actual landing for better accuracy.

Interior stairs

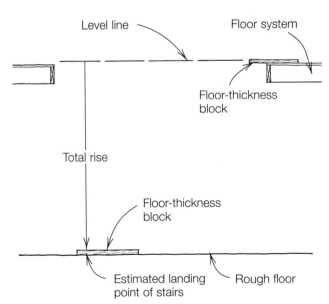

A floor-thickness block duplicates the thickness of the finished floor and should be used as shown when measuring the total rise.

Exterior stairs

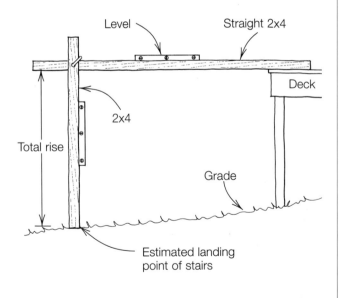

Because the grade can be adjusted, the actual landing point of exterior stairs may have to be estimated.

How Floor Finishes Affect the Total Rise

While the framing and subfloor configurations in the examples below are identical, the total rise is different in each one and is dependent on the thickness of the finished floor at both the base and the top of the stair.

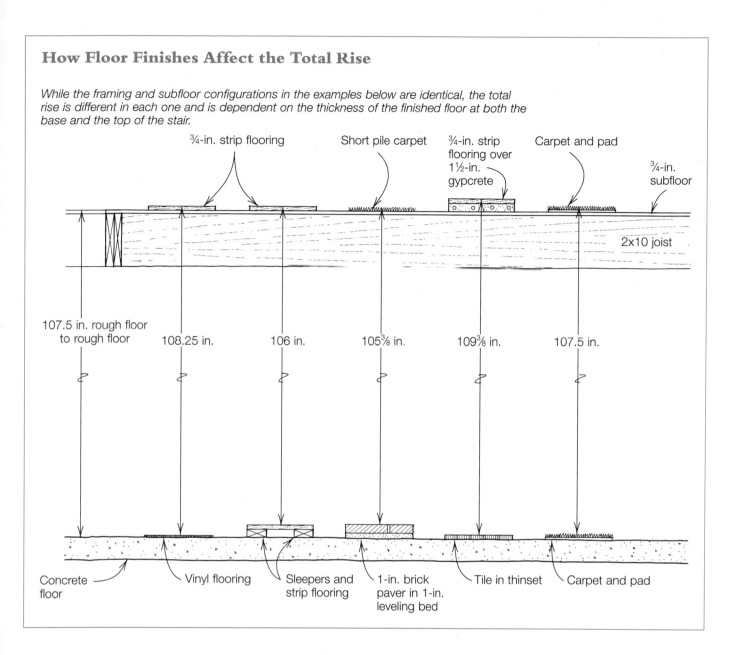

¾-in. strip flooring   Short pile carpet   ¾-in. strip flooring over 1½-in. gypcrete   Carpet and pad   ¾-in. subfloor

2x10 joist

107.5 in. rough floor to rough floor   108.25 in.   106 in.   105⅜ in.   109⅜ in.   107.5 in.

Concrete floor   Vinyl flooring   Sleepers and strip flooring   1-in. brick paver in 1-in. leveling bed   Tile in thinset   Carpet and pad

sented by a scrap of 1x4. It's important to measure carefully the total rise where the stairs will actually begin and end. On outdoor structures the grade must be taken into consideration, while inside the house, floors should never be presumed to be level.

2. Find the number of risers

After determining the total rise, it's necessary to divide that number into equal increments to represent the stair risers. Since the ideal riser is 7 in. high, first divide the total rise by 7 to get a general idea of how many risers

will be needed. For example, if the total rise is 106 in., divide that sum by 7 to get 15.14, which means you can use 15 risers for this particular stair. By dividing the total rise (106) by this potential number of risers (15), you'll find that the actual riser height would be 7.06 in. (or about 7¹⁄₁₆ in.).

You don't necessarily have to use 15 risers, however. You could shorten the stairway by one step to save space and use 14 risers (106 ÷ 14 = 7.57, or 7⁹⁄₁₆ in., which is an acceptable riser height). Where space is an urgent consideration, you might try 13 risers (106 ÷ 13 = 8.15, or 8⅛ in.). A riser height of 8⅛ in. is pretty high and barely passes code here in North Carolina. Of course, if there is plenty of room for the stairway, you could divide this total rise by 16, which yields a very mild 6⅝-in. riser. One occasion when I opted for a riser about this height was when I had a client who had difficulty climbing steep stairs due to severe arthritis.

3. Examine total run options

The total run of a stairway is the horizontal distance from the beginning to the end of the stairs. This figure is affected by the number of risers and by the size of the treads, as well as by the way in which the stairs are attached to the upper floor. A stairbuilder can usually divide a one-story flight of stairs into three or four acceptable riser sizes. Thus, the number of risers and, correspondingly, the number of treads can vary (see the drawing below).

The size of the treads can vary as well, which will also affect the total run of the stairs. Oak treads are available in 11½-in. widths; southern yellow pine treads measure 11¼ in. wide. Of course, these treads can be ripped down to any width as long as they meet the code minimum (usually about 10 in.). Hence, like riser size, neither the width nor the number of treads is absolutely predetermined. Stairbuilders are confronted with an array of possible tread/riser combinations that affect both the pitch of the stairway and its overall length. As the plan of the stairway is beginning to take shape, carefully weigh the advantages and disadvantages of these riser and tread options, keeping in mind the design limits established by your local building code.

4. Determine how stringers will be attached

Before deciding which riser/tread combination to use, you should also think about how the stringers will be connected to the upper floor. While this may seem like a minor detail, the choice can affect the total run by several inches and plays an important role both in

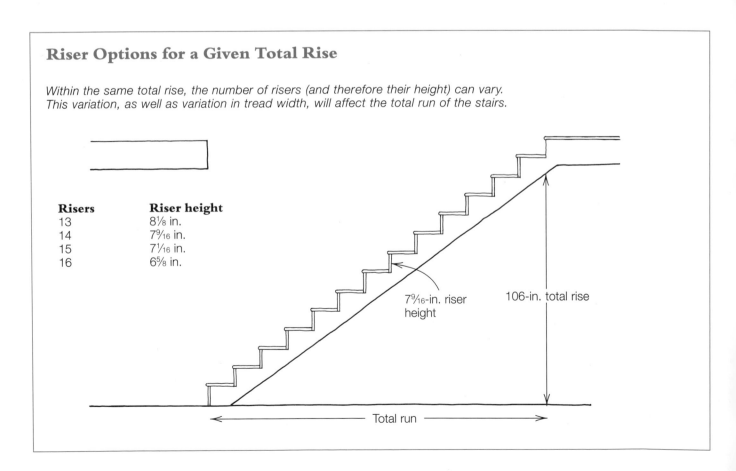

Riser Options for a Given Total Rise

Within the same total rise, the number of risers (and therefore their height) can vary. This variation, as well as variation in tread width, will affect the total run of the stairs.

Risers	Riser height
13	8⅛ in.
14	7⁹⁄₁₆ in.
15	7¹⁄₁₆ in.
16	6⅝ in.

7⁹⁄₁₆-in. riser height

106-in. total rise

Total run

the level of craftsmanship and in the structural integrity of the job (see the drawing below). In fact, mishandling this detail is one of the most common mistakes in stair construction.

A widespread practice in stairbuilding is to attach the stringer one full riser height down from the top of the upper floor. Depending on the circumstances, this can be either a perfectly acceptable way or a sloppy and inappropriate way to install stringers. Dropping the stringer one riser is an acceptable practice when the staircase will be supported by (or bear against) a wall or solid posts or when the staircase is hung with suitable hardware (see the drawings on p. 162). Dropping the stringer one riser is not an acceptable practice, however, when none of these structural components is used.

In most traditional houses, the staircase is amply supported by the framed walls that run under and alongside the stringers. In these cases, you can drop the

How Stringer Attachment Affects the Total Run

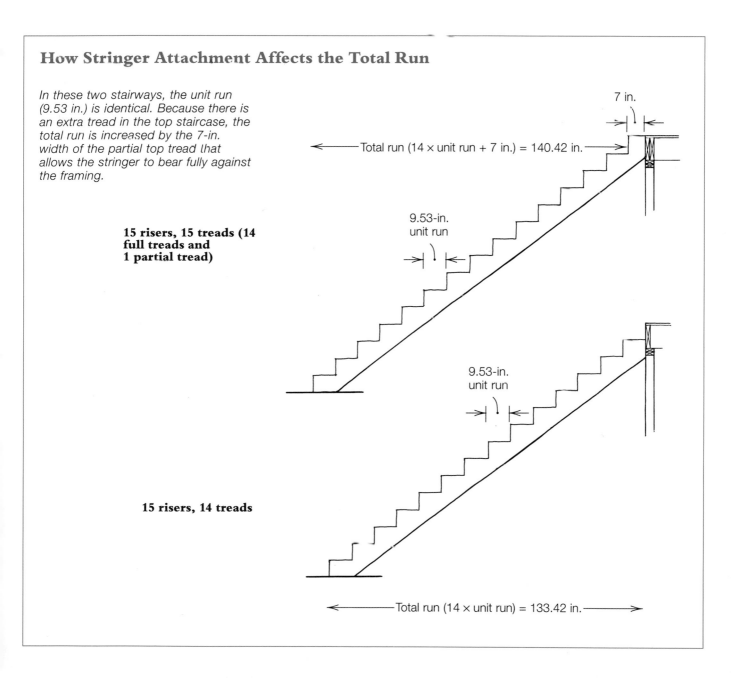

In these two stairways, the unit run (9.53 in.) is identical. Because there is an extra tread in the top staircase, the total run is increased by the 7-in. width of the partial top tread that allows the stringer to bear fully against the framing.

15 risers, 15 treads (14 full treads and 1 partial tread)

7 in.

Total run (14 × unit run + 7 in.) = 140.42 in.

9.53-in. unit run

9.53-in. unit run

15 risers, 14 treads

Total run (14 × unit run) = 133.42 in.

Supported Stringers

When the staircase will be supported by or bear against a wall or solid posts, there are no special structural concerns.

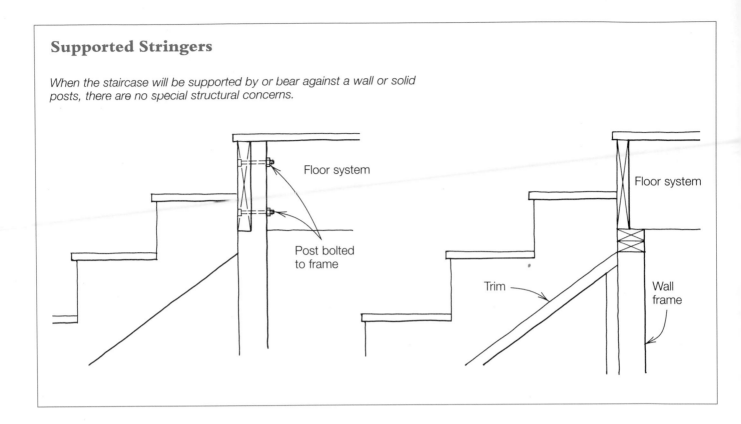

Floor system

Post bolted
to frame

Floor system

Trim

Wall
frame

stringer one riser if you want without worrying about structure. Contemporary designs and exterior decks, on the other hand, often feature free-spanning stairs—that is, stairs supported entirely by their points of attachment at the top and bottom. In these cases, you must be very careful because stairs are quite heavy and subject to sudden concentrated loads (such as that which might occur when two teenagers race downstairs to answer a ringing telephone).

To meet the structural requirements for free-spanning stairs, you have two basic approaches (see the drawings on the facing page). In the first, you can treat the stairs the same way you might treat a standard, stick-built roof. To counteract the thrusting forces of gravity, which want to pull the stairway down and forward at the top and simultaneously force it to slide out along the floor at the bottom, securely anchor the bottom and provide a stable surface to bear against at the top. In these structures, the full width of the stringer must bear against the framing; it can't usually be dropped one riser.

In the second approach, you can use appropriate hardware to hang the stringers, just as you might hang a joist or beam. This approach can be problematic, both because there is no standard hardware available for this task and because the necessary steel and bolts are often unattractive and difficult to hide. These hanging systems are unusual enough that they should be designed by a structural engineer (instead of jerry-rigged) and because of the bother, expense, and ungainly appearance of the fasteners, I use these systems only as a last resort. The primary circumstance that would force me to use a hanging system would be when I needed to build a free-spanning stairway that had to be dropped one riser because of space limitations on the run of the stair.

Unless your hand is forced by existing conditions, I always recommend attaching the stringers of a free-spanning stairway to the upper floor system. To anchor the bottom, install a thrust block and notch the stringers around it. To provide sufficient thrust resistance at the top of the stairs, build the stringers into the upper floor system, which allows them to bear fully

Stringers for a Free-Spanning Stairway

Stringers built into upper floor system

Ideally, a free-spanning stairway bears fully against the upper floor system. A thrust block firmly anchored to the lower floor counteracts the lateral forces imposed by the weight of the stairs.

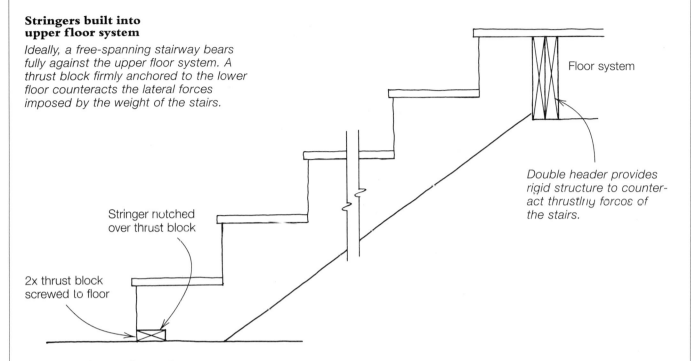

Floor system

Double header provides rigid structure to counter-act thrusting forces of the stairs.

Stringer notched over thrust block

2x thrust block screwed to floor

Stringers dropped one riser

When a free-spanning stair must be dropped one riser, only a small portion bears against the upper floor system. Without appropriate hardware to hang the structure (left), the staircase won't be structurally sound (right).

Hanging system (used as a last resort)

Structurally unsound method of attaching free-spanning stair

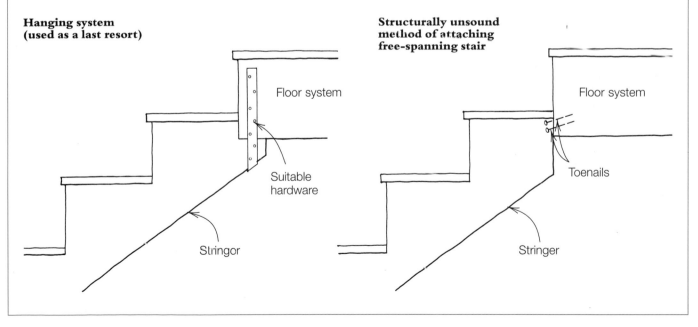

Floor system

Suitable hardware

Stringer

Floor system

Toenails

Stringer

against the floor system, and it's neat and craftsmanlike in appearance. The only problem is that it is often installed in a clumsy manner.

When a floor system (or a deck) is completed and then a staircase is attached to it, the uppermost tread ends up level with the floor but stands proud of the edge. In this case, the top tread looks tacked on and often sticks out like the proverbial sore thumb. This circumstance cannot be categorically dismissed as a flaw, for it is sometimes a deliberate design feature, like a window installed at an unusual height. Having said that, however, I would add that this detail is rarely done by design. Usually, it simply reflects a lack of planning on the part of the carpenter. In these cases, it is simply a mistake, and efforts to transform it into a design feature require creativity and advanced "wordworking" skills.

To avoid having the top tread project awkwardly from the edge, build an inset into the band joist while framing the floor or deck. By building this inset about 10 in.

deep or so, you can attach the stringers securely to the framing and eliminate the projection of the first tread. Then you can incorporate the top tread into the floor system and cover it with finishing materials (see the drawing below).

As I mentioned, the way a stringer is attached to the upper floor affects the total run of the stairs. When the stringer is dropped one riser, there is one less tread than riser; a 15-riser staircase, in other words, would have 14 treads. When the stringer is built into the upper floor, on the other hand, there are an equal number of risers and treads. The top tread, the one that runs flush with the upper floor, can be either a full or partial tread.

5. Choose the riser/tread combination

When choosing one riser/tread combination out of several possible options, try to arrive at the one with the optimal amount of comfort and safety. In other words, you want the stairs to be as close to the 7-11 ideal as conditions will permit. Sometimes there is plenty of

Integrating the Top Tread into the Upper Floor

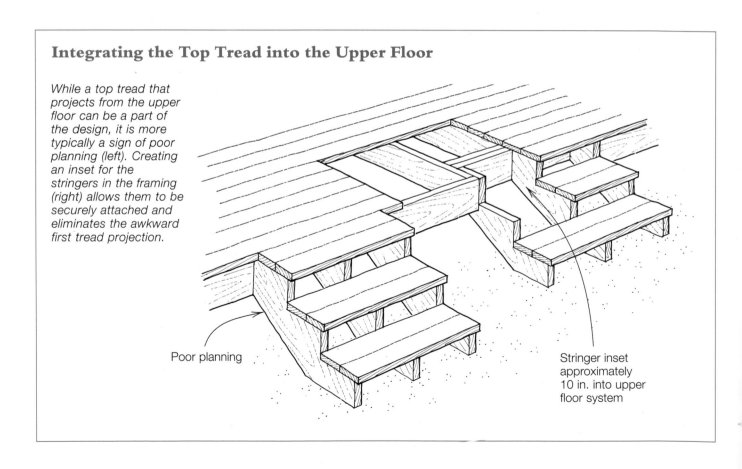

While a top tread that projects from the upper floor can be a part of the design, it is more typically a sign of poor planning (left). Creating an inset for the stringers in the framing (right) allows them to be securely attached and eliminates the awkward first tread projection.

Poor planning

Stringer inset approximately 10 in. into upper floor system

room for the stairs, and the size of the unit run—that is, the width of the tread minus the nosing—can be arbitrarily chosen. In those cases, make the unit run about 1¼ in. smaller than the width of the tread stock you'll be using, which is generally about 11¼ in. to 11½ in. wide. This way you can rip off any small variation in the width of the stock and end up with a very comfortable 11-in.-deep tread with a 1-in. nosing.

More often than not, however, the total run of the stairway is limited. There are all kinds of factors that might restrict the total run: the location of a door, window or wall, or (on outdoor structures) the position of a tree, heat pump, or a property line. When there are preexisting restrictions, the very first thing you want to know is whether the stairway will fit in the available space. To do this, take the lowest possible number of treads and divide it into the space available for the total run of the stairs. For example, if you've calculated (as you did in step 2) that the lowest number of risers you can use is 13 (with a height of 8⅛ in. per riser) and you plan to drop the stringer one riser, you know that the lowest number of treads you can use is 12. If the total available run equals 133½ in., divide the run by the number of treads to find the unit run (133.5 ÷ 12 = 11.125). Adding a 1-in. nosing to the 11.125-in. unit run would produce a very large 12⅛-in. tread—larger, in fact, than readily available tread material. The 8⅛-in. riser is also far from ideal, so you should reject this option.

Next, try a 14-riser/13-tread combination. Dividing the run by the new number of treads gives you a new unit run of just over 10¼ in. (133½ ÷ 13 = 10.269). Adding a 1-in. nosing allows a luxurious 11¼-in. tread along with a very acceptable 7⁹⁄₁₆-in.-high riser (as figured in step 2). While this is an attractive riser/tread combination, don't stop here. A 15-riser/14-tread combination yields a 9.53-in. (or 9⁹⁄₁₆-in.) unit run, which, with a nosing, produces a nice 10⁹⁄₁₆-in. tread; the riser for a 15-riser stair is a near-perfect 7⁷⁄₁₆ in. While the choice here is close, I would select the 15-riser/14-tread combination over the 14-riser/13-tread combination because it provides the safest and most comfortable rise/run ratio possible in this situation.

Sometimes it's necessary to figure out what would be the shortest possible stairway in a given rise. This, of course, depends on the building code. In North Carolina where I live, an 8¼-in. riser is acceptable, and 13 risers could be used in a total rise of 106 in. With 12 unit runs at the code minimum of 9 in., the stairway would have a total run of only 108 in. I'd allow 2 in. more to account for the thickness of the risers and the projection of the first nosing, giving me a total run of 110 in.

6. Make sure there is enough headroom

Most building codes require at least 80 in. of headroom above the nosing of the treads. It's important to keep in mind that the stairs end flush with the finished upper floor and that this 80-in. requirement is measured from the bottom of the upper floor structure. If the floor system is made of 2x10 floor joists with ½-in. drywall on the underside, a ½-in. plywood subfloor, and ¾-in. hardwood flooring on top, the total finished thickness will be 11¼ in. The stairs need to drop at least 91¼ in. (80 + 11¼) then before there is sufficient headroom.

It's easy to figure out where this point will be. In the case of a stairway with a 9.53-in. unit run and a 7.06-in. riser (like the example above), for every 7.06 in. the stairs go down, they go out 9.53 in. To get to the point where there is enough headroom, you would have to go down 13 steps (91.25 ÷ 7.06 = 12.92). If you were walking down those stairs, 13 steps would bring you 123.89 in. forward (13 × 9.53). Adding 3 in. for the trim or drywall along the inside rim of the stairwell, the thickness of the risers and the nosing of the treads, you know you need at least 127 in. for the rough stairwell (see the drawing on p. 166). If you intended to build the stringers into the floor system, of course, you'd have to allow for an extra full or partial tread. Another way to approach this problem would be to set up a proportional equation, where 9.53 is the unit run, 7.06 is the unit rise, 91.25 is the required fall (from the upper floor), and x is the run required to achieve that fall:

$$\frac{9.53}{7.06} = \frac{x}{91.25}, \text{ where } x = 123.17.$$

Suppose you found that there would not be enough headroom because of a framing error. You should first see if the stairwell could be made larger. If this proves impossible or prohibitively expensive, go back to step 5 and try new riser/tread combinations until you find one that allows for the required headroom.

Determining the Minimum Size of the Rough Stairwell

To descend the minimum 80 in. below the bottom of the upper floor requires 13 steps from the top landing (13 × 7.06 = 91.78 in.). Here the cumulative run is 123.89 in. (13 × 9.53 = 123.89), and adding 3 in. to the framed opening to allow for drywall and stair trim results in a 127-in. framed opening.

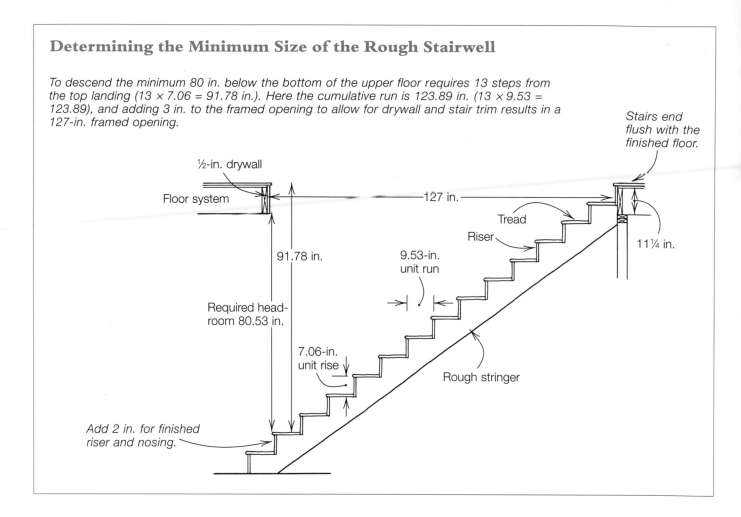

½-in. drywall

Floor system

Stairs end flush with the finished floor.

127 in.

Tread

Riser

11¼ in.

91.78 in.

9.53-in. unit run

Required head-room 80.53 in.

7.06-in. unit rise

Rough stringer

Add 2 in. for finished riser and nosing.

7. Lay out risers and treads on the stringers

After determining the best possible riser/tread combination, it's time to lay out the stringers. The conventional way to lay out both open and closed (or housed) stringers is to step them off with a rafter square. There is one important difference, though: Open stringers are laid out from the top side, while closed stringers are laid out from the bottom.

Open stringers To lay out an open-stringer stair with a riser of 7¹⁄₁₆ in. and a unit run of 9⁹⁄₁₆ in. (like the example above), first find these measurements on the two tongues of your rafter square. Then hold the square so that those numbers align with the edge of the stringer and mark the triangle formed by the outside of the

square. Next, move the square up the board to the end of this first triangle and lay out the next step, repeating the process until all of the required steps have been marked (see the top drawing on the facing page).

When I started building stairs, I quickly discovered two problems with this time-honored method. First, I had trouble holding the square consistently in the same position on the stringer. Second, I usually ended up with cumulative error. Part of the problem was that I was trying to make precise measurements along an edge that was anything but precise. The edges of lumber are eased to protect people from splinters, and along these edges there are also the usual lumber irregularities, like wanes, knots, and nicks. Under these conditions, it's difficult to

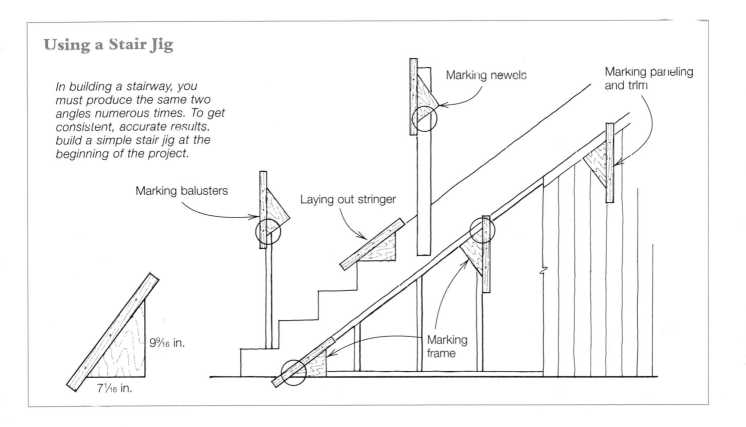

Laying Out an Open Stringer with a Rafter Square

Hold the rafter square so that the rise and tread numbers align with the edge of the stringer. Mark the triangle formed and move up the board until all of the required steps have been marked.

7 1/16 in.

9 9/16 in.

Rafter square

7 1/16-in. riser   9 9/16-in. unit run

Using a Stair Jig

In building a stairway, you must produce the same two angles numerous times. To get consistent, accurate results, build a simple stair jig at the beginning of the project.

Marking newels

Marking paneling and trim

Marking balusters

Laying out stringer

Marking frame

9 9/16 in.

7 1/16 in.

determine precisely just where the edge of framing lumber actually is sometimes.

Many carpenters use stair gauges—little knobs that clamp on to the edge of the rafter square—to hold their square consistently in the same position when laying out stringers. I've always found stair gauges difficult to set precisely, however, and my pair has been gathering dust for years. Instead, I use a site-built stair jig that is

very similar to the rafter jig discussed in Chapter 6. While any scrap wood can be used to make this jig, if the factory-cut corner of a sheet of plywood is handy, I grab it because it's already straight and square (though I do double-check this with my rafter square).

To make a jig for the example here, first measure and mark 7 1/16 in. up and 9 9/16 in. across from the corner, then draw the hypotenuse between those marks. Next make a parallel line about 2 in. out from the hypotenuse and cut off the triangular piece along that second line. Finally, nail or screw a 1x2 fence along the hypotenuse on both sides of the plywood. To use the stair jig, hold the fence against the stringer and scribe the risers and treads along the edge of the plywood. While it takes only a few scraps of wood and about ten minutes to make, a stair jig produces very consistent risers and treads, and it can also be used for several other tasks as the job progresses (see the bottom drawing on p. 167).

Whether you're using a rafter square or a stair jig, you also face the second problem mentioned at the beginning of this section: cumulative error. For example, an error of as little as ¹⁄₁₆ in. when laying out each tread would add up to a cumulative error of ¹⁵⁄₁₆ in. by the end of the layout. This, of course, would produce an unacceptable final step. To avoid cumulative error, always divide the stringer into equal increments, each one representing the hypotenuse of the riser/tread combination.

To do this, first calculate the overall length of the stringer layout, which is the hypotenuse of all the risers and an equal number of treads. Even if you drop one tread from the stringer layout, you must calculate the overall length using an equal number of treads and risers. In this case, 15 risers = 106 in., and 15 unit runs =

143¹⁄₁₆ in., so the hypotenuse is 178¹⁄₁₆ in. After marking this total length on the stringer, set your divider to a distance equal to the hypotenuse of each individual stair. While this can be figured mathematically, it's easier to take it directly off the stair jig. Now, march the divider up the edge of the stringer, adjusting it as needed (see p. 29) until the overall length is divided equally (see the drawing below). After marking equal increments on one stringer, transfer these marks to the other stringers with a square. With the stringer equally divided, you can now lay out the risers and treads without the risk of cumulative error. As you move the stair jig up the stringer, you'll see immediately if you're running ahead or behind the increments and be able to adjust the risers and treads accordingly.

Closed stringers To my eyes, closed-stringer stairs—which are made by mortising the stringers to accept risers and treads—aren't nearly as handsome as open-stringer stairs. From a practical point of view, however, the former are better in several regards. Closed-stringer stairs are built by routing tapered mortises (traditionally called housings) in thick finished stringer stock. Finished risers and treads are then fitted into these housings and driven tight against the upper edge of the mortise by glue-soaked wood wedges installed behind and under the risers and treads. This is unibody con-

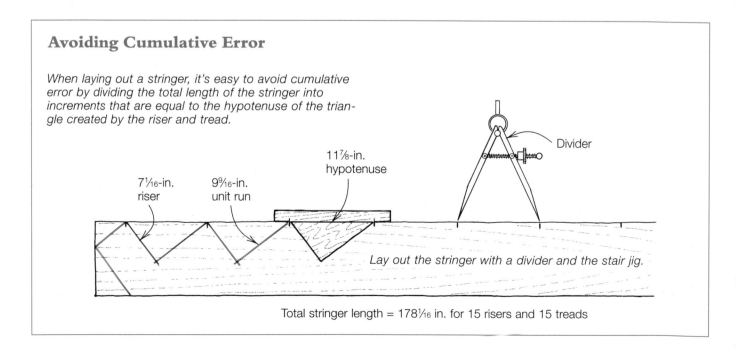

Avoiding Cumulative Error

When laying out a stringer, it's easy to avoid cumulative error by dividing the total length of the stringer into increments that are equal to the hypotenuse of the triangle created by the riser and tread.

7¹⁄₁₆-in. riser

9⁹⁄₁₆-in. unit run

11⁷⁄₈-in. hypotenuse

Divider

Lay out the stringer with a divider and the stair jig.

Total stringer length = 178¹⁄₁₆ in. for 15 risers and 15 treads

Laying Out Open and Closed Stringers

While open stringers are laid out from the top on rough framing, closed stringers are laid out from the bottom directly on the finished stair-stringer material. Note how the closed stringer must be integrated with the baseboard.

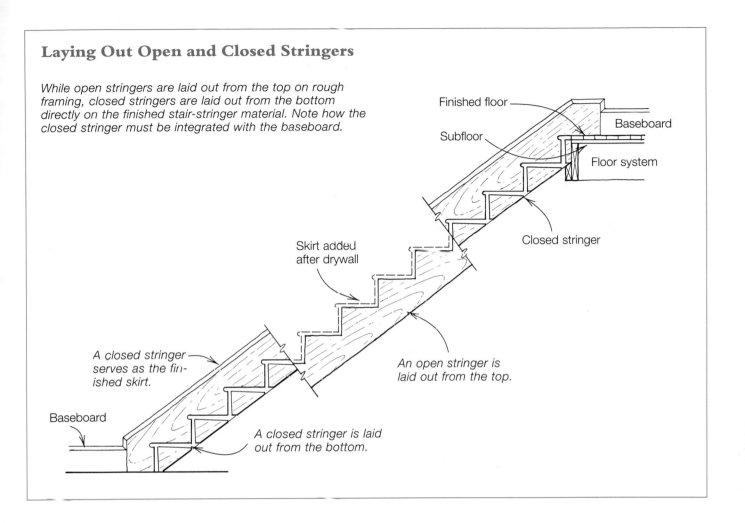

Finished floor

Subfloor

Baseboard

Floor system

Closed stringer

Skirt added after drywall

An open stringer is laid out from the top.

A closed stringer serves as the finished skirt.

Baseboard

A closed stringer is laid out from the bottom.

struction in wood: The materials that provide the structure are also the finish materials, resulting in significant savings in both materials and labor. Closed-stringer stairs are also strong, because the stringers aren't weakened by the deep cuts that characterize open stringers.

As I've already mentioned, the big difference between laying out closed and open stringers is the fact that closed stringers are laid out from the bottom rather than from the top. Avoiding cumulative error is still important though, and closed stringers should be divided into equal increments using the same technique described earlier. Nowadays, housings are almost always made with a router following a commercial or shop-built template. I have an adjustable template manufactured by Porter-Cable. A 1-in. guide collar mounted on my router base rides along the inside of the template as a ¾-in. straight bit inside the collar cuts the profile of one riser

and one tread (with enough room for glue wedges). After routing each step, I realign the template for the next step by using an index mark stamped on its edge. With equal increments already marked off, I can make minor adjustments as I proceed to stay on my layout— exactly the same as if I were laying out an open stringer with a stair jig.

Closed stringers are usually installed so that they bear fully against the structure of the upper floor. This means that a full or partial tread will be installed flush with the finished floor, and therefore there are an equal number of risers and treads. Along the stairwell walls, the stringer serves as a skirt board and normally needs to extend beyond the stairs at top and bottom. Here, it can be integrated aesthetically with the baseboard (see the drawing above).

8. Lay out the top and bottom of the stringer

Before cutting the stringer, check and recheck your measurements to make sure they will yield finished top and bottom risers that are equal to the rest of the risers in the stairway. This detail is easy to botch. In fact, it may well be the most confusing detail of stairbuilding because treads are usually a different thickness than the floor coverings at the top and bottom of the stairs, which also often differ from one another. Because of the different thicknesses, the stringer needs to be dropped one tread thickness at the bottom, and then the thickness of the finished floor covering has to be added. At the top, the last tread of the stringer has to be adjusted to reflect the difference between the tread thickness and the finished floor-covering thickness.

These differences can be reconciled mathematically, but that kind of ciphering befuddles my feeble mind. I find that it is much easier to draw the whole thing out right on the stringer. Begin by drawing in the bottom (or first) tread, then measure down 7¹⁄₁₆ in. (to continue with the example we've been using) from the top of that drawn-in tread and mark to represent the top of the finished floor. Next, scribe the thickness of the floor covering using the finished floor-thickness block you made way back in step 1. Now you have the level of the rough floor, and this is where you make the bottom cut on the stringer (see the left drawing below).

The technique for laying out the top of the stringer differs depending on how the stringer is attached at the top. If you're going to install the stringer flush with the upper floor, draw in the second-to-top tread, measure 7¹⁄₁₆ in. up from the top of it, and mark. As the drawing shows, this mark represents the top of the finished floor. After scribing the thickness of the upper floor—this time using the upper finished floor-thickness block from step 1—you're ready to cut the top of the stringer.

If the stringer will be attached one riser height down, the only difficulty is installing it at the right height. To

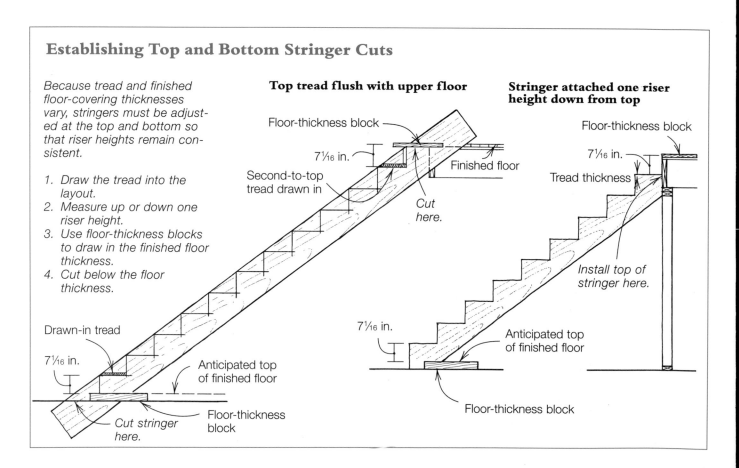

Establishing Top and Bottom Stringer Cuts

Because tread and finished floor-covering thicknesses vary, stringers must be adjusted at the top and bottom so that riser heights remain consistent.

1. *Draw the tread into the layout.*
2. *Measure up or down one riser height.*
3. *Use floor-thickness blocks to draw in the finished floor thickness.*
4. *Cut below the floor thickness.*

Drawn-in tread
7¹⁄₁₆ in.
Cut stringer here.
Anticipated top of finished floor
Floor-thickness block

Top tread flush with upper floor

Floor-thickness block
7¹⁄₁₆ in.
Second-to-top tread drawn in
Finished floor
Cut here.
7¹⁄₁₆ in.
Anticipated top of finished floor
Floor-thickness block

Stringer attached one riser height down from top

Floor-thickness block
7¹⁄₁₆ in.
Tread thickness
Install top of stringer here.

do this, place the floor-thickness block on the upper subfloor, measure down 7 1/16 in. from there, and mark (see the right drawing on the facing page). The mark represents the top of the uppermost tread. Measure down the thickness of the tread and mark again to represent where the stringer should be installed.

Deck builders should watch out for one potential error at this point. If the stringer is installed against the finished band joist of the deck and closed risers are going to be used, as shown in the drawing below, then the top unit run will grow by the thickness of the riser material unless an adjustment to the stringer is made. To avoid ending up with an oversize tread at the top of the staircase, the top tread on the stringer should be shortened by the thickness of the riser material.

LAYING OUT LANDINGS

If a stairway will have a landing, it needs to be as precisely planned and built as the rest of the stairs. The finished floor of the landing should be at the same height as the top of a tread would be if a straight set of stairs were being used in the same total rise. In other words, the landing should be treated as one big step. In some cases, the landing of an L-shaped stairway should also be the same finished depth as the finished width of the stairs so that the stairs remain the same width as they turn the corner. As an example, let's take a look at how to lay out the landing for an L-shaped stairway planned for a space that measures 126 in. from the edge of the floor system to the face of a wall and that has a total rise of 106 in. (see the drawing on p. 172).

Determining the size of the landing

The first order of business here is to decide on the finished size of the landing. If both the upper and lower stairs are going to be a finished 36 in. wide, the finished landing needs to be 36 in. square. But the rough landing needs to be larger than the finished dimensions.

In the first place, the finish materials along the walls —drywall and baseboards, for example—enclose the

---

Allowing for Riser Thickness at the Top of a Stringer

When closed risers are planned for an outdoor stair, stringers need to be cut short at the top to avoid an oversize tread. The depth of the cut off the end of the stringer equals the thickness of the riser stock.

Cut stringer here.

11 in.

11 in.

8 1/2 in.

1 1/2 in.

1 in.

10 in.

1 1/2 in.

10 in.

Establishing the Landing Height

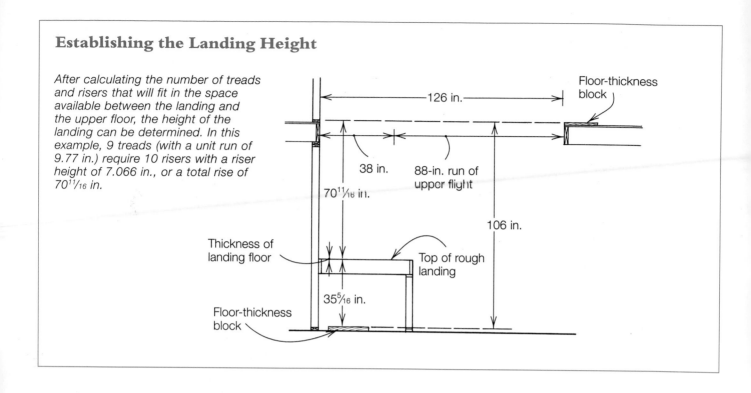

After calculating the number of treads and risers that will fit in the space available between the landing and the upper floor, the height of the landing can be determined. In this example, 9 treads (with a unit run of 9.77 in.) require 10 risers with a riser height of 7.066 in., or a total rise of 70¹¹⁄₁₆ in.

126 in.

Floor-thickness block

38 in.

88-in. run of upper flight

70¹¹⁄₁₆ in.

106 in.

Thickness of landing floor

Top of rough landing

35⁵⁄₁₆ in.

Floor-thickness block

landing slightly and diminish its size. Second, the upper run of stairs rests on the landing, so 10 in. extra or so must be included for this purpose when the rough landing is laid out. This can get confusing, and I've found that the best way to sort through the various contingencies is to draw the whole business out on the lower floor before framing the landing. In the example shown in the top drawing on the facing page, the rough landing turns out to be 36½ in. wide by 48 in. deep.

Determining the height of the landing

By making a drawing that includes details like the drywall and baseboard, you can also determine precisely how far the upper stringer will end from the wall where the landing is located: 38 in. (36-in. landing width plus ½-in. drywall plus ¾-in. baseboard plus ¾-in. riser). Because the available space for this stairway is 126 in. and the stringer ends 38 in. out from the wall, you now know that you have 88 in. available for the upper run of stairs (126 – 38 = 88). Dividing 88 in. by 9 gives you an acceptable unit run of 9.77 in.

If you've decided to attach the stringers one riser height down from the upper floor, there will be one more riser than there are treads, and therefore the top of the landing must be located 10 riser heights down from the upper floor. With a total rise of 106 in., then, the top of the finished landing should be 10 × 7.066 (the unit rise) or 70.66 in. down from the top of the finished floor.

After converting 70.66 in. to 70¹¹⁄₁₆ in., measure this distance down from the line representing the top of the finished upper floor, mark, then measure down the thickness of the landing floor covering (usually ¾ in.), then mark again (see the drawing above). This second mark represents the top of the rough landing. To check the accuracy of your calculations, measure up from the top of the lower finished floor-thickness block to the mark representing the top of the finished landing. This measurement should be 35⁵⁄₁₆ in. (106 – 70¹¹⁄₁₆ = 35⁵⁄₁₆).

Although the rise for these stairs remains the same as for the previous examples, the addition of the landing has changed the run, so you now need a different stair jig

Planning a Landing

A full-scale drawing of the landing right on the subfloor helps to account for details like drywall, risers, and trim. The width of the stairway determines the size of the landing, which in turn determines the precise location (and therefore the run) of the upper stringers.

Landing drawn out on floor

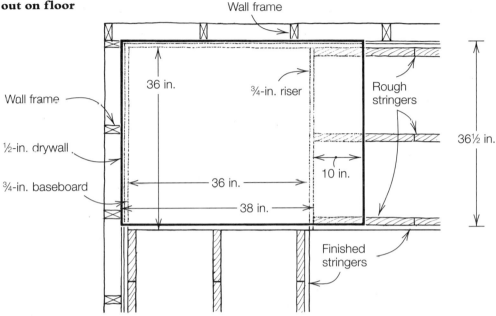

Wall frame

¾-in. riser

Rough stringers

36 in.

36 in.

38 in.

10 in.

36½ in.

Wall frame

½-in. drywall

¾-in. baseboard

Finished stringers

Finished landing

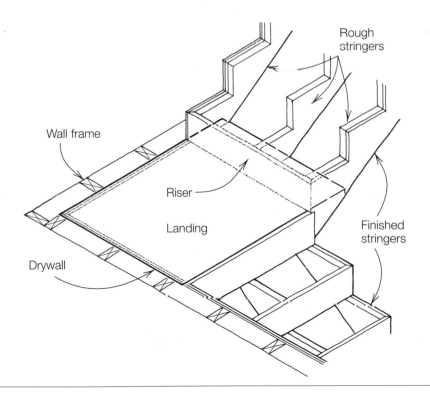

Rough stringers

Wall frame

Riser

Landing

Finished stringers

Drywall

to lay out and fit the upper and lower sets of stringers (as described in steps 7 and 8 on pp. 166-171). The finished stairway should have uniform risers and treads for all of the steps, and the landing should be located exactly 7¹⁄₁₆ in. above and below adjacent steps.

LAYING OUT BALUSTRADES

This chapter would be incomplete, as would many stairways, without a balustrade. A full discussion of the art of making a continuous, over-the-post balustrade could easily be a chapter unto itself. This section, therefore, must be limited to the simpler post-to-post balustrade.

There are three basic parts to the post-to-post balustrade: the newels (vertical posts that support the handrail), the rails, and the balusters. The newels are installed early in the game and require some patience, visualization, and planning to get just right. The rails and balusters, in turn, must be centered on the newels and consistently spaced from the edge of the stairs. In the example I'll be using here, the balustrade will be installed on an open-stringer staircase.

Laying out the newels

The easiest way to figure out the exact location of the newels is to make a scale drawing of the layout in plan view. In this particular stairway (represented in the drawing below), the goal is to position the newels so that they are even with the outside of the (future) treads. This way the finished stringers, risers, and treads will all die gracefully into the newel.

It's necessary to notch the newels carefully before bolting them to the framing. In addition, it's also necessary in many cases to calculate the exact height at which the newels should be installed. If the top of the newel has been milled, that top must be placed at exactly the right elevation, since it can't be cut later after it is installed. But just what is the right elevation? While there is no one answer to this question, generally newels should be high enough to accept the rail as per code (this varies) and project elegantly above it.

For example, let's say you want to attach the rail 34 in. above the nosing of the tread (the maximum allowed in my area), and you decide that the newel top would look

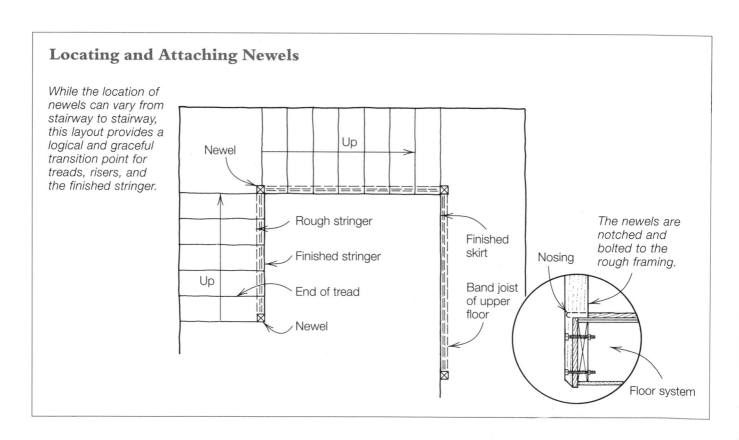

Locating and Attaching Newels

While the location of newels can vary from stairway to stairway, this layout provides a logical and graceful transition point for treads, risers, and the finished stringer.

Newel

Up

Rough stringer

Finished stringer

End of tread

Up

Newel

Finished skirt

Band joist of upper floor

Nosing

The newels are notched and bolted to the rough framing.

Floor system

best projecting 2¼ in. above the rail. Figuring out exactly how high to install the landing newel in this situation can be a bewildering problem. First of all, you have to measure up from a level surface (the tread or landing) to a sloping surface (the future rail). This means that the measurement will be inaccurate if you don't hold the tape measure absolutely plumb. Second, you have to make this measurement in midair. And, third, you have a problem pinpointing where the nose of each tread is, since they haven't yet been installed.

To overcome these difficulties, use a template. The cost is reasonable: a sheet of plywood and about ten minutes' time. To make the template, first mark clearly on the landings where the newel will be installed (see the drawing below). Then temporarily attach two treads (or two tread scraps) in the exact position that the finished treads will be installed. Next, take a sheet of plywood and hold it (it's good to have a helper for this task) so that it runs down the steps, bridging the nosing of the two temporary treads. With the plywood in this position, use a level to make plumb lines on each end. Remove the plywood and take it to a work table, then

mark 34 in. up from the bottom of the plywood along each of the plumb lines and strike a chalkline connecting the two marks. Cut the plywood along those three lines, and you end up with an excellent template for setting and marking newels.

To lay out the newel, simply hold the template to the mark where the newel will be located, take careful measurements, and transfer those measurements to the newels. Later, you can use the template to mark the newel precisely where the rail should be attached (see the drawing below).

Laying out the rails and balusters

After installing the newels, fit and install the finished stringers, risers, and treads. When you're finished with these, mark and cut the rails. Before installing the rails, however, lay out the position of the balusters both on the stair treads and on the underside of the rail. Normally, there are two balusters per tread on interior stairways. To look right, these need to be consistently located on the treads and equally spaced as they march up the staircase.

Making a Newel-Marking Template

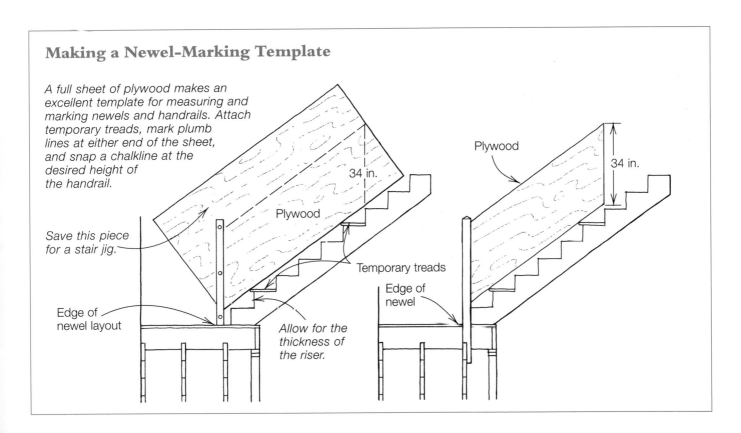

A full sheet of plywood makes an excellent template for measuring and marking newels and handrails. Attach temporary treads, mark plumb lines at either end of the sheet, and snap a chalkline at the desired height of the handrail.

Save this piece for a stair jig.

Edge of newel layout

Allow for the thickness of the riser.

Plywood

34 in.

Temporary treads

Plywood

34 in.

Edge of newel

The first step is to locate consistently the front baluster on each tread. If you've decided that 3 in. in from the front edge would look good, set a combination square at 3 in. and mark that distance in from the nosing on each step. Next, set the cut rail between the newels, resting it directly on the nosing of the treads. Transfer the marks you just made on the treads to the side of the rail. Then take the rail to a work table, turn it upside down, and transfer the marks from the side to the bottom. The layout for the second baluster for each tread is exactly halfway between the marks you've just transferred. After making these intermediate marks, bring the rail back over to the staircase and transfer them to the tread (see the top drawing below).

On the level sections of the balustrade, the layout is much simpler. There is one detail, however, that carpenters frequently mishandle. All of the spaces beside the balusters should be equal; this includes the space between the last baluster in a section and a post, a wall, or

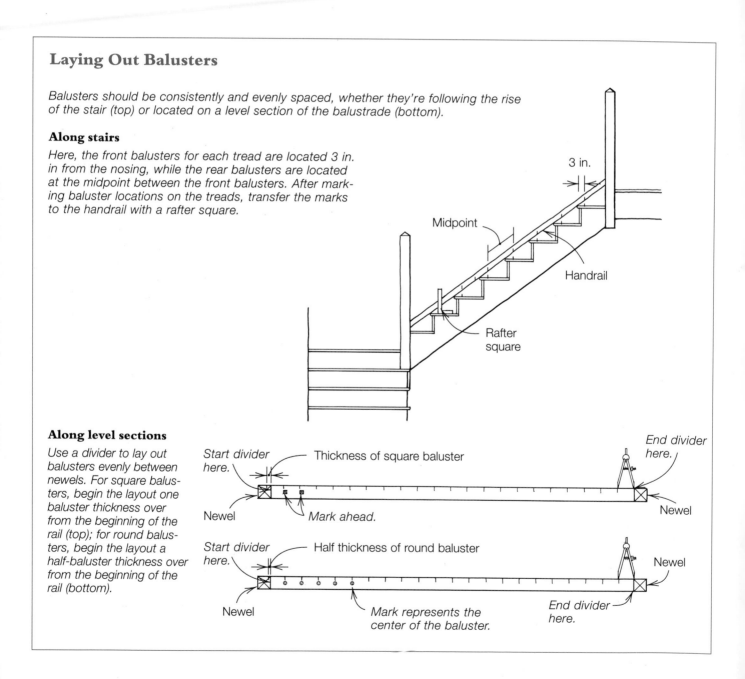

Laying Out Balusters

Balusters should be consistently and evenly spaced, whether they're following the rise of the stair (top) or located on a level section of the balustrade (bottom).

Along stairs

Here, the front balusters for each tread are located 3 in. in from the nosing, while the rear balusters are located at the midpoint between the front balusters. After marking baluster locations on the treads, transfer the marks to the handrail with a rafter square.

3 in.

Midpoint

Handrail

Rafter square

Along level sections

Use a divider to lay out balusters evenly between newels. For square balusters, begin the layout one baluster thickness over from the beginning of the rail (top); for round balusters, begin the layout a half-baluster thickness over from the beginning of the rail (bottom).

Start divider here.

Thickness of square baluster

End divider here.

Newel

Mark ahead.

Newel

Start divider here.

Half thickness of round baluster

Newel

Newel

Mark represents the center of the baluster.

End divider here.

a column (for more on dividing a distance into equal increments, see the sidebar below). When a baluster is crowded against the end point, the balustrade looks amateurish, as if it were bought at a home center and slapped into place. By stepping off the rail with dividers, it's easy to avoid this homely mistake. The trick is to allow for the thickness of the balusters.

To do this, start the layout one baluster thickness before the beginning of the rail if the baluster is square. Fine-tune your divider so that the balusters end up going from that point to the end of the rail evenly, then mark

Xs ahead of your layout. By installing the balusters over the Xs, you end up with equal spaces (see the bottom drawings on the facing page). If laying out the centers of the balusters would make assembly easier (this is often the case when you're installing round balusters into drilled holes), you can use a slight variation of this layout technique. To locate properly spaced center points, start the layout one-half the thickness of a baluster before the end of the rail and end it one-half the thickness beyond the end of the rail.

Dividing a Distance into Equal Increments

The divider is one of my most-prized layout tools. I have several different kinds and sizes of dividers that I use for different tasks. To divide a stair stringer into equal increments, for example, I use a divider about 18 in. tall; to divide a section of the balustrade, on the other hand, I use a 6-in. divider, which is much easier to maneuver. I thoroughly enjoy the simple, quiet, and well-nigh error-proof process of marching the divider up a board, adjusting the spread of the legs, and repeating this process until I get the dividers to land precisely on the end point of the space. Here there are no screaming power tools, no flying flecks of wood, no hidden details, no numbers.

Not everyone enjoys using dividers, however. Some carpenters are bored, not soothed by this quiet, delicate operation. If you're one of *those* people, you can use a calculator with an add-on feature. The add-on feature allows you to add the same number again and

again by simply hitting the = (the equal sign) button.

In the balustrade described in this section, for example, there are two balusters for each step. If each step were 9.77 in. wide (exclusive of nosing), that would mean that the balusters would be about 4.885 in. on center (o.c.). If this balustrade has a level section and the distance you need to divide is 81⅜ in. long (this would be the distance between the newels plus the thickness of one baluster), begin by dividing 81.375 by 4.885. This comes to 16.658 and indicates that this space should be divided into 17 equal increments. To find the size of the increments, divide 81.375 by 17. This comes to 4.7867647. Now, using the add-on feature (the exact process differs from calculator to calculator), begin adding this increment to itself. The cumulative dimensions come to: 4.7867647, 9.5735294, 14.360294, 19.147058, and so on until you get to the 17th dimension (which appears as 81.37499 on my

calculator). You now have all the dimensions you need, but before you can mark them on the rail, you have to convert all 17 of the decimals into fractions.

A simple way to use the add-on feature and avoid these tedious conversions requires an open mind and a metric tape measure. First, convert 81.375 in. to 206.6925 cm (or simply measure the distance with the metric tape measure). Divide the overall length, 206.6925 cm, by 17, which gives you the size of the increments, 12.158382 cm. Using the add-on feature, add this number to itself 17 times in the manner just described. These dimensions can be laid out with no further ado, using the metric tape measure.

Using the add-on feature and metric units saves time, particularly when I have to divide a large space into numerous units. For short spans, the old, reliable divider is just as fast—and a lot more fun to use.

Chapter 8
LAYING OUT MASONRY UNITS

Unlike wood, which is easy to cut and comes in both long boards and wide, flat sheets, masonry comes in small, uniform, and brittle units. There are certain advantages to working with these small pieces. Because they are so hard, people do not expect them to be cut to close tolerances, and they don't expect them to fit tightly together. Masonry units are joined, not by fasteners, but by a conforming, gap-filling, calcinated mixture that we call mortar. The small size of the units in combination with the generous thickness of the joints opens up an almost limitless number of design possibilities. Masonry units can be combined without too much difficulty into almost any shape, and they are particularly well suited to round or curved work.

The adjustable joints are the key to these design opportunities. Unfortunately, the joints themselves are grotesquely large by carpentry standards. Few people would accept a ½-in. joint, no matter how neatly it was filled, between two exposed pieces of wood. In a brick wall, on the other hand, there are thousands of ½-in. joints. These joints are not only accepted, but they're also considered an integral part of the design—like the stitches on a quilt. There are two sides to this bargain, though. The public permits the mason to have ½-in.-wide joints in the wall, but the mason is expected to make the joints as neat and orderly as possible.

PRINCIPLES OF MASONRY LAYOUT

An effective and productive mason needs to plan his jobs carefully and develop good habits of workmanship. In this section, I've distilled the main considerations of this process into four general principles. As you'll see, these principles have a practical side: The measures masons take to make their work more attractive generally increase both productivity and the long-term integrity of the structure.

Measure from the top down

Everyone knows that masons work from the ground up. We first learn this principle as children when we stack one wooden block on another, and it's reinforced every time we watch a mason at work: First he lays one course, then he moves his line up for the next. But while masons may *build* from the bottom up, they generally *measure* from the top down.

The first step in most masonry projects is establishing a top line. From the top line, masons measure down and mark in equal increments the location of the top of each course of brick or block. By working to these marks, masons arrive at the top of foundations, the bottom of windowsills, or at other predetermined landing places with evenly spaced courses. The rest of this chapter returns again and again to the same starting point: the top line.

Avoid unnecessary cuts

Bricks and blocks are difficult and expensive to cut. Like carpenters, masons distinguish between cuts made along the length of their units and those made across the width. Cutting units lengthwise (the masonry equivalent of ripping) is called splitting, while cutting units to length (the masonry equivalent of crosscutting) is usually just called cutting. It is much more difficult to split masonry units than it is to cut them to length. A crude comparison might be to think about how much harder it is to rip a 2x4 than it is to crosscut it.

Split bricks and blocks are not only scourges of productivity, but they also look bad. In unit masonry, the horizontal lines dominate visually. Split units interrupt the orderly progression of those lines and stick out like the proverbial sore thumb, so masons try to steer clear of these time-devouring and homely split units during the layout phase of the job. Fortunately, masons are generally successful at doing this, and it isn't uncommon for a crew to lay a foundation or veneer an entire house without having to split a single brick or block.

Units cut to length are a different matter, though. Because every house has windows, doors, and corners, bricks and blocks inevitably have to be cut to length. That doesn't mean bricklayers don't try to avoid cutting them whenever they can. By adjusting the non-critical dimensions of a structure so that they work to even (uncut) blocks or bricks, masons can save time and produce a better-looking job. Masons are particularly keen on getting even brickwork on tall, narrow structures— like chimneys—where a cut brick on every course can kill productivity.

Keep joints consistent

Masons adjust the height or length of their courses by altering the thickness of mortar joints. This is a basic part of the masonry trade, and it allows masons both to make up for inconsistencies in the size of the units and to fit whole units into a given space (between windows, for instance). This device can be overused, however. The joints in a standard brick wall account for close to a quarter of its surface area and have a surprisingly large impact on how the wall looks. Masons can't alter the color or texture of the units they lay; instead, their craftsmanship shows up in the joints. Because fat joints and abrupt changes in the thickness of joints can look terrible, masons need to alter the thickness of mortar joints carefully.

The size of the joints also affects the performance of the wall. Head joints (those between two masonry units in the same course) that are less than ¼ in. thick can be difficult to fill completely (especially the last brick set in a course) and can potentially allow water to penetrate the wall. Joints that are over ¾ in. thick can cause problems, too. For one thing, they shrink excessively, which sometimes results in leaky hairline cracks. And because masons tend to use a stiff mix when making thick joints, the bond ends up being a poor one, which can result in both leakage and structural compromise. Here in North Carolina, the building code requires that the joints in a

How Big is a Standard Brick?

The inelegant term "standard modular" (see the facing page) may have attracted your attention. This term is a product of two different efforts to impose modern standards on an ancient material. As many builders along the Eastern Seaboard have discovered, the bricks that were laid during the colonial period varied in size. This is because there were thousands of different brickmakers with thousands of different molds in the 17th and 18th centuries (the first English brickmakers arrived in Jamestown in 1610). The size of building products became increasingly uniform with time, and by the end of the 19th century, a standard brick was 8 in. long.

This standard 8-in. brick, unfortunately, did not quite fit the format of modular coordination that was developed in the 1930s because, with a mortar joint, it totaled an awkward 8⅜ in. long. While an 8-in. brick is still officially called a standard brick, it normally has to be special-ordered, and today the most common brick size by far is the modular 7⅝-in. brick. Because it is now, in fact, the standard brick size, the 7⅝-in. brick is often called a "standard modular" brick.

Both the old standard brick and the new standard modular brick are 2¼ in. in height. This means they are identical when it comes to laying out courses, and either can be laid out using the same standard brick spacing rule. For the rest of this chapter, therefore, the term "standard" will refer to both the old and new standard (modular) brick in regards to height.

In addition to the standard modular brick, there are several other modular brick units that are usually laid in conjunction with blocks on commercial buildings. One other brick that is fairly common in residential construction is the oversize brick. This brick is 2¾ in. high (½ in. higher than standard modular bricks) and a full 8 in. long. This brick doesn't work well with block, but it saves money on residential veneer and, in some applications, is more appealing to the eye than the standard modular brick.

Brick types

Standard modular

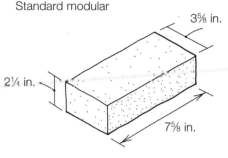

3⅝ in.
2¼ in.
7⅝ in.

"Old" standard

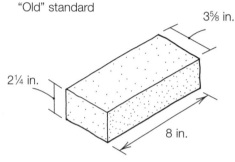

3⅝ in.
2¼ in.
8 in.

Oversize

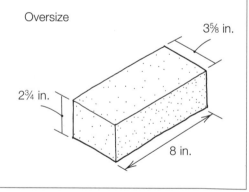

3⅝ in.
2¾ in.
8 in.

---

masonry wall be between ¼ in. and ¾ in. thick. For optimal appearance and performance, however, joints should actually be between ⁵⁄₁₆ in. and ⁹⁄₁₆ in. thick, and they should be as consistent as possible.

Measure in standard modules or in unit sizes

Because masonry units are made in molds, there is an enormous selection of sizes and shapes. My block supplier has no less than 105 different concrete masonry units (CMUs) for sale. My brick supplier has eight different size bricks and a wide variety of special shapes.

Most (but not all) of these masonry units fit into the 4-in. modular format discussed in Chapter 1.

Height increments for concrete blocks are typically 8 in. or 4 in., and like lumber, blocks are smaller than their nominal size. An 8-in. block is actually 7⅝ in. high, while a 4-in. block is 3⅝ in. high. A block with a ⅜-in. mortar joint, then, measures an even 4 in. or 8 in. high. Standard modular bricks average 2¼ in. in height. With tidy bed joints that are just under 7/16 in. thick, three of these courses should equal one standard 8-in. block course. It should be noted, however, that when masons lay standard modular bricks (see the sidebar on the facing page) that aren't backed by block (brick veneer on a frame house, for instance), their layout isn't trapped in 8-in. modules. In such cases, three courses of standard modular bricks might be compressed into 7⅞ in. or stretched to 8¼ in. of height.

When bricklayers lay out masonry courses, they use either of two systems. If they're using bricks and blocks together (as is often the case in commercial construction), they use modular bricks, and their courses con-

form to the 8-in. module of the blocks. If they're using bricks independent of blocks, they can use standard or oversize bricks, in addition to any of the modular brick sizes, and stretch or compress their courses as needed. In these cases, they are free of the 8-in. module, and to lay out their courses, they use brick spacing rules.

I have three brick spacing rules—a mason's modular spacing rule, a mason's standard spacing rule, and an oversize spacing rule—and all three work the same way (see the drawings below). After first establishing a top line, hold the rule so that the end is level with the top line. Then go down the length of the rule and mark at the same number or letter that corresponds to your chosen brick spacing.

To lay out the placement of their units horizontally, bricklayers either measure in 4-in. increments or, when using nonmodular units, they measure in increments that equal the size of the unit plus ⅜ in. It's important to remember that there is often one less mortar joint than there are bricks in a course. For example, a chimney that

---

Brick Spacing Rules

The course spacings on all of these rules indicate the height of one brick and one mortar joint.

Mason's modular spacing rule

This rule provides eight different spacings for modular brick. Residential builders would ordinarily only use the #6 spacing, which measures three even courses for every 8 in.

Standard brick spacing rule

This rule provides 10 different course sizes (indicated by the numbers 0 to 9) for standard 2¼-in.-high bricks.

Oversize brick spacing rule

This rule provides 11 different course sizes (indicated by 11 letters) for oversize bricks, which are 2¾ in. high.

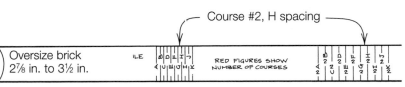

is six standard modular bricks wide should be laid out to 47⅝ in. (six bricks and five head joints). For narrow projects like chimneys, it's often easiest to lay out the units dry to see how they'll fit in a given space. Now let's take a look at how bricklayers might apply these principles to specific layout tasks. (For some useful estimating formulas for masonry jobs, see Tricks of the Trade at left.)

LAYING OUT BRICK VENEER

Prior to World War II, most brick houses built in the United States were "solid masonry" houses, meaning they were made of two or more wythes (a continuous vertical section of a masonry wall) of brick or, more typically, brick backed by block. Today, most brick houses are wood-frame houses that are clad in brick veneer. While the brick provides an excellent exterior shell, it serves no structural function aside from supporting its own weight. Still, the veneer must rest on a solid footing

Plan View of Corner-Pole Setup

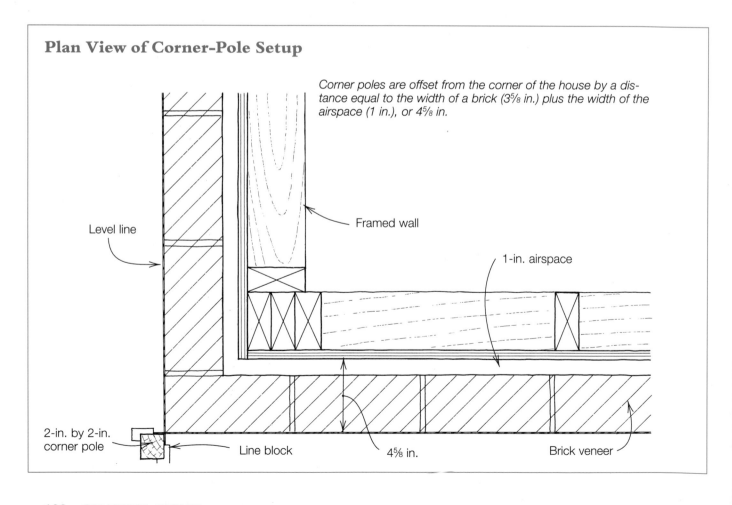

Corner poles are offset from the corner of the house by a distance equal to the width of a brick (3⅝ in.) plus the width of the airspace (1 in.), or 4⅝ in.

Level line

Framed wall

1-in. airspace

2-in. by 2-in. corner pole

Line block

4⅝ in.

Brick veneer

or foundation and be securely attached with wall ties to the house.

Most building codes require a 1-in. cavity between the house and the back of the veneer and a drain system at the bottom of the wall to provide an escape route for any water that makes its way through the brick wythe. A mason has two primary concerns when he begins the layout of the brick veneer for a house. The first is to ensure that the veneer will be plumb and have the requisite 1-in. cavity. The second is to achieve even courses for the entire wall.

Setting up the corner poles and top line

Like most masons, you should begin the layout by setting up corner poles that are plumbed, offset from the corners of the building, and braced at the top and bottom. Because bricks are 3⅝ in. wide, the inside edge of

the corner poles should be set up 4⅝ in. from the outside surface of the framed house to allow for the 1-in. airspace (see the drawing on the facing page). There are several manufactured corner poles available, or you can use a length of 2-in. square steel tubing attached to an L-shaped bracket made out of 2x8 scraps. For an accurate layout, it's essential to plumb the poles carefully in both directions using a plumb bob or a reliable level.

Once the corner poles are in place, you then need to establish a top line (or, in some cases, two or more top lines). On a one-story house, the most important top line is located about 5¼ in. below the underside of the (wood) windowsills (see the drawing below), which leaves enough room for the brick sill that goes underneath the windowsill (see the drawing on p. 187). This line represents the top of one of the courses of brick and serves as a reference or starting point for measuring and

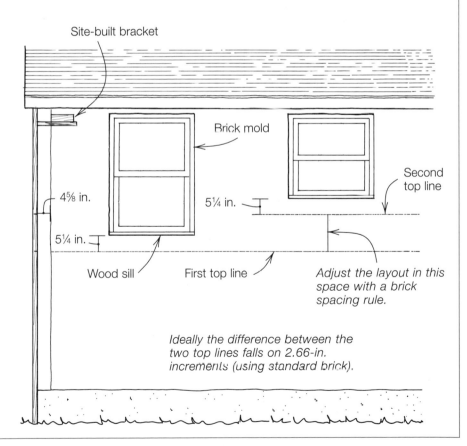

Establishing First and Second Top Lines on a One-Story House

Stringlines stretched from corner pole to corner pole establish the level of each course; their positions on the corner pole are laid out with a brick spacing rule. When a house has more than one window size, a second top line should be established to leave room for the brick sills (see the drawing on p. 187) under the smaller windows.

Site-built bracket

Brick mold

4⅝ in.

5¼ in.

Second top line

5¼ in.

Wood sill

First top line

Adjust the layout in this space with a brick spacing rule.

Ideally the difference between the two top lines falls on 2.66-in. increments (using standard brick).

Setting up Stringlines

The ability to set up stringlines quickly and securely is an important masonry skill. The two most common tools for doing this are line blocks and twigs, which masonry supply houses traditionally provide for free.

To use a line block, pull the stringline through the slot, then wrap it over the back of the block and around the midsection a couple of times. Now pull it from the midsection back through the slot, once from each side. The line block hooks on either the outside corner of the masonry or on the corner pole. It should be pulled tight to remove any sag.

Twigs clip over the stringline and help hold it along the top edge of the unit. After clipping the twig on the stringline, a heavy object, or, in some cases, a small C-clamp, hold the twig—and the stringline—in the proper place. One of the advantages of using a twig is that the line can be pulled taut without exerting pressure on the masonry just laid. Sometimes, instead of hooking a line block on a corner I've just laid, I attach the line to a stake or a heavy object beyond the corner and use a twig, weighed down with a half brick to hold the line even with the top edge of the unit. Twigs should be clamped only to units that are set in fully cured mortar.

A third tool that is sometimes used to affix a stringline to an inside corner is the line stretcher. After the corner has been built and the mortar has set, wrap the stringline around the line stretcher and place the stretcher so that it straddles the girth of the unit. Tension on the line then holds the stretcher in place.

marking all of the other courses (for more on setting up stringlines, see the sidebar at left).

Ideally, from the bricklayer's point of view, windows are all the same size and carefully set at the same height. While main windows usually meet these requirements, there are often a couple of smaller windows in bathrooms and kitchens as well. So, after snapping a chalkline around the house 5¼ in. below the main windows, measure and mark 5¼ in. below the secondary windows, then check with a brick spacing rule to see how the courses between these two levels work out. If they don't work out to the spacing scheme you want to use, adjust the space below the windowsills, since the 5¼-in. space—though ideal—can be fudged ¾ in. in either direction. I usually try to do most of this fudging on the less numerous and less noticeable secondary windows. Of course, this problem can be avoided if the secondary windows are chosen so that they are smaller than the primary windows by an amount that can be divided evenly by the size of a brick course (about 2.66 in.), as shown in the drawing on p. 183.

On many one-story houses, the plans call for a frieze board set so that its bottom edge is even with the tops of the windows and doors. In these cases, the last course of brick can be set higher than the tops of the windows and doors. The frieze board then overlaps the brick veneer (see the left drawing on the facing page). When this detail is in the plan, there is no need for a top line above the openings. When brick is planned above the windows, on the other hand, the courses need to land no more than about ¼ in. above the windows. This means that a third top line is necessary. Usually, there are enough courses between the top line at the windowsill and this third top line to allow for an acceptable course spacing.

Here, a simple principle should be stated: the taller the space, the easier it is to fit courses evenly. The reason for this is simple. The more courses there are, the easier it is to stretch or compress the entire section of brickwork by altering the height of each course a tiny amount. In previous chapters, you fretted over cumulative error. Here, you can harness its power and put it to work for you—as long as there are enough courses to work with.

Frieze Board Aligned with Top of Window

When a frieze board is planned to cover the tops of windows and doors, the brick spacing between the windowsill and the top isn't critical. Otherwise, it should be planned so that there is a ¼-in. caulk gap between the tops of the windows and the course of brick that goes over the windows.

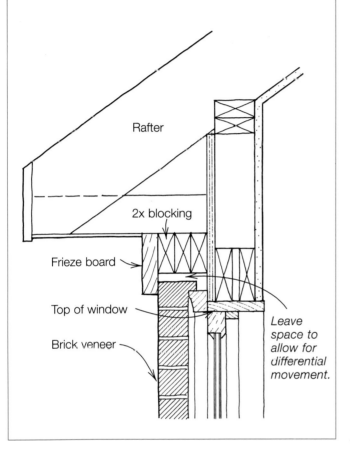

Laying Out Courses with a Standard Brick Spacing Rule

To use a brick spacing rule, mark at the same number to indicate the top of each course. Here the courses are laid out on a #5 spacing.

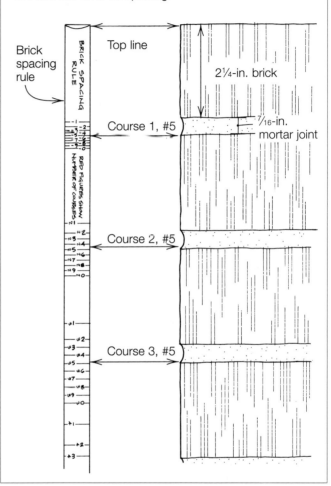

For this reason, tall windows are better—at least from the standpoint of the bricklayer—than short windows.

Marking the courses

The spacing scheme I use can best be understood by first looking closely at a standard brick spacing rule. As you can see in the right drawing above, there are ten space settings. The narrowest increment, the #1, is 2⅜ in. high, while the widest, the #0, is 3 in. high. Since the height of a standard brick is 2¼ in., a #1 spacing yields an impossible ⅛-in. joint, while a #0 yields an unacceptable ¾-in. joint. I've never used these space increments to lay out the courses in a wall, and, in fact, rarely use any of the other course spacings on the rule except for #4, #5, or #6. These spacings equal 2⅝ in., 2¹¹⁄₁₆ in., and 2¾ in., respectively, and yield bed joints between ⅜ in. and ½ in. when using standard brick.

It's often necessary to use a combination of these sizes to lay out even brick courses in a given space. To arrive evenly at the top of a door or a window, for example, it may well be necessary to use a combination of #4s and #5s. While this is perfectly acceptable, as a general rule, don't use three different spacing sizes or jump two sizes at once. The difference between these increments may seem minuscule, but for a mason, the difference between running bricks on #4s and #6s is significant. Even an untrained eye can notice the difference in a finished wall, so I strongly recommend against changing course sizes by more than one number, if at all possible.

To lay out the courses on the corner pole, first transfer the reference line (the line about 5¼ in. below the windowsill) to the pole. Then, hold the rule so that the zero point is on the reference line and mark at the same number (usually #4 or #5) as you go down the length of the rule. If it becomes necessary to switch from one course number to another, move the rule and begin the new brick spacing numbers where you stopped the old ones. To lay out courses above the reference line, just place the rule so that the desired course-number mark aligns with the reference mark, then continue to mark at the same reference number as you go up the pole.

Getting on course as soon as possible

It is very unlikely that these increments will end up even at the bottom. In the drawing below, notice that there is an odd space about 1⅜ in. high at the bottom of the corner pole. How can you dispose of this partial increment? Masons have several ways of "getting on course" as they come out of the ground. One of the simplest ways is simply to beef up or slim down the joints for a few courses. (This is one possible function of the seldom-used extremely wide and narrow space incre-

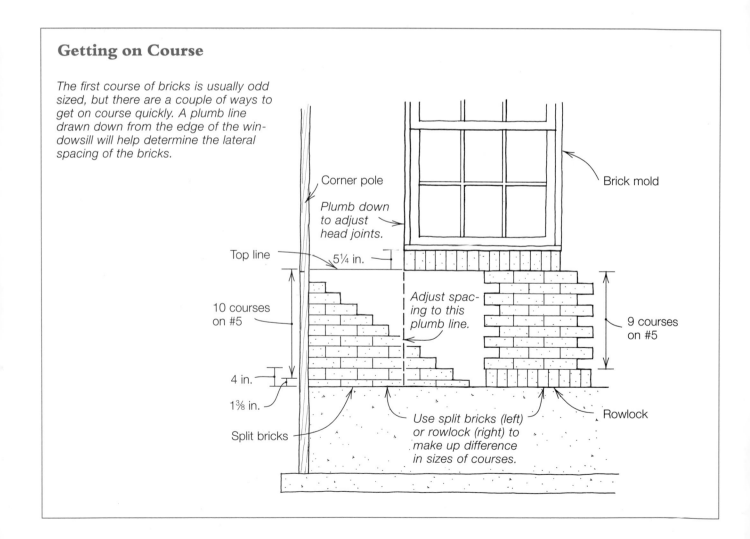

Getting on Course

The first course of bricks is usually odd sized, but there are a couple of ways to get on course quickly. A plumb line drawn down from the edge of the windowsill will help determine the lateral spacing of the bricks.

Corner pole

Plumb down to adjust head joints.

Brick mold

Top line — 5¼ in.

Adjust spacing to this plumb line.

10 courses on #5

9 courses on #5

4 in.

1⅜ in.

Split bricks

Use split bricks (left) or rowlock (right) to make up difference in sizes of courses.

Rowlock

ments on the brick spacing rule.) Sometimes, bricklayers use special 1½-in.-high "split bricks" that are sold by brick suppliers. In other circumstances, they might use oversize bricks. In this case, however, I would probably run a rowlock course (a course of bricks laid on edge with their ends visible) out of half brick to get on course. Whichever method is used, it should be done below grade, if possible.

As you emerge on course above grade, start thinking about the lateral spacing of the units. In doing so, you balance aesthetic issues against gains in productivity. Although the (horizontal) bed joints dominate visually in a brick wall, the (vertical) head joints are also important and should be as orderly and consistent in size as possible. One of your goals at this point is to avoid having to cut small pieces later to fit along the side of the window. I sometimes draw plumb lines down from the edge of the brick molding on the windows and begin fudging

the placement of the bricks well below the windowsills to avoid these ugly and time-consuming pieces.

Laying out the windowsills

After all of the courses have been finished, there will be a 5-in.-high space under each of the windows that will have to be filled with a sill made up of bricks laid on edge and sloped to shed water. To lay these out, use a spacing rule held horizontally. Remember that there will be one more mortar joint than there are bricks in the sill. Mark the brick spacing either on the top course of brick below the sill or directly on the wood sill of the window (see the drawing below). Because there's an extra joint, the layout should end ⅜ in. or so from the end of the opening.

On narrow windows, I've sometimes had to use brick spacings that I would not use on the wall (#3 or #7, for example). I also use the same basic layout technique

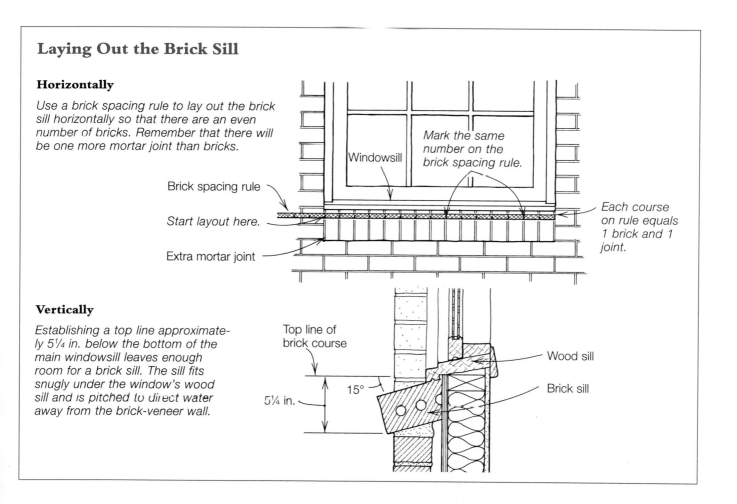

Laying Out the Brick Sill

Horizontally

Use a brick spacing rule to lay out the brick sill horizontally so that there are an even number of bricks. Remember that there will be one more mortar joint than bricks.

Brick spacing rule

Start layout here.

Extra mortar joint

Windowsill

Mark the same number on the brick spacing rule.

Each course on rule equals 1 brick and 1 joint.

Vertically

Establishing a top line approximately 5¼ in. below the bottom of the main windowsill leaves enough room for a brick sill. The sill fits snugly under the window's wood sill and is pitched to direct water away from the brick-veneer wall.

Top line of brick course

5¼ in.

15°

Wood sill

Brick sill

(using the brick spacing rule) if the design calls for a soldier course (brick units set on end, with the long, narrow face vertical on the wall) above the window.

Laying out a brick veneer on a two-story house

So far, I've focused on laying out a brick veneer on a one-story house. But what if you're building a two-story house? Well, laying out courses on a two-story house is just like laying out courses on a one-story house, with one additional challenge: There are two tiers of windows on a two-story house, and the space between them must work out to even courses. This is often a short space, making it difficult to keep uniform course sizes (within one number on the brick spacing rule) and achieve even brickwork at the same time.

When luck dictates that the space is simply the wrong size to make this work, you have no choice but to employ the dreaded split course beneath the second-story windows. For this reason, don't leave matters up to luck. To ensure that there will be even and uniform courses, make sure that the second-story windows are set at the correct height above the first-story windows. One way to do this is to make the rough opening of the second-story windows about 2 in. taller than the specified rough opening. You can then install the windows temporarily until the bricklayer arrives. After he establishes his brick courses, you can adjust the final height of the windows to conform to his layout.

This is a lot of trouble to go through, and there's an easier way. As you've seen, three standard or standard modular brick courses with mortar joints can be laid out to add up to 8 in. This is a very desirable course spacing, between a #4 and a #5 on the brick spacing rule. You've also seen that the space needed for a sill is about 5¼ in. A very good course spacing, then, is 2.66 in., and two of these courses equals the space needed for a brick sill ($2 \times 2.66 = 5.32$ in.). Setting the second-story windows so that the underside of the sills is a distance that is evenly divisible by 2.66 in. from the top of the brick

molding on the first-story windows will assure you of an excellent brick course layout (see the drawing below). If this distance looks like it is going to end up being about 36 in. high, for example, it would be better to make it either 34⁹⁄₁₆ in. ($13 \times 2.66 = 34.58$) or 37¼ in. ($14 \times 2.66 = 37.24$).

Of course, the 2.66-in. increment will not work with oversize bricks, because (with a bed joint) they average between 3⅛ in. and 3¼ in. thick. Two of these courses

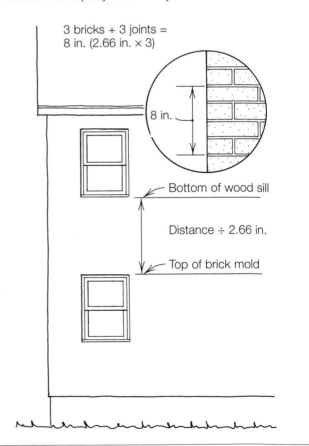

Laying Out a Two-Story Brick Wall

Because 2.66-in. is a good brick spacing that accommodates both brick courses and sills (see inset), a good strategy is to set upper windows so that the distance between the bottom of the upper windowsills and the top of the brick mold of the lower windows is equally divisible by 2.66 in.

3 bricks + 3 joints = 8 in. (2.66 in. × 3)

8 in.

Bottom of wood sill

Distance ÷ 2.66 in.

Top of brick mold

total around 6⅜ in. thick, which is about 1 in. more than would be needed for the sill. To get the right distance between the top of the first-story windows and the bottom of the second-story windows, therefore, multiply 3³⁄₁₆ in. (or 3.1875 in.) by the anticipated number of courses and subtract 1 in. from the total. If the distance is about 36 in., for example, set the top window either 34 in. or 37½ in. above the bottom window:

$$11 \times 3.1875 = 35.057 - 1 = 34.057,$$

$$or \ 12 \times 3.1875 = 38.25 - 1 = 37.25.$$

This dimension can (and should, in my opinion) be specified by the designer, and it should be treated as a critical dimension by the carpenters. This is especially true on houses where the space between the lower and upper windows is short (hence leaving little room for fudging) and oversize bricks are used.

Incidentally, these formulas should be considered whenever choosing windows for a brick-veneer structure, particularly when two different-size windows are planned on the same floor. A window that measures close to a dimension that can be equally divided by 2.66, for example, will work well with standard or standard modular brick. This dimension must be measured from the underside of the windowsill to the top of the brick mold.

LAYING OUT BRICK STAIRS

The common sizes of masonry units are well suited to building stairs. As I noted in the last chapter, stair risers close to 7 in. high are considered ideal, while risers as high as 8 in. are permitted by most building codes. It just so happens that widely available masonry units can be combined to build three different-size stair risers within the range of 6¾ in. and 8 in. high. The key to laying out a masonry stair where the risers and treads are consistent in size and meet code requirements is to have a comprehensive plan before pouring the concrete that will support the stairs.

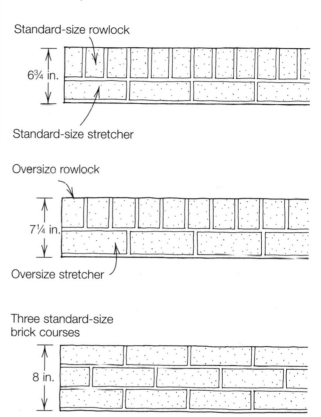

Laying Out Brick Stair Risers

If the exact size of the risers is known, the distance from one level to the next can be evenly divisible by that riser size. These are the three most common brick riser designs. They can be adjusted by varying the thickness of the mortar joints slightly—plus or minus ¼ in. per riser.

Standard-size rowlock

6¾ in.

Standard-size stretcher

Oversize rowlock

7¼ in.

Oversize stretcher

Three standard-size brick courses

8 in.

Laying out the risers

If you know the exact size of the risers you're going to use, you can arrange to have the distance from one level to the next evenly divisible by that riser size. The three most common brick stair-riser designs are shown in the drawing above. They can be adjusted slightly by varying the thickness of the mortar joints, but this device is limited to plus or minus ¼ in. per riser. It's imperative, therefore, to get the total rise correct when you pour the footing or the slab.

Laying Out Brick Stair Treads

Determine the number of treads needed, then measure an equal number of feet out (from the wall you're building the stairs against) before starting the first step. If the stairs will have a nosing, subtract the amount of the nosing. To avoid cumulative error, measure from the starting point out for every step.

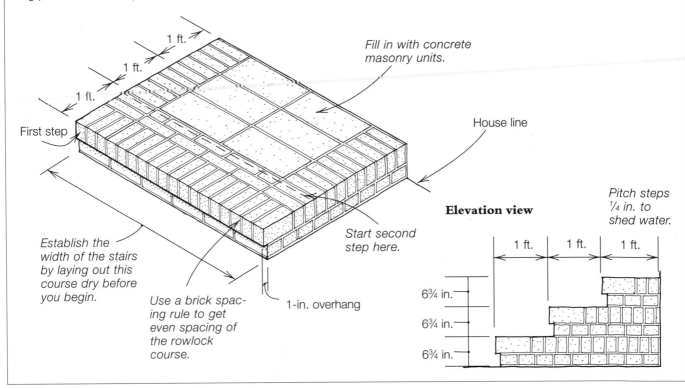

1 ft.

1 ft.

1 ft.

First step

Fill in with concrete masonry units.

House line

Establish the width of the stairs by laying out this course dry before you begin.

Use a brick spacing rule to get even spacing of the rowlock course.

1-in. overhang

Start second step here.

Elevation view

Pitch steps ¼ in. to shed water.

1 ft.　1 ft.　1 ft.

6¾ in.

6¾ in.

6¾ in.

Using concrete masonry units for fill

The structure of most sets of brick stairs is about as simple as it gets in this business: each step is stacked on top of the preceding one. This means that the area behind the first step has to be filled with masonry before you begin the second step. You can save time and money by using concrete masonry units that equal the height dimensions of the brick for this task.

Laying out the width of the stairs

Most of the time the overall width of the stairs can be adjusted to work out to even brickwork. When a rowlock is included in the design, as it often is, you can use a brick spacing rule to get evenly spaced units. If the stairs are being built between two walls, there will be one more mortar joint than there are bricks. If the stairs

are open on both sides, there will be one more brick than there are mortar joints.

Laying out the depth of the treads

On exterior stairs, I find that a comfortable depth of the treads is 12 in. After determining how many treads you'll need, measure an equal number of feet out (usually from the wall you're building the stairs against) before starting the first step. If the stairs will have a nosing, subtract the amount of the nosing. Before starting the first step, square up the entire set using one of the techniques discussed in Chapter 3, or you can simply employ a sheet of plywood as a large square. After completing the first step, again measure from the starting point to lay out the second stair. Do this for every step to avoid cumulative error (see the drawing above).

LAYING OUT FIREPLACES AND CHIMNEYS

The fireplace and chimney should be laid out with care for several reasons. The first and foremost is safety: Because of the hazard of fire, both the fireplace and the chimney must conform to the building code. The second reason is function: They must be built to the proper dimensions to work properly. There are few things that distress a homeowner more than a fireplace that doesn't draw properly. The third reason is economy. A chimney that is well thought out, with as few cut units as possible, goes together faster than one that isn't. And finally, fireplaces and chimneys are both interior and exterior focal points, showcasing the mason's craftsmanship. He would be foolish not to spend a little extra time sweating out the details at the beginning of the job.

Laying out a safe, functional fireplace

There are two general safety concerns when planning a masonry fireplace and chimney. The first is to use approved materials, while the second is to provide proper clearance from combustibles. Building codes make important provisions for chimney and fireplace safety, and before embarking on any project, you should consult and familiarize yourself with the applicable codes in your area.

On more occasions than I can count, I've heard earnest people expound on the art and mystery of fireplace construction. These ruminations always make me smile, though, because they are almost invariably ridiculous. There are, in fact, no medieval secrets involved in building a good fireplace. The firebox, damper, throat, smoke chamber, and flue simply must be built to the proper dimensions, which are widely available in scores of books, magazine articles, publications put out by the U.S. Department of Agriculture (see, for example, U.S.D.A Farmer's Bulletin #1889: *Fireplaces and Chimneys*), and in the literature provided by the manufacturers of chimney components. These dimensions have never failed me. The key to a good fireplace is not to unveil the secrets of fireplace construction but instead to get the mason to build to these proven and widely available specifications (see the drawings and chart on p. 192).

Laying out the chimney to even brickwork

A few minutes of careful layout at the beginning of a chimney project can save hours of work throughout the course of the job. The most important dimension to establish is the depth of the chimney. The determining factor in figuring this dimension is usually not the firebox, as it might seem, but is more often the size of the flue liner and the requirements of the building code. A firebox is typically about 16 in. deep (dimension C in the drawing on p. 192), and in addition to this, building codes usually require at least 8 in. of masonry (including the firebrick) around the firebox. Keep in mind, however, that the firebox often begins at the inside of the wall frame, which means that only about 20 in. of space is needed outside the house to accommodate the firebox. To accommodate a 12-in. by 12-in. flue, on the other hand, you'd have to build a chimney three bricks wide (23⅝ in.).

The width of a chimney varies widely and depends on several factors. These include the size of the fireplace or fireplaces, code requirements, and whether the chimney houses additional flues. If the chimney is built to accommodate a single fireplace, the width can be determined by looking at the requirements of the building code in your area. Where I live, 8 in. of masonry is required on each side of the firebox, so a 36-in.-wide fireplace needs a chimney at least 6½ bricks, or 51½ in., wide. This width can be tapered in above the smoke chamber to three bricks, which is just wide enough to house the single flue liner.

Laying out the fireplace and chimney to please the eye

While it is more efficient to build with full (rather than cut) masonry units, they also simply look better. Neat, orderly, and full bricks make the entire job look good. But there are some other aesthetic issues that must be considered when laying out the fireplace and chimney. Perhaps the most basic one is the location of the firebox. If the fireplace is a couple of inches out of center, it often shows, and it isn't pretty.

The location of the firebox relative to the inside surface of the wall on which the fireplace is located is also important. Sometimes the fireplace surround is supposed to stand in front of the wall. In these cases, the firebox

Traditional Fireplace Dimensions

Each part of a fireplace must be built to the proper dimensions. Match the letters in the drawings to the chart below to find the appropriate size of each fireplace part. Remember that building codes make important provisions for chimney and fireplace safety, so become familiar with the applicable codes in your area.

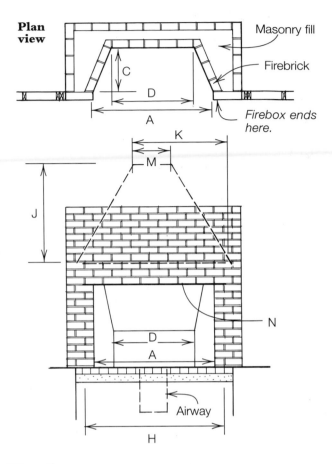

Plan view

Masonry fill

Firebrick

Firebox ends here.

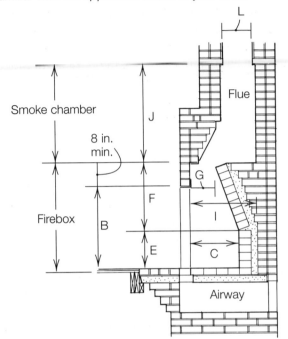

Flue

Smoke chamber

8 in. min.

Firebox

Airway

Airway

Sizing a Fireplace

Finished fireplace opening							Rough brickwork				Flue size	Steel angle size
A	B	C	D	E	F	G	H	I	J	K	L M	N
24	24	16	11	14	18	8¾	32	21	19	10	8 by 12	A-36
26	24	16	13	14	18	8¾	34	21	21	11	8 by 12	A-36
28	24	16	15	14	18	8¾	36	21	21	12	8 by 12	A-36
30	29	16	17	14	23	8¾	38	21	24	13	12 by 12	A-36
32	29	16	19	14	23	8¾	40	21	24	14	12 by 12	A-42
36	29	16	23	14	23	8¾	44	21	27	16	12 by 12	A-42
40	29	16	27	14	23	8¾	48	21	29	16	12 by 16	A-48
42	32	16	29	14	26	8¾	50	21	32	17	16 by 16	B-48
48	32	18	33	14	26	8¾	55	23	37	20	16 by 16	B-54
54	37	20	37	16	29	13	68	25	45	26	16 by 16	B-60
60	37	22	42	16	29	13	72	27	45	26	16 by 16	B-66
60	40	22	42	18	31	13	72	27	45	26	16 by 16	B-66
72	40	22	54	18	31	13	84	27	56	32	20 by 20	C-84
84	40	24	64	20	28	13	96	29	61	36	20 by 24	C-96
96	40	24	76	20	28	13	108	29	75	42	20 by 24	C-108

Dimensions are in inches, except where noted. Match the letters in the top row to the letters in the drawings above.

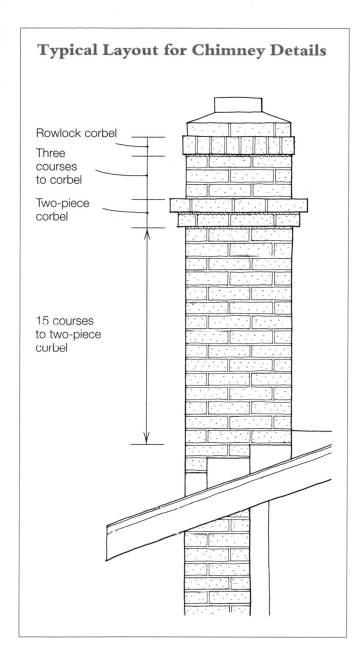

Typical Layout for Chimney Details

Rowlock corbel

Three courses to corbel

Two-piece corbel

15 courses to two-piece corbel

The height of the firebox floor must also be laid out and, in turn, the hearth. There are two basic types of hearths: the flush hearth, which should be laid out even with the finished floor, and the raised hearth, which should be laid out about 9 in. to 16 in., in even brickwork, above the floor. A 12-in.-high hearth is pretty typical and would include three courses of stretchers (8 in.) and one course of rowlock (4 in.). A glaring and annoying mistake is when the hearth ends up one brick off the floor. This blunder is not just an eyesore; it causes people to trip and stub their toes. It usually occurs because the builder fails to provide for the thickness of the bricks when he pours concrete for the hearth.

On the exterior of the house, the detailing of the chimney often elicits admiring remarks. When these details are not well proportioned, however, they're more likely to bring forth snickers—or groans. The best way to avoid these unpleasant sounds is to use a scale drawing. It is usually more effective to indicate details and transitions in terms of numbered courses rather than inches (see the drawing at left).

LAYING OUT FLAT BRICKWORK

The drawings on p. 196 show the two basic systems used for the flat brickwork found in brick terraces, walkways, and floors. The first is a rigid system where brick is set in a bed of mortar over a concrete slab. In this system, the joints between the bricks are about ½ in. wide and filled with mortar. The second approach is a flexible system where the bricks are placed dry on compacted sand or stone screenings. In this system, the joints are only about ⅛ in. wide and filled with sand instead of mortar. The rigid system sheds water off the top surface; the flexible system lets water drain out the bottom of the structure. As its name implies, the flexible system can move and thus ride out things like frost heave and thrusting tree roots.

Choosing the bond pattern and paver size

Like the layout for other brick projects, the layout of flat brickwork is closely connected to the size of the units. The width of a sidewalk, for instance, should be designed to accommodate the size of the brick being used (for example, six bricks wide) rather than to a specific numerical dimension (42 in., for instance). In addition

can begin flush with the inside of the wall. When a traditional mantelpiece is planned, however, the surround should come even with the face of the drywall. This means that the firebox should begin at the outside surface of the wall, as shown in the drawings on the facing page.

Laying Out Brick Arches

A brick arch looks best when it fits into the surrounding brickwork without unsightly and hard-to-cut split bricks just above the arch. So the arch should be laid out so that its height—plus the height of the bricks that form the arch—works out to even brick courses. The most common arches used in residential masonry are segmental and semicircular. An arch that approximates a half ellipse, sometimes called a multicentered arch, is also fairly common.

The first step in building a brick arch is to lay out and build a temporary plywood form that will support the masonry arch until the mortar sets. Segmental and semicircular arches are simply sections of a circle, and they can be laid out on the plywood by rigging up a radius out of a strip of wood with a nail or screw as a pivot at one end and a pencil attached to the other (see the drawings below and the left drawings on the facing page). The multicentered arch (see the right drawings on the facing page) can also be laid out on plywood in a similar fashion, but it requires three

Semicircular arch

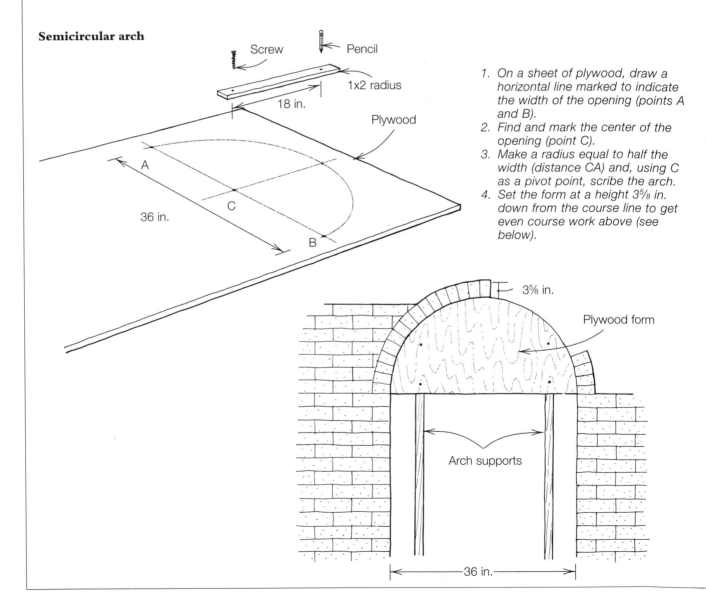

Screw
Pencil
1x2 radius
18 in.
Plywood
A
C
36 in.
B

1. On a sheet of plywood, draw a horizontal line marked to indicate the width of the opening (points A and B).
2. Find and mark the center of the opening (point C).
3. Make a radius equal to half the width (distance CA) and, using C as a pivot point, scribe the arch.
4. Set the form at a height 3⅝ in. down from the course line to get even course work above (see below).

3⅝ in.
Plywood form
Arch supports
36 in.

radii. After drawing the arch on the plywood, cut it out with a jigsaw and then make a duplicate on another piece of plywood using the first one as a pattern. To complete the form, screw in 2x4 spacers between the two templates.

Masonry archways can be built out of half brick, with the mortar joints tapered to conform to the curve of the arch. Another approach is to order brick-arch kits, where the bricks themselves are tapered to conform to the arch. This second path is expensive, requires a willing and able supplier, and early planning. The end result can be well worth the effort, though. If you build the arch with standard or oversize half bricks, you can ensure an even horizontal spacing by using a brick spacing rule, remembering to make allowances for an extra mortar joint.

Segmental arch

1. On a sheet of plywood, draw a horizontal line marked to indicate the width of the opening (points A and B).
2. Find and mark the center of the opening (point C) and draw a perpendicular line through that point.
3. Decide on the height of the arch; this dimension plus 3⅝ in. should be divisible by 2.66 in. if you're using standard brick. In this example, the arch is 4.375 in. high (8 – 3.625 = 4.375).
4. Make a radius the length of DB and swing an arc using D as a pivot. Swing a second arc using B as a pivot.
5. Where these two arcs intersect, mark points E and F.
6. Extend a line through points E and F. Where this line intersects the centerline, mark G.
7. Using point G as a pivot, swing radius GA to lay out the arch.

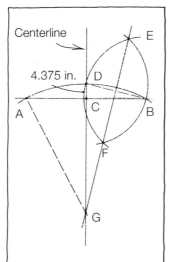

Multicentered arch

1. Draw a line representing the width of the opening (points A and E).
2. Divide that line into four equal parts (points A, B, C, D, and E).
3. Draw a perpendicular centerline through point C.
4. Using A, B, D, and E as pivot points, swing four arcs the length of AB; mark the intersection of the arcs at points F and G.
5. Extend a line from point G through point D to the centerline; mark H.
6. Make a radius the length of GH and swing an arc from point H to complete the arch layout.
7. Set the form 3⅝ in. below the course line.

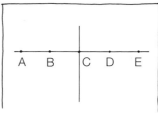

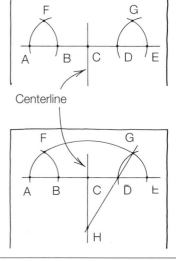

Two Flat Brickwork Systems

The rigid system is designed to shed water. The bricks are set in mortar on a concrete base, and the ½-in. joints are filled with mortar. In the flexible system, bricks are set on a sand and gravel base, the smaller ⅛-in. joints are filled with sand, and water drains through the brick.

Typical rigid design

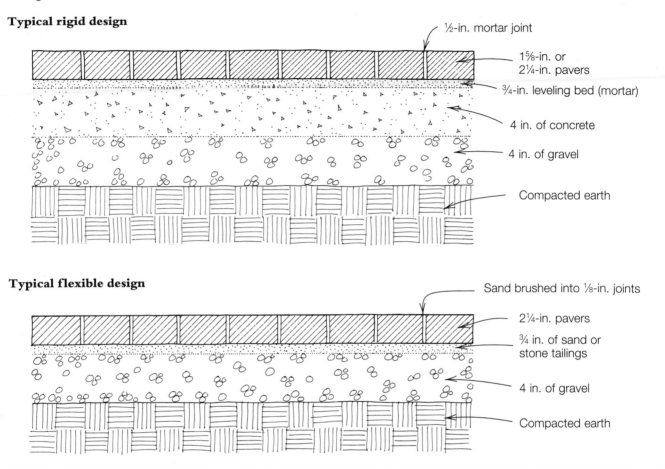

½-in. mortar joint

1⅝-in. or 2¼-in. pavers

¾-in. leveling bed (mortar)

4 in. of concrete

4 in. of gravel

Compacted earth

Typical flexible design

Sand brushed into ⅛-in. joints

2¼-in. pavers

¾ in. of sand or stone tailings

4 in. of gravel

Compacted earth

to knowing the number and exact size of the brick, you also have to know the number and size of the joints to lay out flat brickwork accurately. It's always prudent to have several of the bricks you'll be laying on hand when you plan the structure's dimensions. You can lay out the bricks dry to see how the pattern will fit together and exactly how wide to make the overall structure.

There are three different size brick pavers typically used for flat brickwork: standard (3⅝ in. by 8 in.); standard modular (3⅝ in. by 7⅝ in.); and 2:1 (4 in. by 8 in.). The

system and bond chosen determines which bricks should be used in a particular project. Any size paver can be used for running bond. For basketweave or herringbone patterns, however, you must use standard modular pavers for rigid (mortared) brickwork and 2:1 pavers for flexible (unmortared) designs.

Installing the underlying layers

Both rigid and flexible systems are built in layers. The layout begins with a line that represents the top surface of the brick. From that line, you measure down to es-

Using an Adjustable Screed

When building a walkway, a screed set on forms can be used to establish a smooth and level surface for the brickwork. A piece of plywood screwed to the screed ensures that the various layers of the walkway are at the correct depth below the top line.

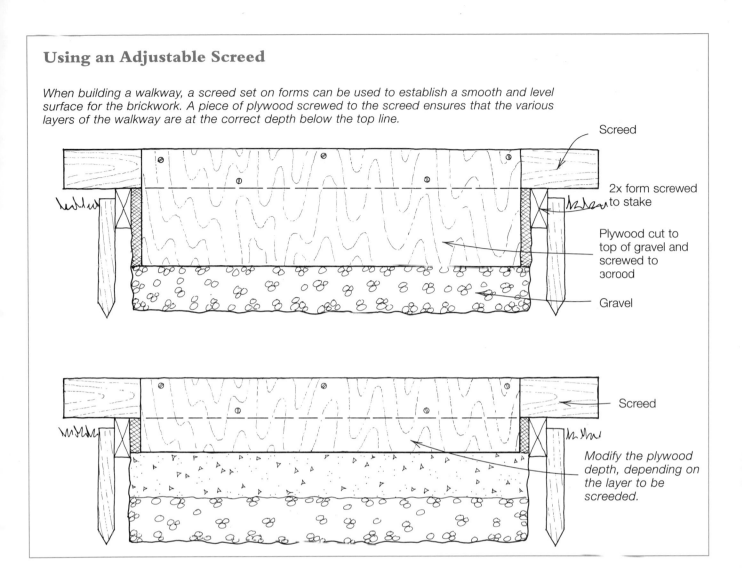

Screed

2x form screwed to stake

Plywood cut to top of gravel and screwed to screed

Gravel

Screed

Modify the plywood depth, depending on the layer to be screeded.

tablish the depth of the excavation and the height of each layer of the structure. On outdoor structures, of course, the top line is rarely level, for it is often desirable both to follow the lay of the land and to pitch the surface to shed water. To ensure that the layers underneath the brick are installed at the right level, you can use a T-shaped screed made of 2xs and ¾-in. plywood that can be modified for each succeeding layer (see the drawings above). The shoulders of the screed ride on a 2x form or a brick border.

Laying out curved walkways

Curved walkways can follow a radius, or they can be drawn freehand and given an organic look. To keep curved sidewalks the same width around the curve, use the same pivot point (a nail driven into a stake works well) for the radii of both the inside and outside curves, making the inside radius shorter by the width of the walk. To get smooth, flowing curves freehand, use flexible plastic molding (the kind used by trim carpenters) as a guide.

Chapter 9

LAYING OUT ROOFING

Roofing performs a variety of functions. Not only does it have to be tough and durable, but it also must form a weather-tight barrier against the elements. But these functions are just part of the equation, because most people are also very concerned that their houses be handsome or, failing that, at least neat and presentable. So the goal of those who install roofing should be twofold: The first is to install the materials so that they will perform like they are designed to perform. The second is to make the installation—and the materials— pleasing to the eye. As you'll see, measuring, marking, and layout play a vital role in achieving this two-part goal, which, in a word, is craftsmanship.

PRINCIPLES OF LAYING OUT UNIT ROOFING

For thousands of years, builders have used small flat units installed in an overlapping pattern to shed water off of buildings. Some of these roofing units are still harvested directly from nature's bounty: slate is quarried from the earth's crust, and wood shakes and shingles are taken from the trunks and limbs of trees. Other roofing units are manufactured, mainly from clay, metals, cement, and petroleum by-products.

People sometimes wonder why builders continue to use these small roofing units when scientifically formulated coatings and large sheets of roofing material are now widely available. At first glance, it seems a bit illogical to nail down thousands of separate units and thus create thousands of punctures and seams in the surface of the roof. But if you look closely at two of the main causes of roof failure, these fasteners and seams begin to make sense. The fasteners, which aren't too hard to waterproof, hold the roof tenaciously to the deck when the house is subjected to high winds. And the fact that the roof is divided into thousands of pieces lets it expand and contract without breaking as the weather changes.

Actually, there are many good reasons why builders continue to install roofs made from overlapping units: They are often considered attractive; some of the units are inexpensive; they are usually easy to install and repair; and they normally don't require special equipment. The main reason why builders, designers, and homeowners overwhelmingly choose these systems, however, is that year after year, generation after generation, century after century, they have faithfully performed their primary function: keeping water out of buildings.

To shed water, unit roofing must be installed in an overlapping pattern, and all types of these units—whether they are shingles, slate, tile, or wood shakes—are installed using the same principles. As a result, it's fairly easy to switch from one material to the other once you understand the basic approach.

Direct rather than seal out water

Whether made of asphalt, wood, sheet metal, slate, concrete, or clay, most roofing units direct water continuously to the outside or top surface of the roof, rather than completely try to seal it out. On pitched roofs, you work in alliance with gravity: While gravity pulls the water ever downward, you use the roofing units as simple barriers to direct it where you want it to go. These roofs are actually waterproof only in the direction that gravity pulls the water, and it's easy to make them leak by using a hose to shoot water uphill against the roof. This is, in fact, why roofs sometimes leak when ice dams form on them. As the dams form, they block water from running down and instead divert it back up the roof and underneath the roofing units.

On a steep roof, water moves very quickly and predictably down the roof. As roof pitches become more gradual, though, water moves slowly, and it becomes more difficult to control its direction. For this reason, roofing units like slate, shingles, or tile aren't appropriate on shallow-pitched roofs. For roofs with pitches between 2-in-12 and 4-in-12, most asphalt shingle

manufacturers have strict (and expensive) installation specifications that essentially require a waterproof layer beneath the shingles. For roofs with pitches less than 2-in-12, most manufacturers recommend against using shingles at all.

The joints between units must be waterproofed

There are two basic methods of waterproofing the joints between roofing units. In the first, the full vertical length of the unit is over two times the exposed length, and the upper part of the unit is overlapped by the unit above it. The vertical dimension of an asphalt shingle, for example, measures 12 in., but the exposed lower portion of it measures only 5 in. The upper 7 in. of the shingle protects the house from water that passes through the joints in the course above it.

For this system to work as it should, it's essential to offset the units. When roofing units are uniform in width, as are asphalt shingles, it's easy to lay out the shingles in a predictable pattern that ensures the units will be consistently offset from one another (this process will be discussed in detail later in this chapter). When wood shingles are used, however, you have to sort through the shingles and occasionally alter the width of them before installation to get the appropriate amount of offset (usually at least 1½ in.).

In the second joint waterproofing strategy, each unit in a course overlaps the one directly beside it, a system typically employed when tile and sheet-metal units are used. On these roofs, the joints are protected not by the units above and below them but by the units to the side. While the seams are often vertically aligned, they are placed so that they are above the flow of water. Water is actually directed to channels in the roofing below the joints, and the strategy here is to prevent water from reaching the joints. In these systems, the full vertical length of the unit is usually just 2 in. or 3 in. longer than the exposed length.

Flashing always directs water onto the top of the roof

One common misconception about roof flashing is that its purpose is to close the crack between the roof deck and the walls, chimneys, or other elements that break the plane of the roof. Operating under this misconception, inexperienced or inept roofers sometimes install and seal flashing to the roof deck before they install their shingles, a practice that directs water underneath the shingles.

Properly installed flashing always directs water onto the top surface of shingles, tiles, or slates. When you install flashing on a wall that runs along the side of a shingle roof, each shingle should get a separate piece of flashing that runs over both the preceding piece of flashing and the preceding course of shingles (see the drawing below). The flashing, in effect, is woven into the courses and continuously sheds water to the top side of the shingles, and usually no sealant at all is required. If you look at a properly flashed wall from inside the house (before the drywall has been hung), you can often see light coming through the overlapping pieces of flashing. While the roof/siding intersection hasn't been sealed off by any means, overlapping the flashing so that water is diverted away from the wall and onto the top of the shingles will prevent the roof from leaking.

Fasteners must be protected from the weather

A 20-square asphalt shingle roof requires about 7,000 roofing nails. But when the roof is finished, there should not be more than a dozen or so nail heads still showing. Any that are showing should be sealed with roofing tar or caulk, because exposed nails sometimes leak and can cause ugly stains on the roof when they erode. Because of these problems, nails are almost always installed in the protected area above the exposed part of the unit.

Water should not be allowed to loiter on the roof

Because unit roofing systems don't seal the house from water but rather direct it to the outside of the roof as it runs downward, water must be able to run unobstructed off the edge of the roof. When large numbers of water molecules congregate in one place, they can create all sorts of havoc. This is particularly true at the bottom of the roof, which receives the accumulated total of all the

Flashing Strategy

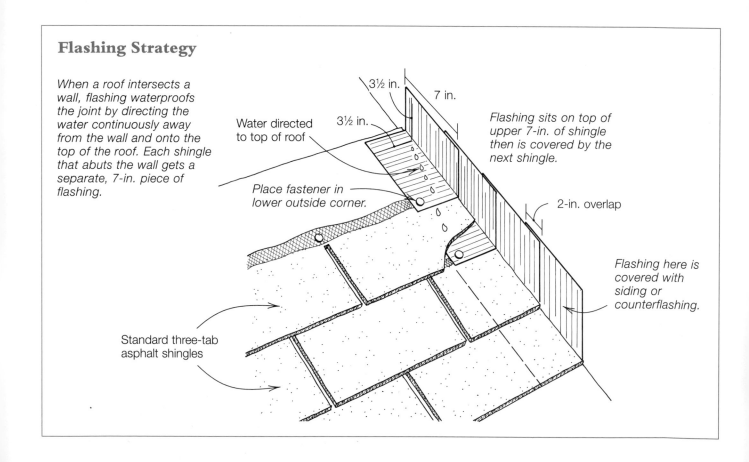

When a roof intersects a wall, flashing waterproofs the joint by directing the water continuously away from the wall and onto the top of the roof. Each shingle that abuts the wall gets a separate, 7-in. piece of flashing.

Water directed to top of roof

Place fastener in lower outside corner.

3½ in.

3½ in.

7 in.

Flashing sits on top of upper 7-in. of shingle then is covered by the next shingle.

2-in. overlap

Flashing here is covered with siding or counterflashing.

Standard three-tab asphalt shingles

water that falls on the roof above it. Architectural features like chimneys at the eaves of a roof or, worse, in the middle of a valley, should be treated with great care. In these cases, the roofer or builder should build a cricket, or miniature gable, to move the water along. An idle water drop is usually up to no good.

A roof does more than shed water

The roof is often one of a house's principal architectural features, and in many cases it helps define the style of the house. Unfortunately, many roofers see their jobs solely in terms of function and don't pay enough attention to the roof's appearance. Thus, when they get aesthetic complaints about their work, their main argument is that the roof doesn't leak. This may be a valid defense when the roof covers a chicken coop, but it isn't what a homeowner who has invested a lot of time and money in a house really wants to hear. It isn't enough to install a leak-free roof; its courses should be straight, and the layout shouldn't look like an afterthought.

LAYING OUT THREE-TAB SHINGLES

Three-tab asphalt shingles are overwhelmingly the material of choice for builders and homeowners across the United States because they are economical and easy to work with. While the layout techniques here are specific to standard three-tab shingles, they should also be helpful for installing just about any type of roofing unit. The primary tools I use are a straight 6-ft. ruler, which looks like an oversize metal yardstick, and a chalkline.

Establishing the overhang

Before starting a roof, it's essential to know how far the shingles should overhang the bottom and sides of the roof deck. Ideally, all the trim has been installed along the edges of the roof and the metal drip edge (if used) is also in place. In these cases, leave a 1-in. overhang along the bottom and sides of the roof. If you install the shingles before the trim has been completed, you need to know how far the trim pieces and drip edge will extend the roof deck and allow for that extension. If a 1x6 rake board and 1 in. of drip edge will be added to the existing subrake, for example, you should leave 2¾ in. over the subrake.

Striking the bond lines

As I just mentioned, one of the basic principles of unit roofing is that the joint between the units must be waterproofed. In three-tab shingle roofing, this is done by offsetting, or "bonding," the shingles. To keep the cutouts of the shingles straight and properly bonded, I strike two vertical bond lines, usually near the left side of the roof. Standard three-tab shingles have three 12-in. tabs and are 36 in. long. If you need to leave, say, a 2¾-in. overhang, extend your ruler exactly 2¾ in. over the edge of the deck and mark at 30 in. and 36 in. (see the drawing on p. 202).

These two measurements are preliminary. To make sure the layout won't result in ugly little pieces at the other end of the roof, measure across it horizontally from the 30-in. and 36-in. marks you just made. You can use a 6-ft. ruler for this, marking it end for end as you walk it across the roof. Each 72-in. mark represents two full shingles. By working this way, you can see exactly where the shingle will land on the far rake by holding it with its tab cutouts aligned on the even-foot increment marks. To help visualize the roof edge better when the trim and drip edge has yet to be installed, you can temporarily tack a shingle that overhangs the rake to represent the trim and/or drip edge's position.

If your preliminary measurements produce a layout that will result in a very narrow or otherwise unsightly shingle at one end of the roof, move the bond lines over to center the layout. Once you get the layout centered on the roof, make identical measurements at the top and bottom of the roof and strike your bond lines. They should be parallel and exactly 6 in. apart. When you install the shingles, begin each horizontal course on a bond line, alternating between the two to create a straight, bonded pattern.

Striking horizontal lines

Standard three-tab shingles are 12 in. wide. To lay out the first course, called the starter course, you need to establish the overhang at the bottom of the roof. Let's say that a ¾-in. fascia and a drip edge that adds another 1 in. are planned but haven't yet been installed. This means you need to leave 2¾ in. of roofing extending past the bottom edge of the roof deck. To do this, hold your ruler so that 2¾ in. extends over the edge of the deck and mark at 12 in. Make the same measurement at

Basic Three-Tab Shingle Layout

Three-tab asphalt shingles are economical and easy to work with. Although this layout is specific to standard three-tab shingles, it should also be helpful for installing any type of roofing unit.

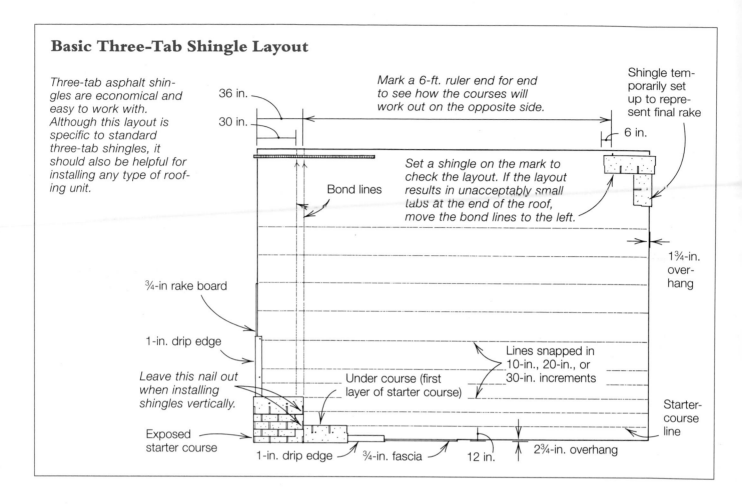

36 in.

30 in.

Mark a 6-ft. ruler end for end to see how the courses will work out on the opposite side.

Shingle temporarily set up to represent final rake

6 in.

Bond lines

Set a shingle on the mark to check the layout. If the layout results in unacceptably small tabs at the end of the roof, move the bond lines to the left.

1¾-in. overhang

¾-in rake board

1-in. drip edge

Leave this nail out when installing shingles vertically.

Exposed starter course

Under course (first layer of starter course)

Lines snapped in 10-in., 20-in., or 30-in. increments

Starter-course line

1-in. drip edge

¾-in. fascia

12 in.

2¾-in. overhang

the other end of the roof, then strike a chalkline across the roof. This is the starter-course line.

As I indicated, the standard exposure of asphalt shingles is 5 in. It's not necessary to strike lines every 5 in., though. In fact, I always strike lines in increments divisible by ten, a pattern that helps me keep things straight when I get into more complex roofs (more on this later). When marking horizontal lines, place the ruler so that the zero point is on the starter-course line. If I'm working with another roofer, I like to strike lines every 10 in. If I'm working alone, though, I often strike lines in increments of 20 in. or 30 in. Remember that the starter-course line is unique among the horizontal lines and that the rest of the lines are measured by tens from it (see the drawing above).

Running the shingles

After you finish striking lines, you can start installing the shingles. This process begins at the intersection of the starter-course line and the bond lines, typically at the bottom left-hand corner of the roof. Place the undercourse of the starter course on the bond line to the left (the undercourse waterproofs the joints on the starter course). I, like most other roofers I know, use a full shingle flipped upside down for the undercourse. Though this is contrary to the instructions of most shingle manufacturers, I've never experienced any problems starting shingles this way, and it eliminates the step of cutting off the tabs of shingles for the undercourse.

The next shingle, the exposed starter course, goes directly on top of the undercourse, but it is offset and placed on the bond line to the right. Because the horizontal lines above the starter course are marked in increments of ten, every other shingle course hits a line

Horizontal, Diagonal, or Vertical?

A neat, professional roof can be installed by running shingles horizontally, diagonally, or straight up the roof (as described in the text).

Inexperienced roofers often run each course horizontally across the roof because this is the least-confusing approach. But many seasoned roofers like to run shingles diagonally, setting up "staircases" with shingles cut into two and one-tab lengths. After the steps are set up, they don't have to lift tabs to slide shingles underneath, which is a necessary part of running shingles vertically, or straight up, the roof. But the trade-off here is that the time gained by avoiding lifted tabs is balanced by the time lost setting up the steps at the beginning of the section and then taking them down at the end of the section. Manufacturers often recommend running shingles diagonally to achieve the best blending of colors, but I've never had a complaint about the blend of color when I've run the shingles vertically.

I prefer to run shingles vertically for three reasons. The first is that I find it easier to keep the layout right when I go around obstructions in the roof. The second reason is that I find it to be easier, because it requires less reaching and less movement. Finally, on hot days I find it more comfortable because I'm sitting or kneeling on the relatively cool shingles I just installed. Working on cooler shingles also decreases the chance of scuff marks (a far more common source of complaints than color blend) and actual damage to sun-softened shingles.

A neat, professional roof can be installed using any (or all three) of the methods shown here.

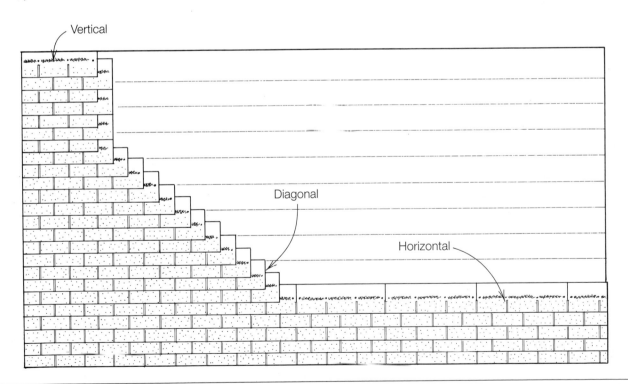

Vertical

Diagonal

Horizontal

and every shingle that hits a horizontal line also hits a right vertical bond line (including the exposed starter shingle). Follow this routine religiously because the resultant consistency is very useful on complex roofs, as you will see.

After installing the undercourse and the exposed starter course, run a vertical row of shingles straight up the bond lines (see the sidebar on p. 203). Install the first shingle above the starter shingle on the left bond line and the next one on the right, repeating this alternating pattern all the way up the roof. The nailing schedule for asphalt shingles is one nail at each end and one nail above each cutout. Because shingles are run straight up the bond lines, it's necessary to leave the far-right nail off every other shingle (the one that falls on the right bond line). This allows you to slip the abutting shingle into place when you run the next vertical row and take care of this fourth nail when installing the next row.

As mentioned above, I sometimes strike horizontal lines every 20 in. or 30 in. To keep the courses in between straight, I use a gauged roofing hammer. This hatchet-like hammer has a steel knob bolted through its blade

5 in. from the face of the hammer head. To use a gauged roofing hammer, place the first shingle on the course chalkline. Then line up the next three (if you're using lines spaced 20 in. apart) with the gauged hammer. The steel knob hooks onto the bottom of the shingle just installed, and the next course sits on the hammer head (see the drawing below).

LAYING OUT SHINGLES ON COMPLEX ROOFS

By adhering to a consistent 10-in. layout pattern and knowing a few simple tricks of the trade, it's easy to keep the courses straight and correctly bonded on complex roofs. Here are a few typical problems and the techniques you can use to solve them.

Laying out courses around dormers

To keep shingle courses consistent as they go around a dormer, first run them past the top and bottom, as shown in the top drawing on the facing page. As you run the shingles over the top of the dormer, nail the first course high on the shingle (within 2 in. of the top edge), which gives you room later on to slide the shingles that go underneath this course into place. Once

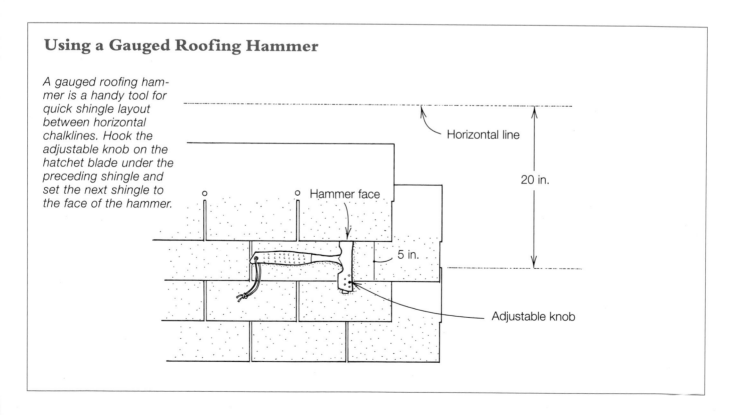

Using a Gauged Roofing Hammer

A gauged roofing hammer is a handy tool for quick shingle layout between horizontal chalklines. Hook the adjustable knob on the hatchet blade under the preceding shingle and set the next shingle to the face of the hammer.

Horizontal line

20 in.

Hammer face

5 in.

Adjustable knob

Laying Out Shingles around a Dormer

To shingle around a dormer or other roof obstruction, follow course lines past the top and bottom. Nail within a few inches of the upper edge of the shingles on the course immediately above the dormer to leave room for the lower course, which will be inserted underneath when the area to the right of the dormer is filled in.

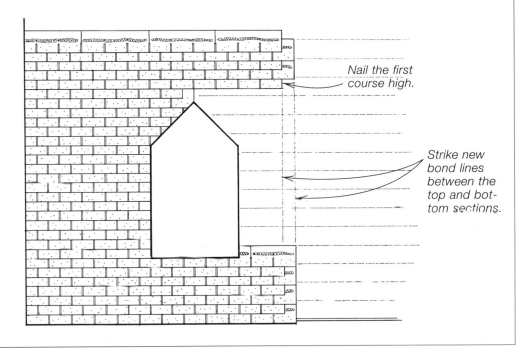

Nail the first course high.

Strike new bond lines between the top and bottom sections.

Reestablishing Bond Lines

Bond lines are always parallel with the rakes and can be reestablished by transferring the upper measurement (x) to the bottom and snapping new vertical bond lines. When all of the horizontal chalklines are 10 in. apart, every shingle that hits a horizontal line will be on the same bond line, and consistently placing the exposed starter shingles on the right bond line makes it easy to reestablish the layout when an obstruction interrupts the roof.

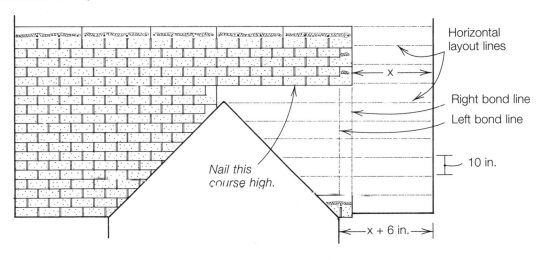

Horizontal layout lines

Right bond line

Left bond line

10 in.

x

Nail this course high.

x + 6 in.

Measuring Down

Holding a ruler vertically with the 12-in. mark aligned with the bottom of the shingle accounts for the 12-in. depth of the shingle; then mark every 10 in. along the length of the ruler to establish horizontal course lines.

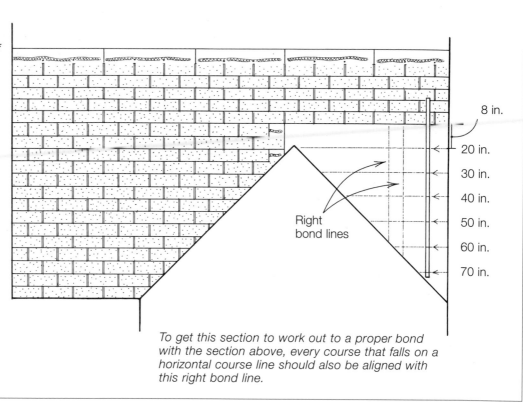

8 in.

20 in.

30 in.

40 in.

Right bond lines

50 in.

60 in.

70 in.

To get this section to work out to a proper bond with the section above, every course that falls on a horizontal course line should also be aligned with this right bond line.

you've cleared the dormer on both the top and the bottom, strike another pair of bond lines on the other side of the dormer to help keep the shingles vertically aligned. Now you can fill in to the right of the dormer following the restruck bond lines and the horizontal layout lines.

When large dormers or intersecting roofs interrupt the bottom section of a roof plane, you can't strike through. In these cases, you must run the shingles across the top until you've cleared the entire obstruction, again making sure to nail the first course high on the shingle to leave room for the shingles that will eventually have to be inserted underneath. Now measure the distance from the end of one of the right bond shingles to the edge of the roof deck and transfer this measurement to the bottom of the roof. Measure and mark 6 in. to the left of this mark, then strike two new bond lines to reestablish the vertical layout (see the bottom drawing on p. 205).

You're now ready to run shingles from the bottom of the roof up the bond lines. But, the question is, which bond line do you start on? If you pick the wrong one, you'll eventually end up with two shingle cutouts aligned one above the other, a roofing abomination. Fortunately, you've struck horizontal layout lines every 10 in. and started (as I always do) with the exposed starter on the right bond line. Once again, put the undercourse of the starter course on the left bond line and cover it with the exposed starter course on the right bond line. As you lay shingles up the bond lines, you'll notice that every shingle that hits a horizontal line also hits a right bond line, so you know that the bond will work out perfectly. How sweet it is!

Sometimes, as in the drawing above, there's no starter course on the far side of an intersecting roof or dormer. In this case, after running the top section over to the rake, you still measure and mark the bond lines to the right of the intersecting roof the same way as before. But

Dividing Courses with the Slant-Rule Trick

In some situations, it's necessary to fit shingle courses into a space that's not divisible by 5 in. For example, in the drawing below, the distance between the starter-course line in the lower section and the starter-course line on the main section is 63½ in. In a situation like this, some roofers will install one narrow 3½-in. course and the rest of the courses at the standard exposure of 5 in.

A better way is to divide these courses equally by placing a 6-ft. ruler on the bottom line and slanting it until the 65-in. mark engages the upper starter-course line. With the ruler in this position, mark every 5 in., repeat on the other side of the roof deck, and then snap chalklines between the marks. This will divide the 63½-in. space into equal increments that are close to 5 in. apart.

After striking these horizontal lines, you have to strike bond lines and then decide which bond line to start the lower section of shingles on. To do this, mark every other horizontal line starting with the top line. I usually mark these with an equal sign because the shingles that hit these lines will be on the same bond line as the shingle on the top line. In this case, because there are an odd number of courses (13), the exposed shingle of the starter course in the lower section is on the opposite bond line (the left one) from the exposed shingle in the starter in the upper section.

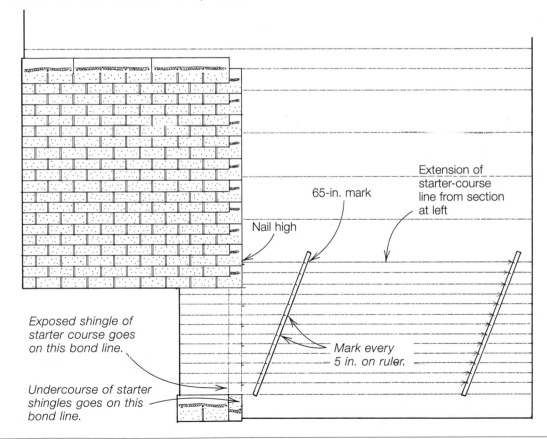

Marking every other course down from the top line indicates that the exposed starter course should be on the opposite bond line from the starter course in the top section.

Extension of starter-course line from section at left

65-in. mark

Nail high

Mark every 5 in. on ruler.

Exposed shingle of starter course goes on this bond line.

Undercourse of starter shingles goes on this bond line.

let's say that there are no horizontal lines in the triangular section created by the intersecting roof. How can you measure down, and how do you get this section properly bonded?

To measure down, hold a 6-ft. ruler so that the 12-in. mark is aligned with the bottom of the first shingle in the top section. Because the shingle is 12 in. high, this puts the zero point of the ruler even with the top of that shingle. With the ruler in this position, mark every 10 in. until you get to the bottom of the triangular section of the roof. Because the bond returns to its starting point every 10 in., every course that hits one of these 10-in. marks should line up with the bond of the first shingle in the section above. It usually requires a bit of finagling at the very bottom of the triangular section, but I always manage to get the bond of the shingle that hits the first marked course in line with the bond of the first course above. If you need to fit shingle courses into a rectangular space that's not divisible by 5 in., use the slant-rule trick (see the sidebar on p. 207).

Moving bond lines

As a right-handed roofer, I prefer to run shingles left to right. On some sections of roofs (such as the roof shown below), there is no rake on the left side. In these situations, the best place to start laying out bond lines is on the right side of the roof. When this is the case, lay out the bond lines with the appropriate overhang on the right side of the roof, then move them to the left in 36-in. increments—the width of one shingle. If you use a 6-ft. ruler, you can simply mark it end-for-end to move the bond lines over two increments at a time. Then, if necessary, add a final 36-in. increment at the end (see the drawing below).

Moving Bond Lines

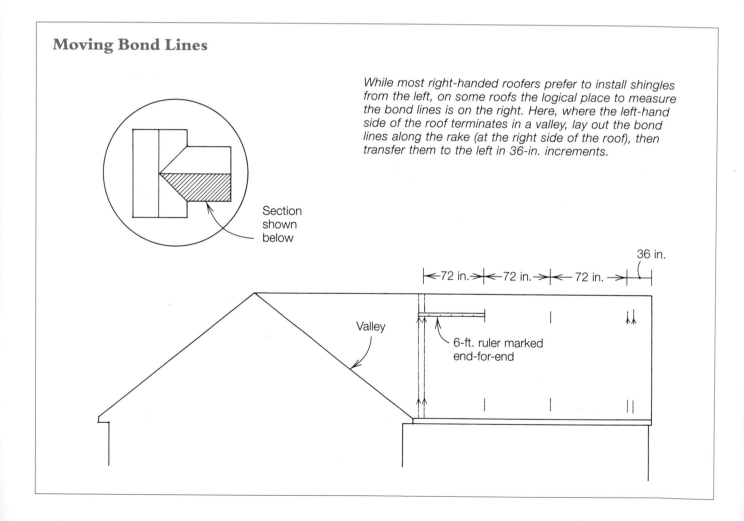

While most right-handed roofers prefer to install shingles from the left, on some roofs the logical place to measure the bond lines is on the right. Here, where the left-hand side of the roof terminates in a valley, lay out the bond lines along the rake (at the right side of the roof), then transfer them to the left in 36-in. increments.

Section shown below

36 in.

|←72 in.→|←72 in.→|← 72 in. →|

Valley

6-ft. ruler marked end-for-end

Laying Out Bond Lines on a Hip Roof

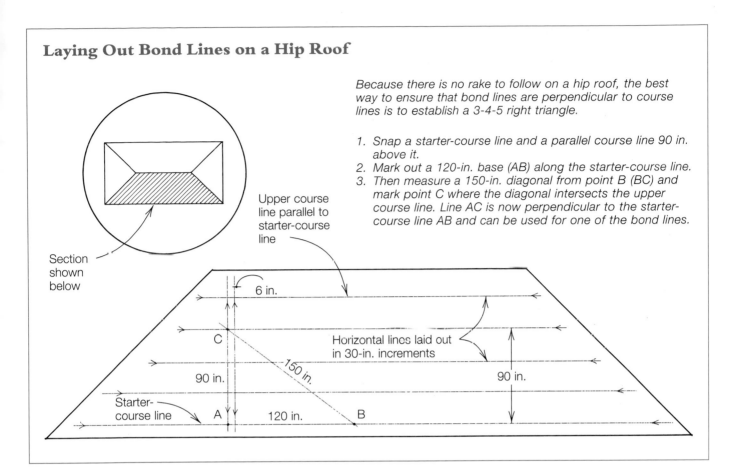

Because there is no rake to follow on a hip roof, the best way to ensure that bond lines are perpendicular to course lines is to establish a 3-4-5 right triangle.

1. Snap a starter-course line and a parallel course line 90 in. above it.
2. Mark out a 120-in. base (AB) along the starter-course line.
3. Then measure a 150-in. diagonal from point B (BC) and mark point C where the diagonal intersects the upper course line. Line AC is now perpendicular to the starter-course line AB and can be used for one of the bond lines.

Section shown below

Upper course line parallel to starter-course line

6 in.

C

150 in.

90 in.

Horizontal lines laid out in 30-in. increments

90 in.

Starter-course line

A   120 in.   B

Laying out bond lines on a hip roof

So far, all of the bond-line layouts that I've described have been measured off the rake of the roof deck. Since a hip roof doesn't have a rake, bond lines can't be laid out this way and instead must be squared up from the starter-course line. To do this, you can use the 3-4-5 right-triangle method.

First, measure and mark a parallel horizontal line 90 in. up from the starter-course line. This line can also be used later for one of the horizontal courses of shingles. Next, mark where you want the bond lines to start on the starter-course line, then measure down the starter-course line 120 in. from the left bond line and mark.

Then pull a measurement of 150 in. diagonally from that mark back up to the second horizontal line and mark where it intersects. This completes the 3-4-5 right triangle, and you can then strike a chalkline from the first mark on the starter-course line through the mark on the upper 90-in. line, confident that this line (your left bond line) will be exactly perpendicular to the starter-course line. Strike a second line 6 in. away and parallel to this line to complete the bond-line layout (see the drawing above).

APPENDIX A

CONVERTING DECIMALIZED INCH TO SIXTEENTHS OF AN INCH

If decimal is between:	Round to:	If decimal is between:	Round to:
0 - 0.031	0	0.469 - 0.531	½
0.032 - 0.093	1/16	0.532 - 0.593	9/16
0.094 - 0.156	1/8	0.594 - 0.656	5/8
0.157 - 0.218	3/16	0.657 - 0.718	11/16
0.219 - 0.281	1/4	0.719 - 0.781	3/4
0.282 - 0.343	5/16	0.782 - 0.843	13/16
0.344 - 0.406	3/8	0.844 - 0.906	7/8
0.407 - 0.468	7/16	0.907 - 0.968	15/16
		0.969 - 1	1

APPENDIX B

CONVERTING DECIMALIZED FOOT TO INCHES

Decimalized foot	Inches	Decimalized foot	Inches	Decimalized foot	Inches
0.01	1/8	0.34	4 1/16	0.67	8 1/16
0.02	1/4	0.35	4 3/16	0.68	8 3/16
0.03	3/8	0.36	4 5/16	0.69	8 1/4
0.04	1/2	0.37	4 7/16	0.70	8 3/8
0.05	5/8	0.38	4 9/16	0.71	8 1/2
0.06	3/4	0.39	4 11/16	0.72	8 5/8
0.07	13/16	0.40	4 13/16	0.73	8 3/4
0.08	15/16	0.41	4 15/16	0.74	8 7/8
0.09	1 1/16	0.42	5 1/16	0.75	9
0.10	1 3/16	0.43	5 3/16	0.76	9 1/8
0.11	1 5/16	0.44	5 1/4	0.77	9 1/4
0.12	1 7/16	0.45	5 3/8	0.78	9 3/8
0.13	1 9/16	0.46	5 1/2	0.79	9 1/2
0.14	1 11/16	0.47	5 5/8	0.80	9 5/8
0.15	1 13/16	0.48	5 3/4	0.81	9 3/4
0.16	1 15/16	0.49	5 7/8	0.82	9 13/16
0.17	2 1/16	0.50	6	0.83	9 15/16
0.18	2 3/16	0.51	6 1/8	0.84	10 1/16
0.19	2 1/4	0.52	6 1/4	0.85	10 3/16
0.20	2 3/8	0.53	6 3/8	0.86	10 5/16
0.21	2 1/2	0.54	6 1/2	0.87	10 7/16
0.22	2 5/8	0.55	6 5/8	0.88	10 9/16
0.23	2 3/4	0.56	6 3/4	0.89	10 11/16
0.24	2 7/8	0.57	6 13/16	0.90	10 13/16
0.25	3	0.58	6 15/16	0.91	10 15/16
0.26	3 1/8	0.59	7 1/16	0.92	11 1/16
0.27	3 1/4	0.60	7 3/16	0.93	11 3/16
0.28	3 3/8	0.61	7 5/16	0.94	11 1/4
0.29	3 1/2	0.62	7 7/16	0.95	11 3/8
0.30	3 5/8	0.63	7 9/16	0.96	11 1/2
0.31	3 3/4	0.64	7 11/16	0.97	11 5/8
0.32	3 13/16	0.65	7 13/16	0.98	11 3/4
0.33	3 15/16	0.66	7 15/16	0.99	11 7/8
				1.00	12

APPENDIX C

CONVERTING DEGREES TO ROOF PITCH

Degrees	x-in-12 pitch	Degrees	x-in-12 pitch	Degrees	x-in-12 pitch
1	0.20946	**30.26**	**7**	**57.72**	**19**
2	0.419	31	7.2103	58	19.2040
3	0.6289	32	7.4984	59	19.9714
4	0.8391	33	7.7929	**59.04**	**20**
4.76	**1**	**33.69**	**8**	60	20.7846
5	1.04986	34	8.0941	**60.26**	**21**
6	1.2613	35	8.4025	61	21.6486
7	1.4734	36	8.7185	**61.39**	**22**
8	1.6865	**36.87**	**9**	62	22.5687
9	1.9006	37	9.0426	**62.45**	**23**
9.46	**2**	38	0.3754	63	23.5513
10	2.1159	39	9.7174	**63.43**	**24**
11	2.3326	**39.81**	**10**	64	24.6036
12	2.5507	40	10.0692	65	25.7341
13	2.7704	41	10.4314	66	26.9524
14	2.9919	42	10.8048	67	28.2702
14.04	**3**	**42.51**	**11**	68	29.7010
15	3.2154	43	11.1902	69	31.2611
16	3.4409	44	11.5883	70	32.9697
17	3.6688	**45**	**12**	71	34.8505
18	3.899	46	12.4264	72	36.9322
18.43	**4**	47	12.8684	73	39.2502
19	4.1319	**47.29**	**13**	74	41.8490
20	4.3676	48	13.3274	75	44.7846
21	4.6064	49	13.8044	76	48.1296
22	4.8483	**49.40**	**14**	77	51.9777
22.62	**5**	50	14.301	78	56.4556
23	5.0937	51	14.8188	79	61.7346
24	5.3427	**51.34**	**15**	80	68.0554
25	5.5957	52	15.3593	81	75.7650
26	5.8528	53	15.9245	82	85.3844
26.57	**6**	**53.13**	**16**	83	97.7322
27	6.1143	54	16.5166	84	114.1724
28	6.3805	**54.78**	**17**	85	137.1606
29	6.6517	55	17.1378	86	171.608
30	6.9282	56	17.7907	87	228.9736
		56.31	**18**	88	343.635
		57	18.4784	89	687.4795

APPENDIX D
THE PROPORTIONS OF RIGHT TRIANGLES

To enlarge any of these triangles without changing the angles or proportions, multiply all three sides by the same number.

Degrees	Base	Altitude	Hypotenuse	Degrees	Base	Altitude	Hypotenuse
1	1	0.017455	1.00015	24	1	0.445229	1.09464
2	1	0.034921	1.00061	25	1	0.466308	1.10338
3	1	0.052408	1.00137	26	1	0.487733	1.11260
4	1	0.069927	1.00244	27	1	0.509525	1.12233
5	1	0.087489	1.00382	28	1	0.531709	1.13257
6	1	0.105104	1.00551	29	1	0.554309	1.14335
7	1	0.122785	1.00751	30	1	0.577350	1.15470
8	1	0.140541	1.00983	31	1	0.600861	1.16663
9	1	0.158384	1.01247	32	1	0.624869	1.17918
10	1	0.176327	1.01543	33	1	0.649408	1.19236
11	1	0.194380	1.01872	34	1	0.674509	1.20622
12	1	0.212557	1.02234	35	1	0.700208	1.22077
13	1	0.230868	1.02630	36	1	0.726543	1.23607
14	1	0.249328	1.03061	37	1	0.753554	1.25214
15	1	0.267949	1.03528	38	1	0.781286	1.26902
16	1	0.286745	1.04030	39	1	0.809784	1.28676
17	1	0.305731	1.04569	40	1	0.839100	1.30541
18	1	0.324920	1.05146	41	1	0.869287	1.32501
19	1	0.344328	1.05762	42	1	0.900404	1.34563
20	1	0.363970	1.06418	43	1	0.932515	1.36733
21	1	0.383864	1.07114	44	1	0.965689	1.39016
22	1	0.404026	1.07853	45	1	1	1.41421
23	1	0.424475	1.08636	22.5	1	0.41421	1.08239

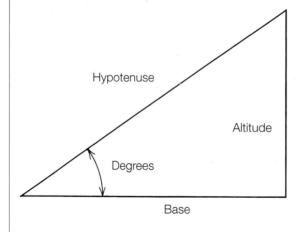

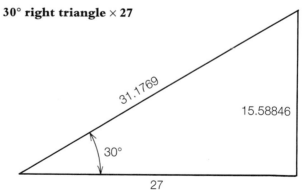

30° right triangle × 27

Base: 27 × 1 = 27

Altitude: 27 × 0.577350 = 15.58846

Hypotenuse: 27 × 1.15470 = 31.1769

APPENDIX E

REGULAR POLYGONS

A regular polygon is a multisided shape in which each angle has the same measure and each side has the same length. The most common regular polygons have names based on the number of sides.

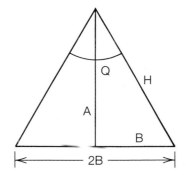

Polygon name	# of sides
Triangle	3
Quadrilateral (square)	4
Pentagon	5
Hexagon	6
Octagon	8
Decagon	10
Duodecagon	12

APPENDIX F

THE PROPORTIONS OF VARIOUS REGULAR POLYGONS

Regular polygons can be divided into a series of equal isosceles triangles, which are arranged in a radial pattern around a center point. The number of isosceles triangles is equal to the number of sides in the polygon. These isosceles triangles can, in turn, be divided into two equal right triangles. The proportions of these triangles, listed below, can be enlarged by multiplying them by the same number, as shown in the drawing of a 10-ft.-wide hexagon (see Appendix G).

# of sides in polygon	Q: 360° / # of sides	A: Altitude	B: Base	2B: 2 × base	H: Hypotenuse
3	120	1	1.73205	3.46410	2
4	90	1	1	2	1.41421
5	72	1	0.726543	1.45309	1.23607
6	60	1	0.577350	1.15470	1.15470
7	51.4286	1	0.481575	0.963149	1.10992
8	45	1	0.414214	0.828427	1.08239
9	40	1	0.363970	0.727940	1.06418
10	36	1	0.324920	0.649839	1.05146
11	32.7273	1	0.293627	0.587253	1.04222
12	30	1	0.267949	0.535898	1.03528
13	27.6923	1	0.246478	0.492956	1.02993
14	25.7143	1	0.228243	0.456487	1.02572
15	24	1	0.212557	0.425113	1.02234
16	22.5	1	0.198912	0.397825	1.01959
17	21.1765	1	0.186932	0.373865	1.01732
18	20	1	0.176327	0.352654	1.01543
19	18.9474	1	0.166870	0.333741	1.01383
20	18	1	0.158384	0.316769	1.01247
21	17.1429	1	0.150726	0.301451	1.01130
22	16.3636	1	0.143778	0.287557	1.01028
23	15.6522	1	0.137447	0.274894	1.00940
24	15	1	0.131652	0.263305	1.00863
25	14.4	1	0.126329	0.252659	1.00795

APPENDIX G

THE DIMENSIONS OF A HEXAGON 10 FT. WIDE

A: $5 \times 1 = 5$

2B: $5 \times 1.15470 = 5.7735$

H: $5 \times 1.15470 = 5.7735$

Helpful hint

The overall height of a regular polygon with an even number of sides, such as the hexagon shown here, is 2 × A. The overall height of a regular polygon with an odd number of sides, such as a pentagon, is A + H.

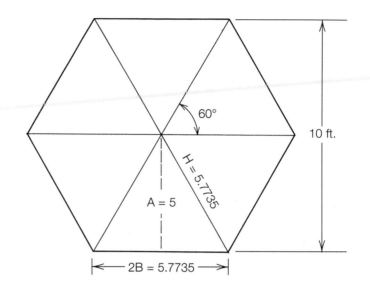

60°

H = 5.7735

A = 5

10 ft.

2B = 5.7735

APPENDIX H

UNITS OF MEASUREMENT

Linear measure
12 in. = 1 ft.
3 ft. = 1 yd.

Square measure
144 sq. in. = 1 sq. ft.
9 sq. ft. = 1 sq. yd.

Cubic measure
1,728 cu. in. = 1 cu. ft.
27 cu. ft. = 1 cu. yd.

Metric units
1 in. = 2.54 cm
1 ft. = 30.48 cm (0.3048 meters)
1 yd. = 91.44 cm (0.9144 meters)

APPENDIX I

FORMULAS

Hypotenuse of a right triangle
(Pythagorean theorem):
1. $a^2 + b^2 = c^2$
2. $c = \sqrt{c^2}$

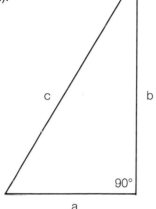

Side of a right triangle:
1. $a^2 = c^2 + b^2$
2. $a = \sqrt{a^2}$

Area of a right triangle:
$(a \times b) \div 2$

Diagonal of a square:
$a \times 1.41421$

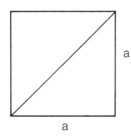

Area of a rectangle or square:
$a \times b$

Volume of a cube
or solid rectangle:
$a \times b \times c$

Circumference of a circle:
$2\pi R$
$\pi = 3.1416$

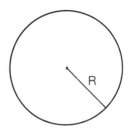

Area of a circle:
πR^2

Volume of a cylinder:
$\pi R^2 \times a$

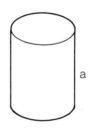

Sides of an octagon:
$x = 0.207 \times a$

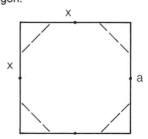

INDEX